Notes from a Turkish Whorehouse

Notes from a Turkish Whorehouse

PHILIP Ó CEALLAIGH

PENGUIN
IRELAND

PENGUIN IRELAND

Published by the Penguin Group
Penguin Ireland, 25 St Stephen's Green, Dublin 2, Ireland
(a division of Penguin Books Ltd)
Penguin Books Ltd, 80 Strand, London WC2R ORL, England
Penguin Group (USA) Inc., 375 Hudson Street, New York, New York 10014, USA
Penguin Group (Australia), 250 Camberwell Road,
Camberwell, Victoria 3124, Australia (a division of Pearson Australia Group Pty Ltd)
Penguin Group (Canada), 90 Eglinton Avenue East, Suite 700, Toronto, Ontario, Canada M4P 2Y3
(a division of Pearson Penguin Canada Inc.)
Penguin Books India Pvt Ltd, 11 Community Centre,
Panchsheel Park, New Delhi – 110 017, India
Penguin Group (NZ), cnr Airborne and Rosedale Roads, Albany,
Auckland 1310, New Zealand (a division of Pearson New Zealand Ltd)
Penguin Books (South Africa) (Pty) Ltd, 24 Sturdee Avenue,
Rosebank 2196, South Africa

Penguin Books Ltd, Registered Offices: 80 Strand, London WC2R ORL, England

www.penguin.com

First published 2006
1

Copyright © Philip Ó Ceallaigh, 2006

The moral right of the author has been asserted

Set in Monotype Dante
Typeset by Palimpsest Book Production Limited, Polmont, Stirlingshire
Printed in Great Britain by Clays Ltd, St Ives plc

A CIP catalogue record for this book is available from the British Library

ISBN-13 978-1844-88046-1
ISBN-10 1-844-88046-X

The lines quoted on p. 107 in 'Walking to the Danube' are from 'Big Two-Hearted River' by Ernest
Hemingway, published by Jonathan Cape. Reprinted by permission of the Random House Group Ltd.

Some of these stories first appeared in *The Dublin Review*, *The Stinging Fly* and *Vivid*.

Contents

Taxi

The sun was getting low and they drove into it and the cars shone hotly and the noise of the city, a machine noise, came through the open window, and even with the open window it was hot and they sweated. They had been sweating for weeks. The taxi driver was talking, and the passenger was listening but was looking straight ahead as if he was not listening. The taxi driver wore shorts and a bright-blue short-sleeved shirt and, most bizarre of all, a pair of wraparound mirror sunglasses. He was in a good mood, it seemed.

'I went off to the coast for a week. Didn't tell the wife I was going. Didn't want to argue about it. She saw the bag and there was women's clothing in it. Presents for your whore, she said. But a woman won't respect her man if he hasn't got a lover. If a man has a lover he can return to his wife relaxed and refreshed. It stabilizes the relationship. This is something that should be apparent to the woman without being flaunted. Should never be discussed with the woman. If you answer one question it establishes her right to enquire and that leads to unnecessary arguments. So I took a holiday with another woman. I work in a particularly toxic environment, you see, constantly exposed to temptation. Especially in this weather. I have beautiful women getting into my taxi wearing short skirts. I see a lot of naked female flesh and it's hard sometimes not to stare. We have the most beautiful women in this country. It's a blessing, but it creates problems too.'

They were driving to the railway station. The driver had

asked if the passenger was going to the coast and the passenger had said, no, he was meeting someone. A girlfriend?
Yes, a girlfriend, said the passenger, and that was when the
driver began to talk about women. They drove past the shell
of the National Library, with its broken windows and dark
hollow interior, and past waste ground with abandoned cranes,
grand projects unfinished over a decade since the fall of the
old regime. After the Palace of the People they followed the
Dâmbovița. Brown-skinned children were leaping off a
bridge into the dirty water. The driver kept seeing women,
beautiful women, and he kept talking. The passenger, who
was nervous, or preoccupied, said very little, but what he said
was just enough to signal that he was interested in what he
was being told. The driver grew confident and spoke about
his conquests, and spoke in greater detail, and his language
became more explicit than would be usual with a complete
stranger, especially a passenger who was really saying very
little. The taxi driver told him about one woman, she had
given him the best blow-job he had ever had. She was able
to do that because she had taken it right back into her throat.
There were very few women who could do that. Perhaps only
5 per cent. Then they could make you come by moving very
slowly, and when you did you exploded.

'Incredible.'

They were stopped at a traffic light and the taxi driver was
leaning back and shaking his head, remembering.

'But what if your wife –' said the passenger. 'If she was to
go with someone else?'

The taxi driver turned his head and the passenger saw
his own face reflected in the mirror glasses, his face red from
the heat, and he saw how puzzled his reflection was, and
he even saw the small nervous movement of his own lip as

he worried he might have offended the driver. It had been a banal thing to say. The kind of thing a teenager might have said.

The driver looked ahead to the road and put the machine in gear and took off from the lights.

'Different if a woman does it,' said the driver.

As they crossed the bridge the driver spoke more thoughtfully than before:

'It's not that men and women are so different. Some people say they are but I don't agree. I think women like to fuck just as much as men. Probably more. I think they get more pleasure from it, the noise they make. I always get a cunt to tell me her fantasies. I encourage them to talk. They always seem shy about it but then you hear the most incredible things. Maybe stuff they won't ever do but they certainly like to think about it. Stuff with other women. Threesomes. Being tied up. Having someone pretend to rape them. And that's just the usual kind of thing. I'm sure there's plenty of stuff they don't say too, because they're ashamed. There's all kinds of kinky dirty stuff they want to do but most of the time they can't. Because the difference between a man and a woman is that we're allowed to try to do whatever we can do. If a woman does it people call her a whore. That's the rule. Not a fair rule. But it's there. It's like driving. There's a few rules or we smash into each other. So if a woman, my wife or your girlfriend, or whoever, fucks around, it means she doesn't care about the rules any more. You can't have relationships without rules. That's why we don't let our women fuck around. Our self-respect depends on it because there's another attitude to the woman who fucks around.'

The driver continued speaking all the way to the station. He had hit on a subject he felt he knew something about. He

3

re-emphasized periodically that he was not a crude chau-vinist, that in fact he had a sophisticated understanding of the female mind. The passenger no longer spoke at all, or even nodded, and sometimes he looked away from the driver, out the side window, at the buildings and the people in the hot street.

They pulled up in front of the station. The driver asked the passenger if he needed a ride back again with his girl-friend and the passenger said, well, yes, he supposed he did.

'Don't bother, pay me at the end, I trust you,' said the driver, turning off the engine and the meter. They had come a long way, from the eastern outskirts of the city, and there was quite a lot of money on the meter.

It was a gesture the driver enjoyed. The passenger would return, he would drive him further, and if anything he would receive more of a tip for his friendliness. He did trust the pas-senger. He had enjoyed talking to him. He knew who he could trust. It had only ever happened once that a fare he had trusted had not returned, and that was a long time ago.

'I'm going to get a cola,' said the driver, getting out and locking the car. They walked into the shade of the ticket hall together. The driver wore light sandals and the passenger wore heavy walking boots, inappropriate for such weather. 'The best fucks,' said the driver, 'are when you haven't seen her for a while. Even if it's your wife, the reunion fuck is always notable.' The driver stopped at a kiosk and the passenger walked on towards the platforms. The back of his T-shirt clung to his back with sweat.

Ten minutes later they were together again in the ticket hall.

'Where is she?' said the driver.

The passenger shook his head from side to side. His misery was now complete.

'Maybe she missed her train,' said the driver, though he knew that this was not what had happened.

'No.'

'I'm sorry,' said the driver. He really did feel sorry for the boy.

'I told her I would forgive her,' said the boy. 'If she got on that train and came back.'

Outside, the light hit them suddenly. The buildings were reddening in the slanting rays and the shadows of the people stretched across the pavement. The boy stopped for a moment and passed his hand over his face once. Then he pulled himself together and got in the taxi.

The taxi driver thought maybe he would take the boy all the way back for free. Then he reasoned that this would be a particularly useless gesture, and perhaps even embarrassing for them both.

He drove. This time he kept his mouth shut the whole way.

In the Neighbourhood

Nic sat up in bed. He was very hungry. He could see the tops of the poplars, swaying outside his eighth-floor window. Beyond the gently swaying trees were other blocks. The trees were newly in leaf and he could hear the agitation of many small birds. He felt there must be something to do on such a morning. He rose and dressed.

When Nic was growing up in the village there was always something to do on spring mornings. In the block, in the city, for a pensioner, there was usually nothing to do. He had lived in the block for twenty-five years, growing old in the neighbourhood.

He made coffee and brought it to Maria, still sleepy in the bed. 'It's very strong,' she said, propping herself with pillows and sipping. He went back to their small kitchen and cracked three eggs into a bowl. The yolks were bright yellow. He scrambled them and crumbled in sharp sheep's cheese and the chopped leaves of green onions and stirred it all into a spitting pan. When it was ready, he brought it to her in bed. He sat on the side of the bed and they ate it together from the same plate with bread left over from yesterday. When they had finished eating he put on his shoes.

'You're lively today,' said Maria.

Nic put on his jacket and went out. Maria heard a thump from the ceiling. The boy upstairs had dropped something again.

★

Alex Duhovi, ninth floor, reached for the alarm clock and knocked over the stool on which it sat. Then he had to get out of bed to turn the clock off. He had to get to the doctor before work. He scratched his head. It was too early and making the coffee looked complicated. He ironed his shirt too quickly, put on his tie, swallowed the coffee and stepped into the hallway and locked his door. An old man was leaving the apartment of his next-door neighbour – the one who drank and sang to himself at night – with a couple of crow-bars. Alex nodded to the old man.

Alex left the building, turned right and walked the small intersecting roads of the neighbourhood. There were maybe fifty blocks, perhaps a hundred, most of them ten storeys high, in an area framed by a quadrilateral of big roads. In the quiet streets between the buildings trees had grown, some nearly as tall as the tallest buildings, and you heard the cool cooing of the pigeons, the frivolous twittering of smaller birds. Alex held to the quiet streets in order to avoid the smoke and noise as long as he could.

He emerged at the intersection. There was a McDonald's on the other side of the road. He crossed the road, skirted the back of the McDrive and crossed a vacant lot covered with broken glass and weeds. Near the remains of a fire made by homeless people was the head of a plastic doll. It had blonde hair and bright blue eyes. He gave it a kick. He walked along a big road. The traffic was heavy and the air was bad. It was like a road on the outskirts of any city: small ware-houses and wholesalers of construction materials and a small textile factory and some anonymous, possibly disused, build-ings surrounded by walls topped with barbed wire.

The clinic was at the next intersection. A man in a dirty jacket sat on the clinic steps, smoking. His hair was greasy.

The clinic building looked like a school for training welders and plumbers. Inside were queues and corridors and doors and rooms like classrooms. Only the smell of disinfectant suggested the practice of medicine. In the hallway Alex queued and said what kind of a specialist he wanted to see and paid and got a ticket. This was the better kind of hospital. In the free hospitals you sat in a queue all day, looking at the wall.

Alex went to the second floor and knocked at door 214. Silence. He tried the handle. Locked. He walked up and down the corridor and looked at rooms. Some of the rooms had instruments. He thought of boys doing science experiments in damp boarding schools, learning Latin and 'Science' and getting caned in an era when Progress was a Fact. Bunsen burners and test tubes and Petri dishes and the periodic table. Everything looked terribly old. A museum exhibit of medieval instruments of torture. Alex walked to the window at the end of the hallway and looked out at what appeared to be a ruined factory.

If you want to see how a city is doing, he thought, you have to see the edge of it. The centre will tell you everything is fine. The periphery tells the rest.

Looking at the factory, thinking of schools and hospitals and warehouses and offices, for no reason he remembered a book he had when he was a little boy called *Podger's Day*. Podger Pup was so naughty, he ran around the farmyard and Daisy Cow chased him and Mrs Chicky chased him, and the farmer's wife chased him when he dirtied her freshly washed sheets, everybody chased poor Podger Pup away. Finally the little boy rescued him and they fell asleep. That was the end of the story.

The dermatologist arrived. He was eighty years old and had trouble getting the door open. He couldn't get the key in. Alex could see the key was upside down, but the doctor kept trying to jam the upside-down key into the door.

Oh good Christ, thought Alex. He knew the day would be very long.

They went inside. They had their usual chat and Alex took out his penis for the doctor to examine. A common candida. It looked like it had been scalded. Week after week, nothing seemed to work. Pills, creams, ointments, restrictions on sexual activity, money down the drain, visits to the dermatologist when he should have been sleeping. And though he had his doubts about the doctor's eyesight, each week he would roll back his foreskin and the doctor would nod and tell him it was coming along fine, give it one more week.

The doctor told Alex how many years he'd been practising; why, before Alex was even born! The doctor always told Alex what age he was. He was very proud of having survived so long, to be still breathing and writing out prescriptions, and he made out a new one for Alex. He told Alex to trust him. Alex felt he had no choice.

Nic went to the ninth floor to borrow a crowbar from a neighbour. Mr Molnar had plenty of good tools but he had not used any of them for about a decade. He had become unsteady on his feet. His watery blue eyes did not focus. He drank and looked out the window. It was early and he was still in a fog from the previous night's drinking. Nic found two crowbars and thanked him. Molnar did not reply. Sitting by the window in an old dressing gown, the light behind him illuminated a long sparse tuft of white hair standing upright on top of his head.

It is not death itself that is terrible, Nic thought, taking the lift down to the ground floor. What is terrible is death in life.

All around him were men who had given up. Everywhere he saw defeated faces. These men had lost more than love, or the spirit of love, they had lost the fight. They were bodies taking up space. If you thought how little of them was left, they were just digestive systems consuming too much, growing fat, inhaling clean air and respiring it foul. Waiting for the sound of an ambulance in the distance. When they actually died there was very little left to remove.

He went outside with the crowbars. He enjoyed the weight of the metal bars pulling on his arms. It had been a long winter and he was glad it was over. He thought how it would be in the country. There was always work to do in the country. In the country you were either dead or alive, none of the confused walking death of the city old. When a peasant gets sick and is stuck in bed he goes quickly. He knows he can't work, and he decides to die.

On the footpath in front of the apartment block was an enormous chunk of concrete, too big for one man to lift. Perhaps four men could make a go of it. It had been part of the footpath. Several months before, a digger had ripped it up so that labourers could continue down with picks and shovels to the hot-water pipes. Hot water, heated on the other side of the city. Once a generous present from the old regime, now a liability. The old pipes leaked as much into the cold earth as they gave the apartment buildings.

And the slab had been left like that. A displaced slab and a hole in the ground and a sense that everything was falling apart. He was looking in the hole when Catalin appeared, a gaming board under his arm.

'Morning, Coco. Are you well?'

'I'm well, and are you well yourself?'

'Particularly well. Going somewhere special?'

'Just a game of backgammon.'

Down at the market the retired, and the prematurely retired for medical reasons, passed their time over gaming boards, weather permitting. Some drank, some did not.

'There's a job here. Here's a hole. Here's a piece that plugs it. Been a while since you last plugged a hole, I imagine, Coco.'

'About as recently as yourself, I imagine, Nic,' said Coco.

A commotion in the branches above as one pigeon tried to rape another.

'Well, it's a job for two, if you're physically up to it. What do you say?'

It looked like trouble to Coco. He would have much preferred to play backgammon, or just watch the traffic at the intersection.

Coco put the backgammon board on the ground, under a bush. He hoped it would not take too long.

On the third floor, George Ristache woke to the singing of birds and the rasping of metal on concrete.

Beside his bed was a photograph of his wife, Madalina, deceased, and a glass of water. He sipped some water.

Today, he remembered, I have another funeral.

It was the funeral of a younger man. George Ristache was seventy years old and Andrei had been his student years before, when George had taught French literature at the university. Andrei had raised a family and then his wife had left him. He gave the family apartment to a son who was getting married, then moved into George's block, which consisted entirely of one-room apartments. That was how they met again, after all the years. The difference between them of sixteen years no longer seemed very significant. Of course, they had re-encountered each other in a world different from that

which they had inhabited before. Their youth had been the
era of the construction of socialism, while the new era was
the construction of something else, and the falling apart
of something else again. They had been very happy to see
each other like that, faces from a time that was the start of
something. They had both lost their women and were now
living in small rooms and sometimes they would meet in the
evening. Not so very often. They talked about the past but
also about other things. They were both readers, and they
exchanged and discussed books.

Andrei had never mentioned to George that there was anything wrong with his heart.

Alex left the hospital. He had one more place to go before
he went to work. He had to walk around for a terribly long
time. There was a lot of noise and smoke and ugly people,
and roads to cross. There would be a road, then another road
just like the one before, maybe a little worse or a little better,
but substantially the same.

He passed the country people at an intersection where on
the ground they had laid out eggs and bunches of parsley and
scallions and radishes and big plastic bottles of milk. One of
the peasant women was arguing with another, arguing over
a piece of footpath. There seemed to be plenty of space but
they both wanted the same piece of concrete. The first woman
said the second woman was in her place and the second
woman said no, she was always there.

Finally, after many such roads and hundreds of cars and
faces, very few of them pleasant, Alex arrived at the office of
the electricity company. There was a long line stretching all
the way down the stairs and out the door, and it was not
moving. They were mostly old people.

Alex asked the last man in the line what the queue was for, though he had already guessed.

'For paying our bills.' The man smiled. He appeared to think it was amusing. Alex got in line. The man was still smiling at him. He seemed friendly, ready to get into conversation. He stank. Alex looked away until the man lost interest. Then another man came along and asked Alex what the line was for and Alex told him. The man got into line behind Alex. He stank too.

Ah, fuck it, thought Alex. Fuck it to hell.

He stepped out of the queue and walked away fast.

He knew he had done an unreasonable thing, as the next day he would have to get up early again and go pay his bill, and there was always someone who was mad or stank, or both, and that was just the way it was. But the immediate feeling was one of relief, to be walking and not standing.

He went down into the metro station and the train did not come for ten minutes, and then when it did, and everyone had boarded and was ready to go, it did not move.

Some days you had no luck. Some days it was stacked against you.

The big things you could see, and struggle with, and perhaps you would win or perhaps you would lose. But you could also be defeated by an accumulation of little things, without even realizing it. So many little things that you could not count them.

Too many in one day, you felt shitted on.

The train remained motionless, and there was no particular reason. Or if there was, it was not given, so there might as well not have been. But if there had been a reason and if it had been given it might not have made much difference anyway. After fifteen minutes you began to wonder if perhaps you would be there for fifteen minutes more after that. Why not? How long would people sit without an explanation, waiting? That was the underlying principle of faith. Faith was a shot of vodka to ease the strain of waiting. He was going to come. And if you abandoned faith just before He did, or left the metro car after twenty minutes of paralysis and just then the doors closed behind you and the train disappeared off down the tunnel, why then you'd feel worse than ever!

Waiting twenty minutes in a metro car was certainly different from sitting at a café terrace in Montmartre on a sunny afternoon. There was nothing to look at. There were the other people, but you did not want to look at them. It was like watching your life drip away, watching it plip plip plip from your wrist and gather in a pool on the floor. And as the minutes passed, and became perhaps twenty minutes, the people, who each had their own individual problems, began to feel restless, and though no one spoke many people wanted to scream. None of them would, not now. Later perhaps. Somewhere in Mongolia a straw set on a camel's back sent the poor beast sprawling in the sand, tongue hanging out, legs splayed to the four points of the compass. What was the last straw for a human being? If you beat them, they took it if they had no choice, and if you beat them every day they kept on living because that is what human beings try to do. But what was going on inside people while they were made to wait on nothing?

Something that was not good, that was what.

There was nobody reading a book except a fat woman and it was something cheap about love, and anybody else who read had a copy of a newspaper called *Freedom*.

Freedom could be extremely funny if you were in a good mood, you laughed along with the crowd, but on days when the crowd looked a shade putrid *Freedom* was just more evidence of something rotten in the state of Denmark. MAN CHARGED! said the headline. Apparently Jonni Bozovici would stick a couple of nails in a 220-volt socket to sober up whenever he had had too many. There was a rather blurred picture of Jonni. He looked like he had not done well at school and his ears stuck out. Then there was something about a television presenter who had invested in a new pair of tits.

The great thing about *Freedom* was that you could try to forget who you were, and who was around you, while you rode to work. The other great thing about *Freedom* was you could wipe yourself with it.

There was a story on the back about the world's cleverest monkey. Apparently he knew in excess of 200 words and by pressing buttons could order any drink he wanted.

They teach that monkey any more words, thought Alex, I'll be out of a job.

Dorin woke and sniffed himself. Today he would definitely wash and leave the apartment. The sun was coming through his tenth-floor window and the colours were rich, objects solid, angles angular. Everything was very itself. He arose from his mattress, a strip of foam a little too short for him on the bare floor. Today was the day to sort out which paintings to sell and which to burn. Call it spring-cleaning. He went to the window. Below, two men were beetling about with crowbars and a lump of stone. He went to the bathroom. He pissed, gasped with satisfaction as the stream was released and the loud frothy slash churned the bowl. He put his head under the tap and drank, slopping and slurping the cold water.

Barefoot, he surveyed the scene. He had been productive, if nothing else. Along with the older stuff there were many new paintings, some of them astoundingly good, most of them abortions.

All the paintings were of the same thing: the view of the apartment blocks opposite his own. Yet no two were alike. It had occurred to him one day that he could devote his entire life to the view from his window. Every time he looked, the light, the weather, the season, his disposition threw up something new. In one painting the trees were shivery wet and the skies leaden, in another the sun glinted on windows while the trees turned mellow autumn colours. There were suffocating monochrome blankets of winter mist, there were enormous foreground snowflakes around which bits of buildings peeked, there were tropical trees asserting themselves greenly, there were pictures where the metal flash of the tangle of aerials on the flat rooftops of the blocks was the most significant thing, there were night-time pictures where the apartments were random squares of lighted windows, gaudy as Manhattan. And then there was the arbitrary frame to be thrown around what he had chosen to represent.

Alex worked in a big new building. You went past security guards, used an electronic card to gain admission through a stainless-steel turnstile, got into a big shiny lift, got out at the sixth. *EMPLOYEES ONLY PAST THIS POINT*. Another swipe of the card, and he entered a huge open-plan office. People were working at desks, dazed by electronic screens. Alex took his seat and turned on his computer. He was thirty minutes late. Not that anyone would comment, it was not that kind of place. You were judged, in the end, on performance. Very sophisticated. Primitive systems of discipline depend on the prisoner, or worker, being continually watched. But if the prisoner or worker never knows when he is being watched, he has to watch himself. And then when he has got into the habit of being permanently on his toes, the result is an office worker. Serve him a bowl of shit, he grins and asked for seconds. No beatings necessary because he was self-beating. He had convinced himself he needed a wide-screen TV and a washing machine. Or he wanted a woman, and she wanted the washing machine. Like the one Dorin liked to tell about Adam and Eve. One day Eve says to Adam, buy me a washing machine. But baby, says Adam, we don't wear clothes. Yeah, says Eve, but if you got a job you could buy me some.

And of course a car so they did not have to use public transport. That would keep them busy for years.

A lanky man walked past Alex's desk. Edgar was from northern Europe. His skin was pink and his blond hair had just a touch of dirty nicotine-yellow. Edgar was a manager and he kept finding problems in the texts Alex edited and it would filter back to Alex that he was unhappy, but the meeting to resolve the problems was always forgotten or postponed as Edgar uncovered new problems with other people. Edgar was nervous because he was a senior manager and it was make or break for being made a partner. He was nearly forty and had a couple of young children. He had been sucked into the job and could not imagine anything else. He had to become a partner. So in the meantime he had the jitters and was out to score points and find problems everywhere, which he would then fix, proving his indispensability. Alex thought of the two peasant women arguing over their scrap of concrete. Same game.

But the air was certainly an improvement on the world outside, Alex had to admit. The windows did not open but the environment was atmospherically controlled. And the people, if they smelled at all, smelled rather good.

Adina, a paragon of fragrance, approached with a sheaf of papers for his attention. He was sure she coordinated her clothes with her scent. Today she was pale lilac towards icy blue and smelled of peppermint flowers. Amazing. And an excellent body. She handed him a document to edit. It was full of words.

And it was not true about the monkey, either. Alex's job was pretty safe. The world was full of monkeys that had learned lots of words. It was so easy to get words wrong. When words came out right, the right ones and the right amount, you didn't notice the words so much as the effect they had. The magic essence departed from the substance, the music played. Yet when the instrument was out of key and the dancer tripped you saw how many ways there were to do it wrong. Dentistry and plumbing were doing excellently but in the use of language, and several other key aspects of civilization, the human race was stuck in the dirt, foot on the accelerator, the wheels spraying mud. Alex scanned the document on his desk. *In respect of the provisions of the applicable relevant existing legislation currently in force* . . . Alex was master of the red pen and the delete button; he put a red line through the clause and wrote: *By law* . . . His days were spent wading through verbiage, slashing redundancies, detonating the foundations of the architecture of misconceived sentences, salvaging the sense and reassembling the basic blocks of meaning so that the text could be read, if not with pleasure, at least painlessly.

Nic and Coco used the crowbars to shift the concrete slab back to from where it came. It was frustrating work. All the pushing and scraping hardly moved the thing. The slab was rounded underneath and, when raised from one or other of the edges that it rested upon, preferred to revolve rather than shift laterally. They were both sweating. Their first sweat of the year. Nic felt a little nauseous from the sudden exertion and by the look of him Coco did not feel well either.

'It's no good,' said Coco. The two or three metres it had to move were rather too many.

Five minutes later Nic had the solution. He placed a fence-post under the slab as a roller and both of them levered from the other side. Progress was painstaking using this method – a few centimetres at a time – but linear.

'You see,' said Nic, 'now we are using the stone's own weight to move it forward. We lift it slightly and gravity does the rest. That's how the pyramids of Egypt were built, using rollers.'

'And slaves.'

In less than an hour they had the slab in the hole.

It did not fit.

Perhaps the water company had displaced rocks or dirt into the hole. The slab sat slightly above the level of the pavement and tilted upwards like the prow of a ship. It was perfect for tripping over when drunk or breaking your toe on.

Coco believed it was fine. It was a great improvement.

'We can't leave it like that,' said Nic.

'Too late now.'

Nic decided the only way to go was to get the slab back out, dig deeper, then replace the slab and even out the difference by laying some cement. In order to get the slab back out one man would have to lever it while the other dropped small stones in underneath, causing it to slowly rise.

The work had just begun when Maria called down to Nic from their window.

★

Nic's walls were wet and various concerned neighbours were now in Nic's apartment, as was Mr George Ristache, the vice-head of the residents' association, a proper old gentleman in a jacket and tie. Walls were already soaking all the way to the fifth floor and the problem was getting worse. Nic figured that a pipe had burst somewhere on the ninth or tenth and water was pouring down the utility shaft. The head of the residents' association was in hospital and Ristache looked confused as to what to do. He looked like he had not slept for a month. There were deep black circles round his eyes. Nic said he would go down to the basement and turn off the water supply for that column. Narcisa Tudor, a fat garrulous woman from the seventh, went to call for a plumber.

Ristache visited the ninth floor. Nobody was home. He headed for the tenth.

Dorin's coffee had hardly brewed when there was a knock on the door. An old man with deep black circles round his eyes like a racoon wanted to know if his walls were wet.

George Ristache took in the pictures as best he could, without wanting to seem nosy. It was a strange room and the strange paintings covered the walls and were piled in stacks on the floor. A mattress and an easel and a stool were the only furniture. A large French flag draped the wall above the mattress. George entered the little kitchen and could hear the burst pipe hissing behind the wall. The hissing eased off and stopped, meaning Nic was down in the basement with a spanner, sleeves rolled up, turning a valve – the correct one. George knew he was not such a practical type. It was good to have a neighbour like Nic, who knew what to do and did it. It was a block of incompetents and complainers, and quite a few nuts. And now this artist type. Every morning George put on his shirt, and put on his tie, like he did when he still taught at the university. He felt he was defending something with a core of decency to it. Something that was surely, very surely, slipping away. Something that had to be done to hold back the mounting pressure of a world of burst pipes and rising bills and falling standards and children with foul mouths who stood around on corners, spitting. Well, he wasn't wearing his glasses but some of these pictures by the fellow with the beard were not bad, not bad at all. But they all showed essentially the same thing, the view from the tenth floor, showed it in different ways. 'It all shows essentially the same thing,' said George, expressing a polite interest, though he would rather just have looked without speaking. 'No,' said the artist type. 'It shows essentially different things.' George thought it better not to get into the ramifications of such a statement, as the argument was an old one – shall I be Parmenides today while the man on the tenth does Heraclitus? Meanwhile a plumber had to be found because the imme- diate choice was inundation or no running water. 'As you wish, essentially different, from the same perspective,' said Ristache, finding himself unable not to speak.

'The same perspective,' said the painter, pulling his beard, head framed, from where Ristache stood, by the French tri- colour. 'But, as Flaubert said, "For something to become interesting, it is enough to regard it at length."'

'Yes, yes,' said George. 'By which he meant with attention. And care.'

Walking down the tenth-floor hallway to the lift, George remembered. He looked at his watch. Soon they would be here to remove the body.

He promised himself that before the day was over he would pick up Flaubert. It had been a long time. You had to keep a moment sacred and free for the good things, the things made with care.

Dorin found it a bit rough, at that hour, for his apartment to be filled with nutty neighbours. Shortly after old Ristache had cleared out they began to arrive. A cross-section of the building's inhabitants – those who lived below him, right down to the second floor – were now intimately bound to him thanks to the defective pipe in the shaft behind his kitchen wall. Sweet solitude murdered by bad plumbing. Nic from the eighth arrived up from the basement, spanner in hand. Old Mr Carol from down the hall had noted the commotion and had barged in without knocking and was now arguing with another of the neighbours about some piece of history. The conversation about how to proceed in the absence of Mr Popa, the head of the residents' association, kept veering into political disagreements about past events. 'Let's not dig up the dead,' said Narcisa Tudor, the fat woman from the seventh, to Mr Carol. When Carol got into a conversation with the woman from the fourth, Narcisa leaned in to Dorin and told him how Carol had taken money from everyone to repaint the hallways, but the paint was cheap stuff, it came off on your clothes when you brushed against it, it couldn't have cost that much.

Narcisa was delighted with Dorin. She told him that she too had wanted to be a painter when she was young, she had been very good at school, but her parents had made her do accountancy instead. The firm she worked for had gone bankrupt six months ago and now she wished she had something to do, it was just her at home all day, and her dog. Dorin did not respond. He knew two categories of people. The majority thought playing with paint was a stupid activity for a grown man, while a small group had wanted to be painters them-selves. Members of the second group always had a reason why they did not paint. Usually a member of the first group had stopped them.

Narcisa had called a plumber and Dorin promised to stay in and wait for him. He then took the sole available seat, a wooden stool. He sat facing the wall, crossed his arms and chewed his lower lip. He sucked his beard, scratched his arm, jigged his leg. They got the idea and began to leave.

He could hear them still talking as they moved down the hallway. They would say it was because he was an artist. Like that explained it. He did not want to be rude. But so much talking was hard to take. He had a problem with men talking, but women talking really put him on edge. It was the sound rather than anything specific about the content. It sounded like chickens, the words ran together and it was just chickens gurgling and clucking, noise against noise.

After all the squabbling, Nic was glad to be heading back to work. On the way down he called at Coco's room. There was no decent way Coco could get out of it, as getting the slab back out of the hole required two men: one to use the crowbar while the other threw in little stones. No, he had committed himself and he would just have to go down and sweat and battle with the concrete like his crazy neighbour, who seemed to enjoy the whole thing.

Nic and Coco took turns straining and grunting with the crowbar and there were long rests to discuss strategy. Though progress was at first imperceptible, by lunchtime they had the satisfaction of having made an impossibly large piece of concrete float upon a lake of little rocks and stones. This basic engineering was for Nic a triumph over a substantial obstacle. Now they could think about rollering it aside and excavating.

It was quiet again and Dorin made some tea. He moved the stool so he could see the sky out the window, and the light shone through the golden glass of tea. Tea had to be drunk from a glass. Russians and Turks drank their tea from glasses. Those nations that drank from cups or muddied it with milk missed the point.

He was thinking about this, and watching the coils of steam rising in the clean light, patient and sinuous like the thoughts of a sage on a rock in India, when he heard a tiny sound at the door. He was unsure if someone had knocked. It could have been a small rodent scraping on wood.

He opened the door. It was the woman from the sixth. A little woman, a confused woman, a woman who rubbed her hands together, and was sorry, but her walls were leaking, and could he tell her, please, what was going to happen?

She was the humble type, sorry to disturb, regretting greatly the intrusion, et cetera. Yet her questions and apologies did not allow sufficient pause for an answer. She knew in advance what Dorin was going to say and was so eager to agree with him that she did not permit the response to be given. It was not possible for him to explain that a conference had just been held, and the plumbers were coming, and until then the water was off, and he had no idea who was going to pay.

She had missed the party. Probably all her life she had missed parties. Or not been invited to parties, because she was simply too annoying and did not realize what she herself was proof of – that people much prefer to speak than to listen.

Humble, yes, but not enough to ever shut up. Only stupid enough to talk.

Dorin closed the door in her face and went back to his seat by the window.

His tea was cold.

I'm living in a nuthouse, thought Dorin. A place confounded with speech. The Tower of Babel. Babble-onia. Baba-lonia. Hubba dubba. Yabba dabba.

He needed to wash, but of course the water was off. He looked around at his creations and remembered the spring-cleaning. There was crap that needed to be burned and the remainder needed to be stacked and the floor properly swept. He needed to hang around bars doing caricatures for some food money.

He went into the kitchen. There was nothing but a bag of rice, a few onions, some loose tea and half a bottle of vodka.

The vodka was good news.

Nic ate lunch with great appetite. The first spring greens of the season were in the market and he ate hunks of bread with a salad of lettuce and crunchy radishes and scallions, then a sour soup of root vegetables and meaty bones, and finally some fried potatoes. He talked Maria through the morning's job as she served. On the television planes screamed from the deck of an aircraft carrier and battle-ready troops bristling with technology smiled and waved to the camera. The scene changed and dark-skinned men with moustaches jumped about in a dusty street, shouting and gesticulating like angry monkeys. Yes, the good weather was back, Maria said. Soon there would be new potatoes, cherries, strawberries, green beans and tomatoes, all the things they had spent the winter without, and the price of the tomatoes would drop week by week until they were almost giving them away.

Nic was ready to go back to work when he heard a commotion. Cars were pulling up outside the block, people getting out. The women were dressed in black. He remembered. The fat man from the seventh. He had seemed healthy enough. But you never knew. A white van pulled up. He could not read, without his glasses, what was written on the side. They opened the back of the van and removed a coffin and carried it into the block. Well, he couldn't be messing around with a crowbar while they were carrying the corpse out to its final rest. It wouldn't be right. He remembered an exchange he had with another boy in his village. He had been perhaps seven years old. You have to have respect for the dead, said the older boy, no laughing or running. Why? asked Nic. Because if you don't, said the older boy, they'll come and get you.

The sons arrived and shook hands with George. That wasn't done before, thought George. You never used to shake someone's hand at a funeral. Perhaps nobody has told the young people. Or perhaps it was possible that such things, which he had considered immutable, were in fact subject to fashion, in which case he was out of step. The priest and the driver of the van did not attempt to shake hands with George. They each nodded to George. The driver of the van wore a white T-shirt, tight over his large belly.

The driver and another man carried the coffin up the stairs. The two sons got into a lift and George got in the other lift with the priest. They rode to the seventh. The priest looked away from George, at a corner of the roof of the lift, and tapped his foot. He held the book and cross to his chest.

'It's much simpler when they pass away in hospital,' said the priest. 'Less trouble all round for everyone.'

The sons opened the apartment and the coffin was brought

in. George waited outside on the landing. He looked out the window at the small group of people gathered below. He knew none of them. After several minutes the men carried the coffin out, preceded by the priest. The coffin was open and Andrei was covered by a white transparent veil. They began carrying the box down the stairs. The turn in the stairs was too tight for the length of the coffin. There was not enough room between the railings and the wall. Snagged, the men discussed what to do. The coffin would have to be lifted above the railings. They tried the new manoeuvre. It was difficult for the men on the lower steps, who had to take the weight of the coffin while raising their arms above their heads. It did not look stable. The corpse lurched as the box tilted. George turned away.

Andrei, like most, was from the country. In the country you removed the body from the house, put it on a cart. Now, they were struggling to get the corpse of an overweight man to his final rest down seven flights of stairs.

George took the lift down and waited with the others. The bearers appeared with the coffin, sweating. They began to load the coffin on to the back of the van, feet first. 'No,' cried the priest, 'head first.' They reversed and revolved 180 degrees, like a clumsy crab, all legs. The coffin slid in nicely. The priest arranged the flowers and the icon.

From the windows of the apartment block many people were watching. It was not interesting, but there was nothing else to do. Mr Zacarias, in a white vest, rested his elbows on his second-floor windowsill, smoking. His wife did not allow him to smoke in the house.

The doors at the back of the van were shut. *Electronic parts and fittings* was written on the side of the van, and a telephone number.

George took a lift with some younger people he did not know. He believed they were friends of one of the sons. He rode in the back. Nobody spoke.

Something is broken, thought George. Nobody knows how to behave, or what to say. Everybody is afraid. This city is wrong. These buildings are wrong. We are all here together but none of us know what we are doing. We don't even know how to bury a man.

George thought of his own body being carried down from the third and Zacarias, unshaven, bored, leaning out the window, smoking.

But George did not want to die in hospital either. He wanted to die in a house.

Pavel Popa, head of the residents' association, minutes after being discharged from the hospital, was squeezing onto an overcrowded bus. Another route with too many people and not enough buses. He put his hand into his left pocket, over his wallet, and held onto the overhead bar with his right hand. Though nobody around him smelled particularly bad the air was stale from too many people. An old fart with cotton wool in his ears and skin the colour of ash stood right next to Pavel, making a wet sucking sound in his ear. A few seconds, *chomp*. A pause, *slurp*. A sickening sensation of being inside a wet old mouth. They were jammed right up against each other, Pavel turned his face away so he didn't have to breathe the old fart's breath, slobbery suck every couple of seconds in his ear. It occurred with such regularity that the intervals between slurps were charged with expectation. Pavel set his teeth. He could not tell an old man with cotton wool in his ears to stop slurping. At that rate he'd be just one more nut on a bus. People were always snapping on buses. It was the old, generally, who would just let go. When it was no longer worth the fight to keep it in, that was when you knew you were old.

The bus moved toward the edge of the city, losing passengers.

Forty minutes after being discharged from hospital, Pavel slid into a seat, there being no wreck with a walking stick who needed it more. Immediately a fat man in a tracksuit was standing over him. He had eaten something. Rotten flesh spiced with garlic, perhaps, washed down with a cocktail of bad vodka, sour milk and onion juice. Green waves passed over Pavel's face. The tracksuited man had run for the bus. He was breathing hard.

They levered and rolled the slab back – it was fast, satisfying work after what had gone before – and began emptying the hole of stones. Then they dug down further than they had to. They did not want to fail again.

The plumber and his assistant arrived in a beat-up car. Nic told them the trouble was on the tenth. Coco suggested a rest and a bottle of beer before doing the Egyptian thing again.

Nic fetched some empty bottles from his apartment and took them in a string bag to the shop at the intersection.

While between the blocks set back from the road you could hear the birds and play at being in the country, at the intersection there was no doubt where you were. Each road had four lanes, so the intersection involved eight lanes, and in the busy hours the air got smoky and loud with car horns. Buses, trolleybuses, petrol tankers, dump trucks full of gravel or soil heading to a construction site or a landfill, spewing thick clouds of noxious diesel smoke as they shuddered and jolted from the lights, quaking the earth like metal dinosaurs. And the cars. Shunting and braking and twitching nervously, the drivers nudging ahead and being pushed from behind, each with the sole aim of gaining a little ground in the jam.

Nic bought the beer, then stood waiting to cross the road again, the four bottles in the string bag. He had never owned a car. The horns were honking and squeaking and screaming, and then inevitably there was one who just leaned on it, held the note for seconds.

Forget writing, forget music, after millions of years of evolution there is a man whose signature is one long stupid note.

The longer you watched the longer it repeated itself, and the more truly frightening it became. It is in their repetition that the simplest human acts become terrible.

The lights would change, a new set of vehicles would come to a halt and the machines would repeat the same angry act of smoke and noise. The horns again, a frustrated mechanical swearing chorus.

At the corner where Nic stood was a kiosk where a Gypsy girl sold flowers. A monstrous truck took the corner and the concrete crust of the earth trembled and black smoke filled the nose of a girl selling red carnations and yellow roses and white lilies and lemon and indigo and cobalt cornflowers.

And behind the kiosk, among the trees, before the first row of blocks, the crazy boy who never spoke was working. Often you would see him there, constructing a makeshift fence with pieces of wood and bits of wire, obsessively extending and strengthening. And in this overlooked patch of earth between road and apartment block, among the trees and in the dirt where things were only beginning to sprout since the thaw, he had planted shrubs and saplings and bordered beds with stones and bricks. It was a little too rough to be beautiful, yet the decorative intent, in such a place, was startling. He had even erected a little handwritten sign: *No Trespassing*. Good luck! A digger from the water company was only a hundred metres beyond and had unearthed mountains of dirt, broken roots of ancient trees, to get down to the pipes that leaked away the hot water. It seemed to be digging a line towards the crazy boy's garden. But the boy, digging with a tiny fork, was, as always, oblivious. Yes, the crazy and the sane, each had to find something to settle them, some activity. Some cultivated their gardens, some played backgammon, some wrote bad verse. And any of these made at least as much sense as the surging ambitious anger of the young. To be someone! To go someplace! Nic was glad he was no longer young, chained to the struggle to make something of himself, and trying to find a woman to impress. Whatever he had made of himself time would soon undo. All he wanted was to move a slab of concrete. That would be enough for this fine day, when it was not too hot and not raining either.

Behind a car windscreen in the choked-up intersection the face of a driver twisted into a grimace. He was saying something, swearing, but Nic could only see his mouth move. And then leaning on the horn, the single idiot note. Mouths moving though the swearing could be heard by nobody, arms waving in anger, red yellow green, red yellow green, on and on.

They could not control themselves, their puppet arms jerking on nervous strings. And the boy quietly gardening, mad.

Soon rush hour would begin.

Pavel Popa got off the bus. It was pleasant to turn off the main road, to walk between the blocks and trees. It was good to be back in the neighbourhood. Nic and Coco were drinking a beer outside. They were working on some minor improvements and were pleased with themselves. Well, they hadn't much else to do these days. And he replied that his health was the same, it wasn't the best, but what could you do? And they told him the plumber was in, there was a burst pipe on the tenth, where the odd fellow with the beard lived.

'I saw it,' said Nic. 'Full of strange pictures. No furniture. Not even a television. A bit of an old mattress and a chair.'

Pavel nodded to a couple of old ladies, sunning themselves on the porch in dressing gowns with designs of faded leaves and flowers. Like a couple of lizards on a rock.

'Hello, Mr Popa.'

'Welcome back, Mr Popa.'

'Hello, ladies.'

They asked about his health and he made stoic noises. He was glad to be out of the hospital, hospitals made him feel sick, he said. We missed you, Mr Popa! I know you did, ladies. I'm not noticed till I'm gone and everything starts to go wrong, and then it's, what do we do, where's Popa? That's right, Mr Popa, that's very true. Well, ladies, as a matter of fact I shouldn't stand here talking.

Yes, it felt good to be back in the neighbourhood. He opened a door on which was written, in red marker in his own printed letters, *Please Close The Door*, past the letter boxes where there was a notice forbidding those distributing advertising from using the block's letter boxes unless they had a contract with the Administration allowing them to do so, signed, P. Popa, President of the Residents' Association. Into the hallway where, to his left, was a list of 132 apartments, columns for the sums owed by each for waste-disposal services, gas, hot water, cold water, heating, lift, and maintenance and staff expenses (mostly Aurelia the cleaning lady, detergent, light

bulbs for the hallways and numerous small repairs). The main
expense was heating and hot water, on account of the hot
water being pumped through old pipes from the power station on the other side of the city. The water dribbled into the
ground and the water company had to dig up whole streets.
What arrived to the block was metered but individual con-
sumption within the block was not. So people with faulty
taps let scalding water dribble down the drain. If somebody
was out at work all day, or in hospital, they left their radia-
tors on, they wanted it to be toasty when they got back. The
apartments on the south-facing side of the block would
inevitably be too warm on a sunny day and people would
open their balcony doors and release the hot air into the atmosphere. It was a rotten system that impoverished everybody,
but you could not have the old things dying of hypothermia,
expiring from pneumonia, and so the system creaked along.
People complained of the hardship. The bills, the bills! In the
kingdom of hardship, Popa had become the people's priest.
They came to him with their grievances, their tales of woe,
their ailments, their piles, their indigestion, their discomfi-
ture, their confusion, their disappointment, their melancholy,
their political commentary, their nostalgia, and he took their
money, entered it in the accounts and commiserated, shaking
his head, saying, What can you do? After all, the people were
not going to rise up, carrying pitchforks and axes, and sur-
round the heating utility, demanding justice. The people had
their pensions and were sleepy in the afternoon, and were
just confused why they were not given as much as before,
which was not so terribly much in the first place. Something
was rotten somewhere, they knew that much, and as months
dragged to years, as they cooked their meals and pulled their
toilet chains, clarity was not forthcoming. They theorized,

swore at each other, especially in queues in post offices and queuing to pay at the electricity company, or at the market, or on buses, but mostly they shrugged and said, What can you do?

The plumber and his assistant filled Dorin's tiny kitchen. The assistant was an undersized young man who kept his wool hat on while he worked. It was floppy at the top and made him look like a gnome, or a moron. They removed the sink from the wall, broke Dorin's only plate and smashed a hole in the wall with a lump hammer.

'Hey,' said Dorin through the pounding, 'you're going to fix that?'

'We've got to break it first,' said the plumber.

'But let's get something straight. I don't shell out for this. The cost of fixing the wall is included in the repairs.'

'Absolutely,' said the plumber, pounding.

The hole in the wall allowed the plumbers to see where the leak was. Further down. So they smashed another hole in the wall.

Popa arrived. He gave the apartment a look around. Even stranger than he had anticipated. Then he recovered his air of authority and went straight to the kitchen.

'You the administrator?' asked the plumber.

'Head of the residents' association. The administrator is dead.'

Two years before, after several decades writing receipts in a painstakingly neat hand, the last administrator had been found dead on the floor of his room on the third.

The first week all Alex had wanted to do was run out and get drunk. It was like a school library, everybody clacking away, churning out turgid wads of prose on tax law. But that was then. Now he did not think he would ever manage to escape. He had got used to the collar. Now it seemed normal to shave and iron a shirt. And it was air-conditioned and clean and the coffee and internet were free and the toilets smelled of lemon air freshener and never had splashes of yellow water on the seats. And the excitement of another pay cheque coming up.

And there was Carmen.

He could see her profile and, under the table, her legs. Her profile was not bad but her legs were excellent. She wore a skirt and sandals. She watched her screen and clicked her mouse and checked accounts, and meanwhile her legs had a life of their own. One thing was going on above the decks and something entirely different was happening downstairs. Long slim legs, crossing and recrossing, jigging rhythmically. Her right leg was crossed over her left and the toes of her raised foot started rotating in slow eloquent circles at the end of those shapely legs, the sandals hanging whimsically off the end off the foot. Jesus. Did she know he was watching? It was like she was communicating to him directly. Of course she wasn't. No, but the legs were talking to him, reciting lines of extraordinary erotic poetry. Alex shifted in his seat to ease the congestion in his trousers. Maybe she was sending him a message, but she didn't even know it herself. No, that was the way crazy people thought. Jesus told me to do it, your honour. Then the circles stopped and she started jigging again. Ripples of movement passing all the way up her legs, through her thighs, to her hips. What secret music was she hearing? Alex's modem emitted a little beep. He had a message. There was work to do. But the legs were calling out to him. She was getting random now, her leg moving slowly, the foot flexing outwards with the dangling sandal. Then she held the leg up, pointing straight out, the foot moving to the side. What did it signal? It was a language of some sort. What was it saying? Amusing sex. Gentle sex. Nasty sex. Sexy sex.

While she checked accounts her legs begged Alex for affection.

She stood up, picked up a sheaf of documents and walked away, her hips swaying.

Jesus, thought Alex, I should snap out of this. I'll end up arrested for something.

He read the message.

Dear Mr Duhovi,

I'm afraid our magazine cannot publish any of these stories either. Frankly, the attitude to women becomes more than a little grating.

'On Her Tail', the story where a man has a relationship with the backside of a woman he sees in the street (where he follows her around all day and where they have entire conversations without the actual woman participating in any way), is cleverly constructed and amusing in its way, but ultimately the subject of the stalking of women by mentally unbalanced men needs a sensitive treatment, and you do not give it one. I think you know what I mean.

Should you ever attempt a different kind of story, we would be interested in seeing it.

Yours, etc.

Carmen returned and with a single fluid motion reassumed her place. The legs started up again.

Alex went to the bathroom. Through a glass door, then the door marked 'Toilets', then you chose between doors marked 'Men' and 'Women', and then you were at the wash-basins. Through another door into the toilet area. The last door was the stall. Alex entered and locked it. Lemon air freshener. Five doors to reach the inner sanctum of excretion, far from the keyboard-clacking crowd. Alex opened his trousers and closed his eyes and saw Carmen's legs. He worked it up. A good rhythm established itself. He kissed her instep. He was licking the inside of her thighs when he heard doors open. He kept going. Somebody took the stall next to his. He heard trousers being unhitched, a male backside taking the throne and letting it all go.

It was no good. He could not do it with someone phooting and phutting and grunting next to him.

Imagine, all those people, tapping away at keyboards in corporate bliss, filling up with gas, like balloons.

He zipped up and flushed for the sake of it. There was a sign on the cubicle partition, in English, that Alex always found amusing.

PLEASE USE THE TOILET BRUSH IF NECESSARY
THINK OF THE NEXT PERSON

Perhaps, he thought, that's what this country needs after all. Colonization by a civilization with superior toilet-training. A bit of corporate hygiene. Lectures in Anglo-Saxon potty ethics before you went through the five doors and back to your fart-free work environment. No wonder the employees here felt privileged, being the advance corps of deodorized capitalism. It was not just the relatively high pay, it was being on the winning team. Apart and above another world outside that was rapidly decaying.

But it was the THINK OF THE NEXT PERSON bit

that made Alex smile. Who were you supposed to visualize while you scrubbed your cack stain?

Alex always thought of Edgar.

The plumber and his assistant replaced the broken pipe. The water company had been pumping water too hot, at too great a pressure, and old pipes were giving way all over the city.

They started putting the sink back in place. They were in a great hurry to be somewhere else. 'We'll be back tomorrow to patch the wall,' said the plumber.

Dorin and the plumber and the assistant went down to Popa's office, on the first floor.

It was not much of an office. There was a small table, behind which Popa sat. There was room for one other person to sit at the other side of the table and room then for two people to stand. The plumber and Popa sat facing each other. The plumber's assistant and Dorin stood, and were soon joined by Narcisa Tudor. Arguments were going on in various directions, and meanwhile an old woman arrived to pay her monthly bill. In the confined space Dorin realized again that he did not smell good. Perhaps now that the pipes were fixed the water would be back on.

'Really, that's far too much,' said Popa. 'That's impossible. We had a plumber in last week and it only cost half that much.'

'That's the price that was agreed. We've travelled across town. I had other jobs to take care of and we came here.'

Popa leaned back in his chair and exhaled smoke. Everything with him was a matter of negotiation. He was the calm smoking centre around which storms blew themselves out. There was nothing so simple that it could be resolved simply. Everything had to be teased out, worked up, and the same arguments repeated until the will of the participants to continue was finally exhausted. This was his art. Tempers flared, bad feelings were engendered, and when the passion to disagree was spent some kind of consensus would emerge.

Much breath wasted, thought Dorin, so many unnecessary words. He saw blunt stupid words, all the same colour. Words that did not mean what they meant literally, words that translated into strings of nos or yeses, negatives or affirmatives of various degrees of shrillness and obstinacy. Barely more inflected than the grunts of cavemen. Cavemen that did not hunt or gather, but sat around getting fat and sick and bitter, who could shit and flush it away, and were thrown into confusion and fits of grunting if the pipe blocked or broke. An aggregation of superfluous humanity, herded into concrete cubicles on the rim of a city. People lacking the strength to escape but with just enough to keep niggling each other. How long before such a species became extinct? Surely it would not be long. In the six years Dorin had lived there he had seen people wheeled out on trolleys, their faces covered with sheets. A waiting room for the terminally stupid.

Writing out a receipt for a woman paying her bill, Popa told Dorin that he would have to foot half the cost of the repairs, the problem having emanated from his kitchen. Absolutely not, thundered Dorin, the pipes were not in his kitchen. If they were in his kitchen, why did a hole have to be smashed in his kitchen wall? Was he supposed to pay for a hole to be smashed in his kitchen wall? If that was the case, next time there was a problem to be solved he would not be at home. He would clear out of the block altogether. What kind of a system was this? Yes, said Narcisa, there was no system in place. Things fell apart and there was no system.

Why wasn't a small sum collected from each of the residents on a monthly basis to cover repairs? I won't pay anything, said Dorin, the roof is falling in on me and the association has done nothing. The rain is coming in and the ceiling coming down in chunks. I'm afraid at times to touch the light switch with the water dripping off it.

'Excuse me,' said the plumber. 'The matter in hand?'

'Tomorrow,' said Popa. 'You have to come back in any case to finish up, to repair the wall.'

'I need to pay my assistant.'

'What difference does a day make? In any case, we have no money at present.'

'Somebody had just come to pay you.'

'Hasn't been entered in the books. It would be irregular to just hand over cash like that. That's not the way we do things.'

'The deal was we get paid today. I have no money. No money to pay my assistant, or to buy petrol to get back.'

Poverty, the final, winning argument. Everyone knew it was a barefaced lie, but calling the plumber's bluff would set Popa in the role of oppressor of the poor. Popa handed over the money and Narcisa talked of all the other things that needed to be looked at. There were broken taps throughout the building pouring precious hot water down the drain, a plumber could come along and sort that out. What was needed was a system, a contract with a plumber so that all the breakdowns were taken care of promptly. The plumber made out a receipt. Popa broached the subject. Some kind of a contract whereby the plumber would be paid a fixed sum by the block every month, whether there was something to be done or not. They could discuss a sum that would make it worth the plumber's while. An excellent idea, said the plumber. They would discuss it the next day, yes? When the plumber came to fix the wall, then he could look at the other problems around the block to sort out. The plumber and his assistant shook hands all round and left. It was nice. It had ended on a good note. The sun was coming in the window behind Mr Popa.

Yes, continued Narcisa, some kind of a system to pay for all these things breaking down . . .

The plumber and his assistant left the building with their bags of tools. They did not speak. They could hear through the open window on the first the same agitated conversation, the woman with the huge breasts talking about the need for some kind of system. Some kind of system, things breaking down, some kind of system . . . They passed two old boys fooling around with cement, who hailed them cheerfully. They reminded the plumber of children playing in the dirt, making mud pies. They put the tools on the back seat of the car and got inside. The assistant took out cigarettes and gave one to the plumber and lit the plumber's cigarette and then his own. They were tired and wanted to go home and shower and eat.

'Are you going to make a contract with them?' asked the assistant.

'Not before I grow a pair of tits,' said the plumber.

The assistant laughed. The plumber started the engine.

'It's falling apart and they're insane,' said the plumber. 'I'd be up there for every crazy old lady with a blocked sink.'

'That would be great,' said the assistant. 'Having a pair of tits.'

'You'd get no work done. You'd just sit around playing with your tits all the time.'

'Yeah,' said the assistant. 'It would be great.'

The plumber put the car in gear and drove away.

★

The service was in a small church squeezed between two large blocks, as if inserted as an afterthought. Which it was. First they built all the blocks and moved the workers in. Then the workers decided they had some other needs, when they were not working.

The coffin was reloaded into the van and the funeral convoy travelled out past the edge of the city. They turned right on to the ring road. Looking back across the sick starved fields they could see where the city began abruptly, the first row of blocks like a grey cliff face. Some of the prostitutes were already out, trying to hitch more than a ride. On a happier day some of the men would have honked their horns. The cortége passed the city dump, where Gypsy families were combing the hills of refuse for glass and plastic and metal, and turned left off the ring road after the cheese processing factory.

They parked and followed the coffin into the cemetery on foot. The cemetery was new and appeared unfinished. Its perimeter was made of the kind of reinforced concrete slabs that usually surrounded old factories or rail yards. They passed a pile of sand and then one of gravel, though there was no sign of anything being constructed. At the shell of the junked car they turned left. Vast emptiness, punctuated with gravestones and by a few feeble saplings looking scared of so much open space. They stopped beside the grave and the priest said the words. He sprinkled an amber fluid on Andrei's body from a half-litre plastic bottle, sprinkled dirt from a plastic container that had perhaps held yoghurt or sour cream.

Four labourers stood at the head of the grave. The mourners were gathered on the other side. The labourers had dug the grave and they would lower the body into it. Two of them held shovels. The day had warmed up and they wore long baggy shorts and singlets, and plastic sandals on their feet. They had the faces of men who had experienced nothing but hard labour and expected more of the same. People who could never entirely wash the dirt from their hands. Their bearing was unaffected by the mourners. So many holes that had to be dug, and then filled in again. Steady work, but badly paid.

George watched as two of the labourers placed the lid on to the coffin. The lid did not fit. The coffin was too shallow, or the corpse too big. The lid sat in place at the foot, but would not go down at the head. A ripple of discomfort passed through the crowd. What if they could not get the lid on? Had nobody checked beforehand? The labourers began pushing at the lid, forcing it down on to the face of the deceased. George looked away. He heard an authoritive voice say, 'Drive it in at an angle. That's it.' He heard the blows of the hammer knocking in the nails. When he looked again the problem was resolved.

The labourers used straps to lower the coffin into the hole, directed by the man who had given the advice about the nail. He was cleaner looking than the labourers, wore long trousers and leaned over the grave, giving advice on the coffin's descent, with a cigarette in the corner of his mouth. Ashes to ashes, thought George. Straps recovered, the men began shovelling the dirt back in the hole. It was very workmanlike. There is no special way to shovel dirt. The shovel scraped, the soil thudded on the coffin. People turned and walked away.

At the gates of the cemetery some of Andrei's women relatives had set up trestle tables, covered them with tablecloths and set out refreshments, including many glasses of wine and tiny glasses of a clear spirit. Though George was tired from so much standing, this was cheering after the unpleasantness of the burial. This is how it should be, he thought, observing the people beginning to relax and speak to each other. A man should be commemorated, not dispatched. He drank some wine.

The moment was short-lived. The priest barged through, all skirts and colour and energy. 'Come on now, be reasonable, we can't have you clogging up the cemetery gates. Really now, ladies, you'll have to start clearing up.' George felt disgust. He knew the type. Usually they were in government offices, heads of faculties. People sure of their power. People with the necessary skills for rising in a dictatorship, people with no ideas beyond smiling unctuously to the man above and being merciless to the man below. Then the dictator was gone and they were members of the ruling party, as smug and sure of themselves as ever, because they were on the inside, with their friends, running the show, and everybody else was on the outside. People who were used to the timid, the compliant, the passive. The women began to clear away the drinks and the food. Most of the drinks were untouched. The priest was telling them to get in their cars and drive back to the city. The people began to move. The priest disappeared into the church. People whispered as they left. Something about the priest, and money.

Dorin took the seat that the plumber had vacated. The association wouldn't even fix his roof, leaking for over a year, and now on top of this, was he supposed to pay for holes being smashed in his kitchen? When was the roof going to be fixed? His home was falling apart.

'Yes,' said Narcisa, 'some kind of system is required. Why should Dorin have to pay?'

'This is really not your business,' said Popa.

'What we need is some kind of a system, whereby everyone in the block contributes a little per month for common repairs.'

'People don't have any money,' said Popa.

'It's a matter of a small sum each.'

'You haven't paid your bills in months,' Popa reminded her.

'I've been unemployed!'

Popa shrugged, extinguished a cigarette. 'We all have problems.'

'Our problem is an incompetent administration! If things aren't getting fixed we need to hire a new administrator!'

'By all means.'

Narcisa swept out. Dorin and Popa said nothing for a moment. It was very quiet. It would be a shame to break it, thought Dorin. Let Popa do it. Dorin looked at a spider's web, very bright in the corner of the window. Gossamer threads, thought Dorin. Gossamer threads? What was gossamer anyway? Why did people use words like that? It was a spider's web. Flies got stuck in it and had the juice sucked out of them.

Still, it looked nice there, illuminated from behind. He heard Popa fumbling at the cellophane of a virgin packet of cigarettes. Another man smoking his way through health worries. Sick people smoking, that would be an interesting title for a painting. Amazing what you could do with a good title. Fat people eating, poor people smoking. No, that was more a title for a novel, and he wasn't going to go down that road. Far too much had been written already. The click of the lighter.

'The administration is elected, not hired,' said Popa, tiredly, exhaling the first drag. 'You know, I don't even get any money for this. I'm not paid a penny for all the work I do. They've asked me to take a salary, but I've refused it. I've lived here for a long time, you see. These pensioners, my neighbours, they have no money. I can't take from them.'

Dorin said nothing. There had been conflict, catharsis, and now the softer feelings would be indulged. He was now attending a scene of reconciliation. All he had to do was sit still and not spoil it. He knew Popa's type. Not hard-hearted, simply lazy, wanting to be seen as a kind of social worker. The plumber had played the right card. Of course, Popa was the same as Narcisa, essentially a busybody. Now that he had a position of responsibility he no longer appeared a busybody. Other champions of the people could get as excited as they wanted; Popa would sit behind his desk, unpaid, impassive to their taunts, chain-smoking. It paid to let such people perform their dramas. In exchange they gave you what you wanted.

'You don't have to pay,' said Popa, as if this was what he had intended to say all along. 'We'll take care of it. Of course, we want to help you with the roof too. There's no money at present. After the cost of the winter heating. A little later in the year, when the pressure is off.'

As if on cue, a frail old woman appeared beside them, nodding agreement. One of the many old ladies who adored Mr Popa, so competent and polite and concerned with their troubles. Mr Popa always had time to listen, to discuss health concerns, to commiserate about heating bills, the cost of medicine, the severity of the weather, to agree that politicians were thieves and decent people were poor. A real old lady's sort of a man.

'Yes, no money,' said the woman. She had just been down to the market, and had a parsnip and some parsley, which she would cook with rice. She opened the cloth bag to show them, and Popa nodded as if the parsnip and parsley were the ultimate proof of something. 'I was just passing by,' said the woman, 'and saw you back. How is your health?'

'The treatment does nothing. Still alive, in this dead life. But what can you do?'

'What can you do?' the old woman chimed.

Alex opened a new message on his screen.

It's over between us. I could give you a big long speech but I think you know what is wrong. I need more. More! And you don't want to give it. I want the passion like before. Passion! And you have none. Don't try to contact me.

Alex looked out the window. Dumped by electronic mail. After over a year together. It was going to be quite a century, with the way IT and improved transmission speeds were revolutionizing communication.

The bit about passion was a bit hard on a man with a sunburned member, though. Doctor's orders. It would have been easier to treat had they got it sooner, but both of them had been out of work and could not afford appointments and medicine.

He knew what she meant, though, about passion. She didn't just mean sex, though that was certainly included. He remembered one of their fights. As usual she was giving him a hard time about looking at women everywhere he went. He explained that the important thing was that they were together, that that was a choice, whereas sex was an indiscriminate urge. The fact was you could copulate with just about anybody, it made no difference. He gave her the example of one of her own indiscriminate copulations. Practically the village idiot. You had to deal with it, that your woman had been serviced by a renowned clown and people were discussing it. Be a man, he'd told himself. There were more important things than all those other cocks she'd had.

'That wasn't an accident. I chose him.'

Somewhere a tiger ate a lamb. Somewhere a bridge in a jungle collapsed. Somewhere in India a truck driver fell asleep at the wheel. Somewhere an idiot loaded bombs on to a plane. Somebody dropped a spoonful of paprika into a pot of pork and beans. It all made sense. A man smashed a big glass of red wine against a wall.

It was amazing, the area that could be spattered by a glass thrown with force against a white wall.

'Now,' he said. 'Whenever you look at that you can remember your choice.'

She went and huddled on the floor of the bathroom in the dark. The wine dripped down the walls behind the television where a winner was being announced at the MTV music awards. He went and picked her off the floor. Then they cleaned the glass up. They went to bed and made love, and it was very good.

She was happy. It was passion, and he had demonstrated it.

The bit about 'whenever you look at that' etc. had been rather good, but he knew he had to fix up the wall before the landlady came round for the rent.

The work went swiftly. They could feel it was nearly over. The rollering was done efficiently. The slab sat snugly in the hole. They wiggled it with crowbars. It sat snugger still.

Even Coco looked happy about it. He kept saying how good it looked. They took turns standing on it. It had gone home.

They cracked open the second beers and drank them. The day was without doubt the warmest yet of the year. The leaves had never been younger or greener.

It was an easy job, making some cement and smoothing it over. Nic could have done it alone, but Coco no longer felt like leaving. He had got a nice buzz from the beer also. Nic smoothed over the wet cement with a trowel. Then Coco got down and took a turn smoothing it over.

He smoothed it. Then he smoothed it more, and smoothed it again. Nic said, 'Get off your knees. It's not a girl's thigh.'

Alex found it hard to concentrate on the work, but it kept coming. It was a tired and sad feeling. The sun burned the grass and then the sun drank cheap wine and fell down again. At the same time it was a relief to be freed from the demands of another human being. Whoever he was, something of him had to be held back and saved or life would be impossible. There was the job, which consumed most of your hours and energy, click clack click, millions of words, shovelling shit, and never ended. The faster he could do it the more shit there was to shovel. Then there was travel in overcrowded sewage pipes. And crossing roads. And billboards looking down on you, telling you what to buy. And watching the president of the United States, the perfect puppet, his lip almost quivering with emotion, and realizing that he was actually moved by how his speechwriters had put it. And boy and girl bands performing their dance steps. And being awoken by an argument in the hallway outside your apartment at 4 a.m. and going to the door, and finding that it is just one person, arguing with the walls.

In the middle of this it was good to have some moments in which whatever was left of you could sit in silence. When you could remember. When the evidence that had gathered could be sorted. And it was a difficulty if another person imagined these moments were their property. Your life got sliced from two sides like a supermarket salami until there was nothing left in the middle. You were the bits that had been given away right and left to others. Because they wanted the piece of you that belonged to them. Because they wanted more. Because they wanted passion.

And you did not have it.

'What about your neighbour?' asked Popa. 'She hasn't paid her bills. What about her forwarding address? I thought you'd know.'

He knows I was fucking her, thought Dorin.

'Lili? Said she was going to Holland.'

One day she was just gone. She had mentioned going to Holland, but then she said lots of things. Now that business was resolved satisfactorily, Dorin felt he had better talk a bit of shit with Popa. Didn't do to be too brusque.

'She was back with her husband a few months ago,' said Popa. 'Dropped by to pay up; since then the place is empty.'

Dorin had seen the husband. Big silent lump with a beard and a glowering brow. Perhaps an ex-sailor, few illusions and content to settle with a big healthy imported girl with straight-forward expectations. Perhaps it was a recipe for happiness. Dorin had had a spell of over a year when he could knock on her door whenever he had drunk a bit and needed a woman. She had been very little trouble, but every time he would return to his own apartment and shower he swore it was the last time. Sex made a sucker of you, and then you were back face to face with nothingness, staring at the bathroom tiles, washing away the evidence of another human being.

But now that it was gone, the memory of that body grew magnificent. Large breasts, but solid. You needed both hands and a mouth to do justice to just one of those things. One time in another city Dorin had accompanied a friend to a prostitute's apartment and the doorbell had had exactly the same sound as Lili's – birds twittering sweetly. Lili's twittering birdies and her ample chest. Half drunk, stepping out into the hall and listening to the birds twitter. Erotic nonsense.

'The husband didn't like the city,' said Popa. 'Said it was dirty.'

'Observant type.'

It had been good in a way. They would drink, smoke, talk. One day, drunk, she told him that she loved him. He felt bored listening to her confession, and just a little sad that someone had even less in her life than he had in his.

'She's a simple girl,' said Dorin. 'She didn't want too much. Just to get married. A man with a little money to take care of her.'

He had actually felt some responsibility towards her, and after her declaration of love he decided it was time to stop visiting. So she told him she had not really meant it, about being in love, and he repaid her by removing her clothing again. Then one day he realized he was just a television soap opera to her. They were there watching television one evening and he had said something that she did not like and she was acting offended, and had her head under a blanket. Dorin drank and ignored her. Then the protagonist in the Venezuelan soap opera shot her lover and she emerged from under the blanket, back into the world. For Lili, as for everyone, some cheap drama had to be going on, one had to be manufactured with whatever spare parts you had to hand.

Popa was speaking: 'How can you marry somebody you don't love? I asked her. I don't care, she said, I just want to get married, leave the country.'

Her secretarial job, at the firm where a friend's husband

was the manager, had paid her more than most people earned. But it was never enough, there was always some crisis, a stolen mobile and some overdue bill. Her only interests were clothes and women's magazines and television and the next thing to buy. In the middle of a crisis over a mobile phone bill she would be talking of how she could buy a car in instalments. Poverty, thought Dorin, was loving only the things you could not afford. She was trapped in her room, dreaming of what she could not buy. When he thought of that, Dorin pitied people who did not paint. They were always trapped in their rooms, with the idiot screen for company.

'Maybe she's happy now,' said Dorin.

Dorin left Popa in his den of smoke and got into the lift, pulled the clanky interior doors shut and rode to the tenth. The graffiti were in support of football teams, against football teams. *Anyone who reads this sucks cock.* He had read that one a thousand times. A block full of cocksuckers and a dead administrator. And the one member of the crew who actually was a talented cocksucker had jumped ship. Well, he could not blame her.

He got out of the lift. The door between landing and corridor was locked. He unlocked it and passed through. Old Mr Carol had been listening behind his door and popped up like a jack-in-the-box. 'Did you lock the door? You didn't lock the door!' Obsessed with security. And snooping, and gossip, and interference. What were they going to steal, his false teeth? He did not have false teeth, and nor did his wife, though they could have both done with some. But they had a television, which they say is a marvellous comfort to the elderly. 'Fuck you,' whispered Dorin, into his beard, sweetly, like a prayer. Bless us, Father. For there is not enough space between us, we have gripes, an itchy ring, hard winters, short tempers, rough toilet paper, bad language, fuzzy tongues, monthly bills, damp walls, hairy ears, burst pipes and the water is inexorably rising. Dorin heard Carol muttering behind him, his thoughts gone audible, like in the nuthouse. He imagined Carol had been a tough customer in his day, but in only a few years Dorin had seen the last of his aggression sputter out and now, even after Dorin had closed his door, he could hear Carol toothlessly lecturing the echoing corridor. As people listened less he talked to the walls more.

The day had been a lot of talk about nothing to nobody. Through the hole in the kitchen wall a damp stench now rose up all the way from the basement. The plumbers were not coming back. All that about signing a contract was pleasant yakking. He would have to improvise something to block the hole to prevent rats climbing the shaft and exploring his home. The roof was also a negative phenomenon. Popa, of course, was lying too. But lying was putting it too strongly. Popa was simply talking, and inertia and laziness would win. Any commitment to action was an extravagance of the moment, a little cerebral excitement gone verbal. Popa was an entropic system presiding over an entropic system. The prince of disintegration. The pope of putrefaction. And then autumn would come and it would be too late to fix the roof for yet another year. 'Ah!' Popa would say. 'It's too cold now. In the spring!' You would get angry, he would sit behind his desk, exhale smoke, spread his hands. 'What can we do? We have no money.' And little old ladies would nod. The coloured fungus was an interesting feature, but the plaster was coming off the roof in chunks, and now when it rained the water dripped from the roof and streamed from the walls, and the whole place smelled of damp. It was depressing when it was raining outside, but even more so when it was also raining inside. No, Popa didn't give a shit. He had his old ladies. Dorin could not afford to fix the roof. Maybe if he hired a lawyer he could do something. But he had nothing but some change in his pockets. He had resisted the temptation to buy a bottle of water. Soon the water would be running through the taps again.

Something had to happen soon.

Didn't it?

Then the water came, splashing and sputtering, brown with rust and sediment, then relatively clear. He drank. Then he showered.

And on to other needs. Rice, onions, vodka. Time for a little picnic. He put a pot of water on for the rice, and tipped the bottle for a good chug. Alimentation, always nice, even in the midst of deterioration. Down the hallway old Mrs Carol would be frying some doughnuts for the old fellow, or something else that did not take much chewing. He heard a television go on. The room, having no carpet and being almost empty, amplified the sounds from his neighbours.

Pavel Popa rose and extinguished his cigarette.

It was true what he had said about not being paid for his work. Completely true. But the fact was that he could not be formally employed by the block and still receive his disability pay. Pavel had not worked for the past eight years, since the age of thirty-nine, due to recurring trouble with his liver. He could have worked, it was not such a debilitating condition, but there were too many workers doing nothing so they made it easy for you to leave. You were only slightly poorer on a pension than working for such wages. And he got public transport for free. He had too much time on his hands, though, so it felt good to run the building, to be in charge. What the block could offer would be only marginally more than his disability pay. And it would change things entirely. At present everyone was in his debt for everything he did, for free. If he became their employee he would then be responsible for all the things he did not do. It would be nothing but complaints and bad feeling and obligations to take care of matters that did not interest him. Yes, he had it worked out.

Popa locked the door to the office and went down the hallway to his room.

He opened his door. Two decades in a room. With the curtains drawn everything looked brown. His sofa bed was as he had left it the morning he had left for the hospital, the blanket thrown back, sheets crumpled from where he had slept. His imprint was left in the sheets. He could almost see himself lying there. He never unmade the bed, turned it back into a sofa, as he had no visitors: his social business was transacted outside, in the block. He had to keep the people out of the room. If they knocked on his door, he would step out into the hallway. Dorin, on the tenth, it seemed he had been pretty close to Lili. People tended not to copulate with their neighbours, though. Seemed like an intelligent instinct. Neighbours were good for small- to medium-sized talk, but otherwise you didn't let them into your business. Popa took off his shoes, put on his slippers. Still, you can be too wise, too protective of your space. He wouldn't have turned Lili down. When she came round to pay her bills she always spent a while talking. Not stuck up like Dorin. Last summer Lili had practically suggested they head off to the coast together. It wasn't a joke exactly. Perhaps in the general territory of idle talk. But it had set him thinking. He had been so long without a woman that now any reasonably attractive, reasonably young woman seemed impossibly far away. A gap had appeared and stepping across it was now as unreal as stepping in front of a bus, or taking off your trousers in public. Popa took off his trousers and laid them over the back of the chair. Some things were never going to happen. And then, they were always there, on the other side of the gap, in looks, in words. In the idle words of a woman a year ago who had put in his mind her body, naked on a beach. And he had heard an innuendo that another had had her, and all he had had to do was go next door. Through the wall separating him from her. What magical power had he possessed to do that? No magic at all. The same power that stupid vulgar pimpled teenagers had over pretty sixteen-year-old girls. The luck to be there, and say the right words, that was all. And he did not have that luck. He lay down on the bed. Dorin had smelled bad. He did not like Dorin. Dorin was all right, just an odd sort. But no, he did not like Dorin, lucky and cool with it, not even a wink or a smile at the mention of Lili. Acting superior, and smelling bad and living up there with no furniture and a dripping roof. What was going to get wet? The weather was warming up now. If Dorin wanted, he could put on a loincloth and sit cross-legged on the porch with a bowl and beg alms from the ladies as they returned from the market.

Nic drank a glass of wine. Maria got the dinner ready. It was better than all the days doing nothing.

He ate well.

The television was on the whole time. All the things that were happening in the country. The television made the most of crime, accidents, domestic tragedies, economic hardship. Today he didn't give a damn for their whining. Fuck them, there was only so much you could listen to. He crunched through radishes, sawed steak, forked fried potatoes, washed it down with red wine.

Coco came round. It felt like a different time was coming. The windows were thrown wide open and the bright evening light was falling through the branches of the trees. Having the windows open and the air moving through made everything feel different. On such an evening you couldn't help but feel the future was something good waiting for you. In the middle of the winter you easily got discouraged. Such strange things people were. It didn't take much to scare them. A cloud passed overhead and they felt something clutching the heart. They find some money in the street, they think God loves them.

Still, to fix something gave you a better feeling than watching it fall apart. If you sat around you ended up watching yourself falling apart, feeling like a nice big sack of shit.

They watched the news and played the game of commenting on the things going on. Then news came in. A rocket or missile had not hit its intended target. The bombed-out concrete skeleton of a large building, rubble in the streets, cars burning, ambulances wailing. A crowd of men shout and gesticulate into the eye of the camera, women howl. Then the camera pans around the building. It was hard to say what kind of a building it had been. It had been a big bomb.

Neither Nic nor Coco commented, but they both were thinking the same thing: about how much concrete had gone flying, and about how there would be no way to put it back together again.

Popa arranged the sheets and blanket and reclined and closed his eyes.

There she was again, the Gypsy girl, fifteen years old but practically bursting out of the school uniform. White strips of cloth like bandages bound her arms and feet to his bed, which now had posts at each corner. Her mouth was gagged. She begged with her eyes. She shook her head, brow corrugated with fear, silent tears spilling down her face. As she strained, the binding dug into the tender skin of her wrists. She pulled and moaned and arched her body, then fell back in exhaustion, her skirt now bunched up to her hips, her chest heaving. He lifted the scissors from the table. Her heart pounded beneath the tight white fabric of her blouse. The scissors were huge, rusty, clumsy as shears, but very sharp and they sliced through the fabric of the skirt cleanly until it fell back. Then he cut the blouse off. Her white bra and panties were glowing white against her dark skin, like a stripper he had seen dancing under ultraviolet light in the city of Constanţa in 1991. Her underwear was from a lingerie catalogue he kept in his bottom drawer, under his socks. He touched a scissor blade to her neck, in the depression just above her clavicle, let the weight of the scissors depress there. To see the delicacy of skin it had to be touched by something hard, like metal. All this time she watched him with liquid pleading eyes. A scissor blade eased under her bra between her breasts. She was breathing fast and shallow. He snipped, then with the tip of the scissors flipped aside each half of the fabric. Big breasts flopping sideways and out from each other, big dark nipples like another pair of eyes. Then the scissors snipped the final piece of fabric and she was revealed to him as God made her.

Pavel Popa *was* God.

He brushed his fingers against her neat bush, set down the scissors and disrobed.

He pushed, with difficulty at first, but then he was engulfed with wetness and warmness. As he ploughed her with a very slow circular deepening rhythm her tears turned to something else, her moans and whimpers were transformed, her fear became gratitude for his almighty mercy, for what he had generously granted her. He thrust deeper and finally proved his beneficence through acts, he untied the bonds at her wrists and her hands grasped at him, the bonds at her feet fell away of their own accord and her legs clasped him, and finally he pulled the gag from her mouth. She gasped and his tongue entered her mouth. A kiss, in the end it all came down to something as simple as a kiss.

He reached out for the roll of toilet paper on the table to his right and tore off a wad and wiped his belly. He lay there for a moment. The room seemed to have got a little darker. He looked at the clock. Still early. Perhaps it had clouded over. He could pull the curtains open and tidy the place a little. It needed that. He rose and went to the bathroom and flushed the paper. He arranged the pillows on his bed so he could sit up. He picked up the TV remote control, aimed it and clicked worlds into existence.

Veronica, from the ninth, brought the little fellow down to his grandparents to play for a while before she put him to bed. It was good having Nic and Maria in the same block. Her husband, Dan, was working in Israel, sending money home, and she was always able to leave the little one with her parents for a while. They were very lucky that they had been able to get her a room in the same block.

Nic said it would be good to do something with the land he had got back from the collective. It was just a field, but maybe they could fix up a summer house. He was too old of course, he said, but it would be good for the little fellow, and maybe he could do something with it when he got bigger. It was far away and they had no transport, that was a problem. But maybe when Dan got back from Israel he would have enough money to buy some wood for building and they could fix something up. It would be good for the little fellow to know that there was a world outside the neighbourhood.

Veronica nodded and drank a tea of lime flowers and honey. That's a very good idea, Daddy, it's ours and it's a shame not to use it. I've got strength in me, said Nic, I don't need to be sitting here in a city doing nothing. I worked decades in a machine tool factory and now it's gone, but I'm still here! Outlived their plans! Have a few of my own now, while I'm not too old. That's a very good idea, Daddy, said Veronica.

Nic was in such good form, Veronica did not want to tell him that the last she had heard from Dan was that his boss had cheated them. He was holding their papers and the workers did not know what would happen. It seemed they were not fully legal.

A light rain began falling as Alex turned off from the main road and on to the quiet street where his block was. At least it was quiet where he lived, he appreciated that. But now that he was earning money it was time to think about another neighbourhood. He had been living there for four years. When he had moved in at first the woman who lived opposite him, whose husband was on a building site in Israel, was pregnant. Now he could see the kid running around, growing. People had died and been carted out. The old woman who had begged on the steps had gone. Always sitting there on the steps in the evening. She would start whimpering. He always gave her his change. His granny tax, he called it. And then the administrator had gone.

Aurelia, the cleaning lady, a dull-faced Gypsy, was standing inside the door of the block, watching the rain. They said good evening to each other. When he had moved in first he had said good morning to her as she was mopping the hall and she had looked at him as if he were mad and he never tried it again. But since the day she had borrowed money from him she greeted him with a smile. It made him uncomfortable.

He got into the lift with Picol, a neighbour from a few doors down. Picol was a very small man. Piccolissimo, Alex thought. Didn't speak. Greetings made him turn away. Practically autistic. But Alex knew his story. Gave classes in the civil engineering college, concrete constructions his speciality, and precautions for earthquakes. No doubt he made the eyes of his students water with boredom and they had a name for him.

They took the lift and got out on the ninth. Alex did Picol a favour by not saying goodbye as they separated in the hallway.

Definitely time to get out. To live somewhere a little less marginal, somewhere that did not have the whiff of the asylum about it, and the odour of slow decay. He remembered picking up a girl in a bar years before. When he said the address to the taxi driver the girl announced that she was not going *there*.

He closed the apartment door behind him. He looked at the wet wall. He did not care much. He was tired. He would lie down for a little, then would go to Dorin. It seemed to have come from above. Maybe they would have something to drink.

There was a knock on the door. It was Aurelia, the cleaning woman. Her mouth hung a little open. In childhood she had got in the habit of not closing her mouth and now it was too late to fix. She was holding a banknote. She wanted Alex to change it.

Since Alex had begun working many people had turned up, needy and eager to siphon off any surplus. Old 'friends' appeared from nowhere, urgently needing to 'borrow'. Some intended to repay, some were the other kind. Some neighbours too, seeing him going to work now in a suit, enquired about the possibility of small withdrawals, and Aurelia had been one of them. The first time she was oblique. There was a request for him to help her draft a letter to some television show where people told their sob stories, and Aurelia's involved domestic violence, potential homelessness and a sick child. The second and third times were straight requests for cash, until 'next week'. Alex decided it was time to put a brake on the credit before the news that he was a soft touch spread any further.

Alex looked at the note.

'I'm sorry, Aurelia, I don't think this is worth very much.'

She looked at him blankly.

'You see this man with the moustache? He doesn't have much of a future. He doesn't get out much these days. The Americans don't like him. In fact, they strongly dislike him.'

Whatever was happening in Aurelia's head did not register in any facial expression. The eyes were two zeros. It was the face of someone about to lose consciousness.

'It's like this. You know how in the film Bruce Willis saves New York from the terrorists, just in time?'

She nodded.

'Well, he wasn't there when he was actually needed, so they got New York. And the Americans said that this man had enough bacteriological weapons, nerve gas and uranium to destroy the planet, so before he could do it they decided to take him out. But they've had to bomb his country to shit in the process, which is why this money, while interesting, is probably not worth anything. But thank you for showing it to me.'

She left. Alex took off his shoes and looked at the ceiling for a while.

He did not owe anything to anybody and it was not a bad feeling. He wondered what the story of the banknote was. How had it journeyed into Aurelia's hands? From the rivers of Babylon to his doorway. It was so original he wished he had bought it.

Picol took off his shoes. He had always been a great fan of Elvis and in 1990 had met some Mormons from the United States, the country of Elvis. They were all such big people, fed on meat and milk. Their teeth were perfect and they knew the answer to every question. He was convinced. They had no particular interest in Elvis, but this did not matter. Soon Picol's love of Jesus and his new community became great, and Elvis was just a singer. The greatest singer ever. But he was not Jesus Christ.

Dorin had eaten and finished off the bottle and was lying in the dark, dozing. He was at sea, and he was in a pedal boat. His body was bronzed and it glistened in the sun. He pedalled and the boat moved forward to Tahiti. Palm trees, a long white beach, a wooden pier. The boat was taking in water. He could see women on the pier. He pedalled harder, desperately, but the boat took more water and moved sluggishly. His paintings were bound together and stacked behind him in the boat. The whole back of the boat was full of paintings.

He ripped at the string and began jettisoning the paintings. They floated on the waves. He could recognize some of the paintings, views of concrete, but there were also ones he could not remember doing. He was amazed that he had had so many paintings in him. Well, they were gone now. He pedalled furiously ahead. On the pier, women in bikinis moved. Blue, yellow, red bikinis, one wore a tight sarong, another a bright green bandanna. They were all athletic-looking. Tahiti's women's Olympic beach volleyball team. He pedalled with masturbatory fury. They waved to him. The boat was still going down. The nose of the boat pointed down in the direction it wanted to go. The girls jumped up and down. Come on, Dorin! You can do it!

But he could not do it. A wave hit him in the face. Water was splashing about his face. There was a cracking sound and the boat split in two.

He sat up in the dark. Rain was coming down heavily. There was a flash of light and another crack of thunder. He got up off the mattress and went to the bathroom and washed his face. Soon the water would be dripping from the ceiling and flowing in rivulets down the walls. It would take an hour or so to infiltrate. He arranged the paintings so that nothing was left uncovered.

There was a knock at the door.

George Ristache made tea as it began to rain. He sat with the tea and watched television. He found it terribly depressing. When he was fifty years old, when Madalina was still alive, they had a couple of hours of television per day, and it was awful stuff. Now he had fifteen or sixteen stations and it was awful, but in a new and sad way. All it showed was what people wanted, and did not get, that was what George understood. Beautiful women that you could not sleep with, beautiful houses you could not afford to live in. Lives full of drama, excitement, emotion. It was all canned and processed and unreal, all bright colours and camera angles and shots changing before you could focus. It was made to dazzle you, not to show you anything. Something to fill you with second-hand images, some cheap fantasy of what real life should be, when it finally began.

He remembered what he had promised himself. He extinguished the screen with the remote. As he rose he realized how tired he was. Once that tiredness in the legs might be noticed when taking stairs, telling you that you were having a bad day. Now it happened every evening when you had to get out of a chair. He polished his glasses and looked through the bookshelves. He picked out Céline and opened it.

Our own journey is entirely imaginary . . . It goes from life to death. People, animals, cities, things, all are imagined. It's a novel, simply a fictitious narrative.

Céline was strong, despite his disrespect for elegance and form. All personality, bubbling, caustic. He replaced the book and found Flaubert. He resumed his seat and opened the book at random and began to read.

When he woke he was not sure how long he had been dozing but now it was raining hard and the book was open on his lap. Half a glass of tea was cold beside him. He got up and closed the window. It was dark and the air was turning cold. A flash of lightning lit up the trees, the puddles of water, the apartment block beyond.

It was time for an early night. There was nothing else to do. Reading in French had been tiring. He could not remember what he had read. He had kept remembering the funeral, the men unable to close the coffin, and he had read and reread the same lines without understanding anything. Perhaps tomorrow. Perhaps tomorrow when he was fresh he could read Flaubert. You had to keep hold of the good things, not let them slip away. It was a fight. He remembered seeing an old man in the supermarket the day before, trying to open his wallet and count out his money, and getting confused with the different bits of coloured paper, and what he needed it for. Then remembering what he needed it for and not remembering how much he had, and beginning again, counting out the money. It was a scene from a nightmare, the horror of disintegration. It was a fight to keep it together, for the mind to hold on while the body did. Perhaps Andrei had been lucky. He had got away cleanly.

He undressed and used the bathroom. He got into bed. He looked at the picture of Madalina and turned off the light.

The couple on the other side of the wall started up. Sometimes they woke him at five in the morning. Or she did. He could hear him only as he affected her. She translated him into music. Brief clear notes punctuating the silence, as if something had surprised her, again, and again. Later there were long bending notes as her wonder assumed a discursive, enquiring quality.

But finally it was a sound like no other sound but that of a woman being fucked.

Listening to it made him feel like a ghost.

In the end there was just remembering. In remembering you seek the company of ghosts.

It was a long time before he fell asleep again.

'Give my muscles a rub!'

Nic stretched out in the bed wearing only his pyjama bottoms. Maria rubbed his back the way he liked it.

'I think we got that concrete down just in time.'

She rubbed.

'Any later would have been too late.'

She rubbed. 'You worked so hard.'

He sat up and put on his pyjama top.

'We got it just in time.'

Dorin opened the door. It was Alex. He walked straight in and saw the paintings stacked up.

'Going somewhere?'

'Tahiti.'

'I'm getting out of here too. And I got dumped today.'

'Sorry.'

'What's the stink?'

'Basement. Popa keeps the bodies of his young victims there.'

Dorin showed Alex the damage.

'Better block it up with something. You could have the rats moving in.'

'I forgot about that.' Dorin put one of his paintings over the hole. 'There,' he said. 'Who said art was of no practical use?'

'You have to get out of this place,' said Alex. 'It would do you good to look at some other view. This one is exhausted.'

'The thing is, I am a property owner, unlike yourself.'

'Dorin, I know you have very negative ideas about jobs, but there is a positive side to them.'

'Getting paid.'

'Regularly. Paying bills, getting stuff repaired, getting out of your room. Not having things collapsing around you. Money changes things radically. You become interesting to other people, they smile at you more and want your company. You feel different.'

'Why don't you support me? I can cook.'

Alex went out for something to drink. He came back, his hair wet with rain, with a bottle of vodka and bread and cheese and olives and salami. They ate and drank and listened to the rain. Alex told Dorin about the cleverest monkey in the world, which knew so many words it could order drinks. Drinks? asked Dorin. Like what? Banana Daiquiris? No, said Alex, the monkey would have to evolve for another million years before it could order drinks with umbrellas. Then the plip of rain inside. Dorin put out pots, cups. There was a symphony of drips and splashes.

'It sounds good,' said Dorin. 'If you ignore the reason.'

Veronica put the little one to bed, and since there was only the one room she could not have the noise of the television, so she just watched him, breathing, until she felt sleepy too. It would be strange if Dan didn't come back from Israel, it would be bad, but it would also be strange when he did come back, the three of them in the room, when it seemed just about perfect with the two of them. Before Nic fell asleep he thought of the land, how something had to be done about the land, for the little one, it would be terrible to grow up and only know the neighbourhood. By the time Maria had finished in the bathroom his mouth was open, snoring, and in his dreams he was hammering nails, building a house. Pavel Popa watched a last quiz show. The contestants answered questions for money and Popa answered out loud, and was impressed at how much he knew, and how much it was worth. Picol listened to 'Hawaiian Wedding Song', 'Can't Help Falling in Love' and 'In the Ghetto', and thought about the tragedy of Elvis getting fat in Vegas. And he said his prayers and thought of Jesus on the cross. George Ristache remembered the priest who had buried Andrei and got so angry that he turned on the light, but was still unable to concentrate on *Madame Bovary*. Narcisa Tudor ate vanilla cream biscuits and her dog sat in front of her, begging. No, she said, you're not getting any. And she ate until the dog began to tremble. Then she gave it one biscuit and hugged it and said, You love me, don't you? and it licked the crumbs from her lips. Dorin lay down and though the rain had stopped outside it was still percolating down and raining inside. Something has to happen soon, he thought. I have exhausted the view from the tenth. Or it has exhausted me. At the intersection the cars became fewer. The traffic lights flashed amber and the cars crawled across. Alex thought of how things and people became each other. Imagine a pair of boots that had been worn a year, or a hat. An empty chair pushed back from a desk could speak of the absence of the person who had been sitting there. What about this building, then? If I stay here do I gradually become a part of it? When I leave will it keep visiting me in my dreams? Alex listened to a couple of dogs debating the bones of the night. He was tired but he liked to keep an hour for himself at the end of the day to sort through whatever had accumulated. Not a lot had happened, once again, very much worth commenting on. Perhaps it would, soon, when he finally got out of the neighbourhood.

He began typing, clacking away, just for the hell of it, because there was nothing else to do.

Who Let the Dogs Out?

You'd need to see his place – bookshelves to the ceiling and books piled everywhere, on tables, on sideboards, in stacks on the floor. And little statues with their arms broken off. He's a big fat homo and he's into Greeks. It's Greeks this and Greeks that. But occasionally Romans get a look-in, and Trojans. You'd need to see him too, a big waddling roly-poly type in baggy green corduroy trousers and a brown corduroy jacket. He has leather patches on the elbows of his jacket because he's a professor. He's wheezing a little from the exertion of getting to the door to greet me, and his face is flushed from drink.

'Wayward barbarian youth! Enter!'

He bows and with a sweep of his arm shows me the hallway. He's such a puffed-up piece of theatre you have to wonder what happens when he's alone, if all the air goes out and he just crumples up, deflated, and weeps.

Because he's a lonely old fuck, with his Greeks.

'I have been anticipating our symposium!'

That's what he calls it. As always, I head straight for the fridge.

'I have some exceptional kalamata olives, some artichokes stuffed with truffle pâté . . .'

A woman comes in and cooks and cleans and always the fridge is overflowing and he must have to dump most of it. Pork chops in gravy, mashed potatoes, spaghetti and meat-balls, entire chickens stuffed with spiced rice and fruit and nuts. He didn't get that size on carrot sticks and other artistic nibbles, but he never mentions the real food, he has to talk about his stuffed artichokes and pickled pigeon cunts from Syracuse. I find a beautiful raw steak. I point to it.

'Of course! Whatever pleases you.'

I light the gas ring. Blue fire.

'You must be ravished with hunger, after playing tennis.'

There's no point telling him again I don't play tennis. He is convinced he saw me one dewy morning on a tennis court, when I was but a youth with the first down upon my cheeks.

'When are you going to let me watch you play?'

'Tomorrow.' The steak hits the butter in the pan and hisses.

'Where?'

'Mind your own fucken business.'

'Ooh!'

He needs that, sometimes. While the steak sizzles I dig into some very unusual cheese, some olives, and some very finely sliced smoked Italian ham. I put the steak on a plate and pour the cooking juices over and sit down at the table and eat. My host pulls a bottle from the freezer. He pops the cork and pours mine into a tall water glass, as I'm not a sipper. I take a chug and it hurtles down my throat, so crackling cold it almost hurts, like plunging your head into an icy mountain stream. After a few more dips in the mountain stream I bring my head up and blink and find myself in a better place. The steak is gone and a big fat pompous homo is looking at me and I want to laugh. This is all a scene and I have a role. I pick up the bottle and empty the last of the wine.

'Barbarian! Vile Scythian! Savour the fruit of the vine!'

I grip the edge of the table with both hands and sway and roll my eyes. 'I feel a bit Dionysiac,' I say.

See, I've picked up a bit about the Greeks.

We go into the living room with all the books and muti-lated statues and sit down on his couch. Let the symposium begin.

While I'm here for the job at hand, really he's a sad old antiquity and there's some foreplay in the form of dialectic. There's a certain recurring theme. What the professor wishes me to understand is that the mischief we get up to on this couch is not really what it's all about. It is the intellectual aspect of our relationship that the professor most values. Oh yes. And what is more, the physical dimension of any act is illusory dross, and the essential form is what really matters. But the essential form is only perceived intellectually, if you will. The senses are of no assistance. I'm not me, see, that's an illusion. I am the manifestation of youth and beauty, how-ever. And that's why he'd like me to move in with him. So he could contemplate me on a steady basis. We'd be friends. It would be Platonic.

Plato. Socrates and Phaedrus. Socrates and Alcibiades. Pausanias, Aristophanes and Eryximachus. I know these smooth-talkers and I know their arguments frontways and back. Their names form one long ass-banging daisy chain. They're all homos.

Love, according to this gang, is something between equals, so you didn't have a relationship with a woman any more than you did with an animal. Fields and women had to be ploughed and planted, but you saved all your love for your boyfriend. That's how it worked. Enjoying women was for vulgar types who just wanted to get their rocks off. The refined went for a boy when he was in the flower of youth yet old enough to be a rational creature – a man.

Socrates can't say, Phaedrus, I'd like to ream that puckered nether eye of yours. There are a few philosophical texts to get through first.

Socrates is the professor's favourite. But an interesting thing about Socrates is that he never wrote a word. Everything Socrates is supposed to have said is written by Plato. Plato says everything, but claims he never says anything, because he has Socrates say it. Follow that? That's intellectuals, they can't say anything straight. Plato has Socrates like a ventriloquist's dummy on his knee, talking about reality and telling everybody their business. If anyone disagrees strongly with the views stated he can blame Socrates, who's dead already. That's a nice trick. I tell the professor this. I tell him my doubts about Plato.

'Stratagems must be adopted, don't you see?' the professor explains. 'Look at Socrates. Obliged by the mob to imbibe the hemlock. Plato was displaying prudence by using Socrates as his mouthpiece. He was keeping an eye out for the unruly masses.'

But Socrates wasn't obliged to drink the hemlock. He was invited to accept exile but passed up. I point this out.

'Yes, but an Athenian cast out of his city was no longer a man, he was nothing. The Athenians didn't even have jails, you know, because to be extirpated from the body politic, to be severed from the polis, was such an effective punishment. So Socrates preferred death to exile.'

Still, I can't help thinking he was trying to stick it to the democracy by dying when they all expected him to get on a boat and get lost for a while. I don't trust Socrates either. I don't trust any of that gang. Plato has Socrates condemn the Sophists because they didn't say what they meant or mean what they said. But they were all tricky, the Greeks, and you can't take anything they say at face value. Plato had all the Sophists' tricks, and a few of his own.

As usual, we get to talking about ideas. The idea of ideas, in fact, and I find this very interesting. The philosopher, in Plato's scheme, is the man interested in ideas, as the stable reality behind appearances can only be apprehended intellectually. You see, me and the prof and all these books aren't real, and nor are you. That sounds crazy but it makes perfect sense. There is no permanence outside of Ideas, because the things we perceive through our senses are always shifting and changing. Something that appears to us to exist only partakes of the Idea, in a flickering, momentary way. Whereas now we think of the 'ideal' as being an artificial composite, something imagined and unattainable, to the Platonist the Ideal is the realest thing of all.

At first I thought this was a cockeyed way of looking at things. But one evening I was walking down the street looking at stuff and it all started looking very dreamy and unreal. There was a beggar on the ground, the toes eaten away from his diseased feet, and he was displaying these bloody, grimy stumps, holding out his hand for coins. Cars were swishing by in the street and flies were buzzing around the stumps and these two very hot cunts were stopped dead ahead and gazing in a shop window at jewellery. A convertible with the hood down slowed down to take in the women and it was Mr Fantastic, sunglasses, hair gel, driving one-handed, elbow resting on the door. They didn't see him, just kept looking in the window, dreaming of how beautiful it would be just to reach out and grab the glittering things on display. And I was thinking, as I always do, how good it would be to push one of them face up against the wall, wrench up the skirt and mount. Just to get it like that, once, and die. And the sun was going down, and I was looking at all these people, all these faces, and they looked either completely dead or excited about something very strange, and I was one of them, and I thought to myself, Well, perhaps Plato does have a point, this is a dream, a sick dream, and all these lost people are working and suffering and drinking and puking and fighting and fucking and lying and exchanging possessions back and forth, never satisfied with what they hold, and living in houses and discussing football games, and eating and shitting and worrying about getting fat and getting old, and reproducing and finally getting sick and dying.

I reach over to the professor's trousers. As always he looks shocked. He raises his eyebrows, opens his mouth – 'Well I! Ho! Excuse me but! I! Ho!' But he rapidly accommodates himself to the barbarian incursion on his crotch, his trousers are open, and then the little fellow is out, sitting in a nest of grey pubes upon his crumpled nut-sack, winking at me.

He's leaning back in his cushions, head tilted back, away with Trojan shepherd boys who cavort and play pan pipes on the fragrant hillsides about Ilium. He's away in the gymnasium, where all the boys are toning their abdominals and pectorals and deltoids before heading out for a symposium. He's away in the Olympian highlands of the mind with the gods of perfection.

'My goodness! O heavens! My word! O gosh! You barbarian! You vile thing! Guttersnipe! Scythian! You!'

It would be in my interest to blow his flute but I'm fussy about what I put in my mouth. It's psychological, all in the mind. Of course. Everything is.

Plato explained it like this. Some prisoners are in a cave, shackled, facing inwards, unable to turn round. The only source of light is from a fire behind them. Objects passing by behind, between the fire and the prisoners, cast shadows on the wall of the cave, and the prisoners, seeing these shadows, of people, of things, of animals, believe the shadows to be the sum of reality.

We are those prisoners. This is our condition.

Then someone comes along who can perceive the reality behind the flickering shadows – let's for simplicity call him Jim. Jim tries to explain to us that what we are seeing is not reality. If we understood what shadows were, that would be an excellent start. But because we think the shadows are the whole show, our existence is dominated by illusion. You see, Jim has got the Idea. The Idea of what causes the shadows. You see what I mean now about Ideas being real? I didn't explain it so well the first time. Nor did Jim, because all he has at his disposal are abstract words. Which is why Plato, and I, used this story and this visual image, this appeal to the senses as well as to the mind.

I can see the rest of the story of the cave, though. The prisoners consider that they have it bad enough without Jim chewing their ears. Someone takes out a pack of cards and begins to deal. Jim is not invited to play.

Plato figured he was Jim, who knew it all.

Me, I still have my doubts how much Plato knew. I think he rather too much enjoyed thinking he was the one who knew it all. So, we're all stuck in a cave. Thanks. Now what? Plato had his plans for everybody, though, and if it didn't suit you he had a cup of hemlock with your name on it.

But still, when I'm walking down the street sometimes and I don't feel quite there, I think about the cave. This happens usually on evenings, when the sun is getting low and life is slowing up and the shadows stretching.

I got a hard-on once when I was shaking the professor, but that doesn't make me a homo. I was thinking about something else entirely, about my own cock in fact, which is incomparably more beautiful than the professor's. I have the Ideal cock, you could say. Many women have complimented the aesthetic perfection of my erect phallus – enough of them for me to know they weren't just trying to find something nice to say – and I've come to regard it as something of a work of art. I've got so narcissistic about it that the true joy of having a girl suck me off is seeing her lips upon my own swollen loveliness. It's a very visual sort of thing. I was thinking something along those lines the day I got the hard-on. Even if I was a queer I don't think I'd get it up for the professor.

I always know when he's about to shoot because he switches to the vernacular.

'O you dirty shit! You filthy fuck! Cuntfucker –'

At this point I disrupt the rhythm, just for the fun of watching him jerk about like a spastic puppet, sputtering abuse.

Then Thera erupts, Atlantis sinks, and tidal waves swamp the Minoan palaces, eclipsing the cleverness of Perseus. There is a cloudy volcanic night in which black dust settles on the ruins, and a long dark age when nothing very much, culturally or otherwise, punctuates the stillness. I get up and walk to the kitchen and wash my hands. I dry my hands, then I wash them again, right up to the elbows. I throw water on my face, then open the drawer where the cleaning lady leaves the towels and I pull out a clean one. I dry my hands and face with the towel and throw it in a ball on the sideboard. Then I go back.

The professor has tidied himself up but is still there in his cushions, his big chest heaving, a little dazed at the storm that has blown through his skies. It's the same every time. He is a bit sheepish, mumbling about how I must despise him, unruly behaviour, lack of restraint. What he's trying to explain, it seems, is that it's not this 'gross act' which is the centre of our relationship. What it is really about is what he loves in me. The idea of me, young and perfect and beautiful. And he does adore me, because he's an old fuck washed up on the shores of time and I have absolutely no interest in sitting around with him being adored. The adoring are boring. Much as it has been interesting talking about the Greeks, I have places to go.

'You're a lovely boy. Coarse yet, but raw and pleasing too, and such an attentive listener. Ah, but that my students had your critical cast! Your aptitude for dialectic! You must not think ill of me. See how I hunger for your respect? I am just a silly old man. I was once a boy, much like yourself, starting out in life, full of dreams and hopes. But it is a bad bad world. People do not love each other. There is very little we can hold on to. Youth? Certainly not. Ideas, a taste for beauty, that is perhaps all we have.'

From the Platonic to the Epicurean to the Stoic. But that is life, Professor, hanging on for the next shot of whatever turns you on. Then you have spent your juice and there is nothing left, and it is time for a new philosophy.

Me, I'm a Cynic.

That doesn't mean what you think it means. If you want to know what words mean you have to go back and undo the layers. That's why people like the professor can talk so much; they know all the bits a word contains.

But that's a trap too, because they get to just arguing about the words sometimes and lose the plot.

No, the word Cynic meant canine, because the Cynics lived like dogs. Stray ones. Stoic comes from the word for porch but the Cynics didn't even have a porch. They despised possessions. And didn't trust words. They didn't write stuff down. The vagabond mongrels of the ancient world.

'I'd love to sit around and drink some wine, Professor, and talk about the Greeks some more, but –'

'But must you really go already? Must you? We've hardly talked.'

'I must. I really must.'

He waddles out after me to the hall. I stop at the hall table. Open the little book in which he has his telephone numbers written and remove the money. It is double the usual. Well, thank you, Prof, I know you can afford it but I also know you didn't have to. I am actually quite touched. It will wear off soon, I suppose, and I will feel it is my due, but for now I feel sure I will spend extra time with you next week. As I open the door, I say:

'Prof, next week I would like to discuss the Siren episode with you. There's more to it than first appears. Think of it, Odysseus could have plugged his ears with wax too, but he went for getting tied up to the mast and listening. I want to talk about this, get all the facts of the matter straight.'

Outside, I walk fast through almost empty streets. I am late.

It's a long dim sort of bar, wood everywhere and fake old stuff, but I see her immediately down at the end. It's her legs I see, long and crossed and shining and hard like metal under a full moon. She's got herself up.

People talk about the ethics of certain actions, such as cheating on your wife. They talk a lot of caca. If a woman like Helen walked up and offered herself to any of them you would see what a pack of phoney shits they are.

She's found company, unsurprisingly, and he's telling her something nice, because she's smiling. I walk up to them. The son of a bitch smiles at me.

'This is Yannis. He's from Greece. He was telling me about it.'

I shake hands with Yannis. Yannis is expensively dressed, with a chunky watch and an easy smile. A charming Mediterranean who'll be chatting the panties off your girlfriend the moment you turn your back.

'You can shove off now, Yannis. I have a private matter to discuss with Helen.'

Yannis is still smiling, but the soul has gone out of it. He considers saying something to me but decides it's a bad idea. Helen is looking at the ashtray, tapping her cigarette on it like a little drumstick, and she too has the wisdom to hold her peace. Yannis addresses her, with superior manners: 'It was lovely talking with you.'

She nods at the ashtray and he slips off the stool. I watch him slink away to one of the bar's dimmer recesses. The barman is standing nearby, polishing a glass, grinning to show me how much he liked it. Fuck him too.

'He was just being nice!' says Helen.

'We both know what that leads to.'

'You're crazy.'

'I'm paranoid, too.'

'That's right, you are. And anyway, he's going back to Greece.'

'Grease what? Your shitpipe?'

She staccato-stabs the butt to death in the ashtray, gritting her teeth.

'No. Yours.'

'You're probably right. I know my Greeks. You know how they won the Trojan War?'

'Yeah, I do. That horse.'

'Yes, that horse. By cheating. They were proud of that. It

was their defining moment. Then there was no one else in the Aegean but Greeks, and they spent the next thousand years outdoing each other in sneakiness.'

'The Greeks invented democracy.'

'They invented giving it up the shitter. And that's all they have left. The Turks got Constantinople.'

'It's called Istanbul now.'

'Is that a fact?'

'Yeah, it is, and you'd think you never went in the back way.'

'That was special, for your birthday.'

'Yeah, really special. I couldn't walk properly afterwards.'

'That was funny. You kept bumping into walls. Did you know the Athenians didn't have prisons? They had to shut them down. All the boys were lining up to get in. No one would join the navy.'

'Yeah, I knew that.'

'What do you want to drink?'

I get my wallet out to let her see the paper. Her eyes glitter.

'Where did you get all that?'

'Working extra for the professor. I'm his right-hand man. He has a book coming out and I've been helping him. He's a very bad speller.'

We drink for a couple of hours, then get out of there. We walk down the street together.

She stops in front of a window. There is a long coat hanging from a mannequin.

'I've never seen anything like that,' she says.

She steps up to the window, holding my hand. Her nose is almost touching the glass. I think she has stopped breathing.

'It's not normal skin,' she whispers.

You want to reach out your hand and touch it.

It is made of many pieces of fine suede sewn together. The pieces are every shade of green and brown and ochre and rust, the colour of the earth and plants and the winter sea, and no two of the shades are exactly the same, though there are very many pieces. It must be the skin of day-old lambs, kids, alpacas, or some small almost-extinct animal we have never heard of from the eastern Anatolian foothills. It was tailored in some ancient mercantile city, in Aleppo or Damascus or Antioch, by the last living master of a guild that crafted gowns for princesses and merchants' daughters. It was made for a tall, beautiful woman. It was not made for any ordinary woman.

'I want it,' she says.

She touches the glass.

'I don't want anybody else to have it.'

She looks into me and my heart turns sadly and slowly, like a dolphin under waves at night. You are suddenly nothing, and you can give anything, because it does not matter, because you hold nothing, ever, very long.

'I know how you feel,' I say.

The price tag says I'll be doing extra research on the Siren episode, and Scylla and Charybdis and the Cyclops too. I might work late and have to sleep over.

'I'll put a deposit on it tomorrow. It might take a couple of weeks . . .'

Her mouth goes on mine. She is happy and I am happy. Everybody is happy. It is worth the price.

We get back to my place. It's no palace. She points to a cockroach taking an evening stroll across the floor. I sprayed but this one has munched on radioactive waste somewhere and is bigger and tougher than the rest. It isn't fast, though. I spray it and it runs and I keep spraying it until it does little loops in the middle of the floor, drunk, then flops on its back, twitching its legs.

'Got the fucker!'

She opens the windows for the insecticide to clear. Her hips from behind wrapped in the skirt. Those legs. Royalty. She is Plato's Idea of a woman. My Idea too. The others are shadows. In another era she would have been seized from her village by the Janissaries and brought, at the age of fifteen, straight to the sultan. Any dirty soldier along the road who tried to grab her cunt would have got his head cut off. But it is the twenty-first century and she is mine, for a while.

She heads to the bathroom. If you think women are delicate creatures, you should hear mine piss. While she churns the bowl, I pick up her phone and scroll through the numbers. I get YANNIS. The Greeks used to be Aristarchus and Agesilaus. Now they're Yannis. I instruct the phone to block incoming calls from YANNIS. Then I change a digit in the middle of YANNIS's number.

It's her lucky night, we're going to play her favourite game. A strange man has broken into the apartment and things get a little rough.

She comes out of the bathroom and I shove her on to the bed. She fights and I get my head punched and my neck scratched. I pull her clothes off. She manages both to struggle and to facilitate the undressing at strategic moments. This is inauthentic, but her dainties cost good money and she won't have them getting ripped. I pin her down and wrap my belt round her wrists. I pull it until it pinches her skin white and tie her to the bed frame. She squirms and hisses. I strip.

I look at her tits, the curve of her hips.

Plato believed in the holiness of sphericality. He said the circle was the perfect geometric shape, because it was infinite. The sphere is more perfect still, being a circle in three dimensions. Her tits look good, with her hands tied back like that. I grab a handful and bite her neck and force her legs apart. I grab some haunch. I wish I had more hands. Plato believed God, being perfect, was therefore spherical, and thought about himself all day, that being the best thing around to think about.

Plato said lots of stuff.

My cock goes in.

Our eyes lock. Our souls have a serious talk.

It's not about love, exactly. It's the starry highlands, but the junk from the basement is there too.

You're going to get it now, bitch, say my eyes.

Give it to me, dog, say hers.

It goes into the hilt, and when I thrust it rocks her whole body, tethered to my bed. She bucks back, healthy creature that she is.

I could tell you how good it is. But there are not words.

Honey

'Honey!' Bob sounded irritated.

'Dear?' questioned Mary, busy preparing food in the kitchenette.

'Aren't you done yet?'

'Oh relax. They won't be here for hours.'

'One hour, to be precise,' he grumbled, and went back to his article on political and economic turmoil in Africa.

Bob and Mary Hamilton, in their sixties, having raised a family and been around the world together, were finally settled and alone in Scottsdale, affluent suburb of Phoenix, Arizona. A saguaro cactus stood like a sentinel in the quadrangle of gravel outside their neat suburban home and they had a small swimming pool out back. As they sat there in the cool of evening, after a barbecue perhaps, hummingbirds would come down and hover over flowering shrubs like fat bumblebees. But the interior of their home was transplanted from northern Europe. The floor was covered with deep brown carpet and the furniture was of dark heavy wood. On the walls hung conservatively rendered scenes of nineteenth-century European village life. The largest painting was of a group of small boats in a harbour, awaiting a storm. The sea was slaty grey and the sky was heavy with cloud. Only the loud mechanical hum of the air-conditioner reminded you that you were in the desert. Slatted blinds held back the harsh light.

'Honey, they'll be here any minute.'

Mary had just started preparing the chicken.

'Sweetheart, I know that. It'll be ready.'

Dick and Nancy were coming to dinner. They were new in town. Bob, who was in real estate, had sold them their house. Always after a sale you invited the couple to dinner. It was a matter of courtesy.

'I don't know why you have to leave everything to the last minute, dear. I –'

She placed a bowl of guacamole in front of him and some tortilla chips and he began to eat. An exasperating man at the best of times, he had become worse recently as his medical appointment loomed. The previous weekend, driving in the desert up north in Navajo country, he had fainted.

Initially he was angry with her for having made the appointment. 'Don't know why you have to treat me like a damn baby, honey,' he'd said. 'If I wanted to make an appointment, I could have done it myself.'

'I assumed you were going to, dear, otherwise I wouldn't have tried to save you the trouble,' she had said. 'I can cancel.'

'Oh, don't bother. It's too late now. The doctor would think I've gone nuts. What the hell, it's only a check-up.'

'That's right, sweetheart.'

But his bad humour persisted through the week. If it was because he was scared they would find something wrong, he never said. He could never reveal something like that directly. He could never say, for instance, 'Honey, I'm an old man, getting older, I feel unwell and it scares me.'

Instead, he said, 'Too much salt in the dip, dear. You always go overboard on the salt.'

Dick and Nancy were from Texas. They were in their forties and their two children were at university in far corners of the country. Nancy had thick blonde hair and it was hard to know if her waxy skin shone from a layer of make-up or from long days in intense sunlight. Either way, she didn't look quite real.

'Lovely blouse,' said Mary, and they chatted about what Nancy had in store for the new house. Bob admired her body. I'm not dead yet, he thought to himself. He observed that his own wife was dried out in comparison.

'How are things at Circle K, Dick?' Bob asked.

'Rolling along. Competition is stiff. Always is. Nature of the market. Got to keep fighting to hold our share.'

Dick had come to Phoenix to manage a new supermarket. He'd been transferred from Houston by his company, the Circle K corporation. Scottsdale was a growing area, selected for attention by the company as an important new field of operations. Dick was serving on the front line. Much was expected of him. Bob, chin in hand, issued a long 'hmm', expressive of interest in the supermarket trade.

'But it's a challenge,' concluded Dick. 'And what's life without a challenge?'

'Indeed, indeed,' concurred the host. 'Can't get stuck in a rut. Once that happens in business, once you become a piece of the furniture, you're more of a liability than an asset. And then you're dead.'

'I'm not ready to cash in my chips just yet,' Dick announced, and the assembly chortled at the absurd notion of the boyish Dick prematurely cashing in his chips. The hostess fetched refreshments.

They sat about the coffee table, a great irregular slab of varnished oak, drinking beers from the can and talking about the climate in Phoenix. Comparisons were made between Texas and Arizona, sunshine hours noted and relative humidity reflected upon. Bob, as usual, was a fund of fascinating statistical information, and enlightened the party concerning seasonal variations in temperature and mean annual precipitation. Bob had found a very good listener in Dick. He had a handsome easygoing face and he frequently raised his eyebrows as if to say, 'Really? I hadn't heard that before.' He seemed satisfied to be in the company of someone better informed and travelled than himself. They talked about the trials of celebrities, broadcast on TV, and how the rich and famous got acquitted because they could buy the best lawyers. Disparaging comments were made from all quarters about the legal profession, and Bob related some pertinent anecdotes, from personal experience, attesting to the wickedness of that profession. They discussed the deteriorating crime situation, real-life acts of depravity seen and heard on TV and how impossible Houston had become. Dick and Nancy were enthusiastic supporters of the death penalty. Bob Hamilton, presiding, sat back, crossed his legs and demurred. On casting the dissenting vote, he said, 'In some ways I suppose I'm just an old-fashioned liberal.'

'So, Bob,' said Dick, as Mary served them chicken cacciatore at the dinner table, 'sounds like you've been a few places.'

'A few moves. Of course, I was raising a family then so I had to think in terms of business. Argentina. It was booming then. A great place if you were young. Hong Kong. South Africa – briefly. Beirut.'

Dick raised his eyebrows. He remembered when a crazed Arab fundamentalist suicide bomber drove a truck of explosives into a compound full of marines. Dick had been a marine himself twenty-something years before. He wanted to know what Beirut was like.

'Oh, that was back in the sixties, before it all went to hell. Then back to the States. San Francisco, where Mary's from originally. Then here. I can't see us going anywhere now.'

The air-conditioner went off and the silence struck Mary as suddenly peaceful, even though she had not been conscious of the unpleasant noise. Then Bob started talking again.

'This is one of the fastest-growing cities in the country. A decade ago this was a worthless piece of desert. Now it's prime real estate. Values are going through the roof. Golf courses are springing up everywhere. That's when you know a place is doing well, when they turn dry scrub into an 18-hole. Can't be cheap, getting water to keep it all green. But obviously people are willing to pay. Are you a golfer, Dick?'

Dick admitted to being more of a tennis man.

'There's an Indian reservation just north of here, couple of miles away,' Bob continued. 'It was the usual thing, here's a bit of land, stay quiet and we'll give you a cheque each month to get drunk. Now the land is worth so much they're set to be a tribe of millionaires. Some of them, anyway. I'll be interested to see how they develop it.'

'I hear there's quite a few Indians in Arizona,' said Nancy.

'Native Americans, that's what we're supposed to call them now. Half a dozen tribes. The biggest tribe in the country, the Navajo, are up north, past Flagstaff. Two hundred and fifty thousand of them last anybody counted. Probably a lot more than that by now. They have so many kids. It's appalling, really. They're all on welfare.'

'We were up there last week,' said Mary. 'Just for the day.'

'Yes,' said Bob. 'Four Corners. Canyon de Chelly. There's even a stretch of desert there where the land is red. It's like driving across Mars.'

Dick raised his eyebrows.

'Magnificent scenery. Horribly hot, though. We had to come back early.'

'What a shame!' sympathized Nancy.

'Yes,' said Mary, 'but the car was overheating and Bob wasn't feeling too well. A bit of a bug or something.'

'Honey, I was feeling fine,' said Bob loudly and gruffly as his cutlery clacked to a standstill on his plate. A little too loudly, because Dick and Nancy had to smile to reassure themselves and Mary that they understood perfectly that Bob was only joking, that his angry voice did not really mean that he was angry. But Mary, despite her best attempt at dissimulating, looked embarrassed, and with the passing seconds the guests felt their grins turning stiff.

'Sweetheart –' she began.

'Honey, the problem was the car,' he asserted, as if the conversation could not be permitted to proceed further until the matter was cleared up. 'You cannot go driving around in temperatures approaching 110 degrees with the air-conditioning not working.'

He looked from understanding face to understanding face to ensure the point was well taken.

'And I was feeling fine. A cold, or flu. Some bug.'

The road north of Flagstaff rose beyond the verdant piny hills on to an arid plateau. This dry land was the reservation. Souvenir stands stood at intervals along the road to tempt the occasional passing motorist with their trinketry. Most were empty and those that were manned were doing no business. Mary suggested stopping to take a look but Bob explained that if she were the only customer she would feel compelled to buy something she didn't really want, and he drove on at speed past the sleepy stalls. The landscape was scattered with shacks and wooden hogans and trailers bristling with aerials, and sometimes a litter of these various habitations was clustered under the big empty sky. In places the land was covered with patches of yellow scrub, seasonal nourishment at best for cattle or sheep. In other places the land was baked clay or rock. They passed a sheltered crevice, the pitiful remnant of a winter stream, where rows of maize had been planted. Pick-up trucks crammed with families passed by in the opposite direction. Observing the broad Asiatic features of the tribe, Mary observed that Indians weren't as good-looking as in the movies. Bob noted that many were overweight.

'What I can't understand is how these people survive,' said Mary. 'I mean, look at this land.'

'Welfare, honey. The government gives them money.'

They'd noticed for a while that the air-conditioning wasn't working as well as it should, and half an hour after passing through Tuba City (not a city at all) the car showed signs of overheating.

'Damn it to hell! Well, we'll make it to the next gas station. Where is the next gas station anyhow? Where's the map, honey? You had it last. There it is.'

There was nothing for it but to continue driving towards Shiprock, the next town. There had to be a gas station somewhere along the route. The drops of perspiration dotting the red curve of Bob's brow began to run down to the collar of his polo shirt, which was soon drenched and clinging.

'Sweetheart, you're sweating?'

He looked terrible; the blood was leaving his face and he was breathing in short gasps.

'I know I'm sweating, honey,' he snapped. 'We're in the damn desert with no air-conditioner.'

Though worried, she decided that fussing would make him worse. His lips were a ghastly colour. She hoped there was a station round the next curve.

Smoke, or perhaps only steam, issued from the engine.

'Need water,' he gasped.

An erratic jerk of the steering wheel jolted them off the road and sent them careering down a dusty track towards a group of low buildings. He braked the car to a noisy dusty halt in front of a trailer. Beside the trailer were six dismembered automobile corpses of varying antiquity.

'Well, take a look at that mess,' he said as he angrily slammed the door behind him. 'We seem to have come to the right place. It's a graveyard for cars.'

He managed to open the hood of the car without burning his fingers, releasing clouds of steam. Then he put his hand to his head. 'Honey, I –'

His legs buckled and he fell towards her. She was able to take some of the limp weight by leaning against the hot metal of the car. Then she let him slide down on to the dust.

He raised his head and saw Mary, sitting beside him. She did not speak. He was lying in the shade on a low wooden bench set against a wall, looking out across a dusty courtyard formed on one side by a long trailer home and on two more by an L-shaped bungalow. A colonnade of rough wooden posts supported a shady porch running the length of the building. It was at the intersection of the two wings of the bungalow that Bob lay. At the open end of the courtyard he could see the trailer with the rusted cars and his own paralysed machine. Nothing moved in the grip of the heat except a few chickens pecking lazily in the dirt.

He removed the wet cloth from his head. His voice was a dry croak: 'How did I get here?'

He didn't try to get up.

'The man who lives here carried you. You were out for a couple of minutes.'

He closed his eyes. The idea of being carried like a baby by another man was humiliating. Next he'd be wetting his pants. And now he'd probably have to talk to the man who had carried him. He didn't want to do that.

'Where is he now?'

A door opened a distance from them. A plump Navajo appeared, grey hair falling behind his cowboy hat, bearing a ceramic jug. Indians are the only ones who dress like cowboys any more, thought Bob. His belt had a big silver buckle and round his neck hung an amulet. Bob felt he should say something to the stranger, a greeting of some kind, but he could not think of anything to say. He wanted the Indian to speak first. He wondered how much English the Indian knew and if it would be necessary to speak slowly. His head spun as he sat up. The Indian's face disappeared behind the brim of his hat as he tilted his head to watch the water bubble and swirl until it filled the glass like a living thing. He handed the glass to Bob.

'Honey, are you sure it's sanitary?'

'Shh, drink it.'

He did. It was cool as a mountain stream and immediately he felt better. The Indian poured another glass for Mary and set down the jug on the wooden bench and spoke:

'Best you folks sit around for a while. I'll take a look at your car, see if there's something I can do. Hungry?'

'No, really, thank you so much,' said Mary. The Indian nodded.

'Really,' she continued, 'it's very kind of you.'

'No, it's no trouble.'

He loped away slowly towards the car. She thought about his accent. It wasn't so different. She tried to isolate what made it a little bit strange. The words seemed to come from deeper down in the throat, from the belly even.

The colour was returning to Bob's face. He was sitting up now, with his hands on his knees, gazing blearily at the retreating shape of the Navajo, now wavering in the haze as he approached the car.

'I certainly hope we won't be stuck here all day,' he said testily.

He was recovering.

She was reminded of years before, in Beirut – no, it must have been South Africa because she was pregnant with Andrew, the youngest. That's right, because Charlotte was only a baby and she was sitting in the shade with Charlotte and Alexander. What had they been doing? Just sightseeing in the hills, miles from anywhere, and the car had broken down. She remembered that Alexander, the eldest, was very quiet on account of the heat. Anyhow, they sat still and quiet under the tree while Bob puttered around the car cursing and fuming, in a rage with the inert hunk of metal.

She remembered how he was so absorbed in his fight with the car that he noticed nothing else around him. She sat watching him from beneath the tree and believed that he had momentarily forgotten that he had a wife and that she was pregnant with his third child. Why did she remember that? She remembered above all because, in that moment, she had a clear revelation as to his character. And she realized that they would be tied together, for better or for worse, until parted by death. She would remain by his side irrespective of his faults and failures, and even because of his faults and failures. This would remain beyond his comprehension. In his imagination he was loved for his greatness. For how else was a woman's devotion inspired? He would never realize, she understood, that his own wife could see him as something comical and ultimately futile, as in that moment when he cursed and stamped about a machine that refused to move, or at any other moment. She felt pity for him; such men were vain and useless creatures. He would carry his conceit to the grave.

And then, beneath the tree, with her child and baby falling asleep in the heat, she remembered how she had met him first, on a jetty in San Francisco harbour. The wooden planks creaked on the swells and the boats swayed and bobbed, and she had to shield her eyes and squint because the sea sparkled so intensely behind him. There he appeared, tall and rangy and dressed in white, with a sailor's cap aslant his head. Her older brother had been teaching him to sail a yacht. She was very pretty and was used to men being instantly affected by her presence. His indifference distinguished him. No matter what she tried to talk about, she couldn't shake the impression that his mind was elsewhere. His eyes seemed always focused on a point over her shoulder, in the distance, out to sea.

And the years had passed and still he had never quite seen her. Still his eyes were fixed past her shoulder and somewhere in the distance.

She was distracted from her memories by a door opening. A girl of about eight walked out, leading a naked little boy of about three by the hand. The girl looked away from the old people, smiling self-consciously.

Mary thought about her children, and her grandchildren, whom she very rarely saw. They were scattered from one corner of the country to the other. Alexander, in Chicago, had one child, as did Charlotte in Miami. Charlotte seemed happily married but Alexander was already separating. His son was three years old and she had seen him twice. The children were so busy with their careers that it was hard to get time to visit. Occasionally she phoned them but they always seemed tired or 'in the middle of something'. Once they had driven across the desert to visit Andrew in Los Angeles. The area to the sides of the highway sparkled with broken glass as though sprinkled with diamond dust through the length of the desolation.

She had come to admit to herself that she was lonely. It wasn't enough simply to go to the office each day and return home, or to drive the sterile streets of Scottsdale, deserted in the heat. Hostages to the climate, people lived out their lives in private air-conditioned bubbles, getting into air-conditioned cars and driving to shopping centres, where you would scarper like an insect across the searing parking lot for the refuge of the air-conditioned supermarket. That was their home; street after street that no one walked in, golf courses and super-markets. And her family gone.

The girl, having collected tomatoes in a basket, returned the way she had come. She smiled shyly at the old people and passed back into the building.

'What beautiful children!' said Mary. 'That little girl, her eyes were so beautiful, so black and shiny.'

'Indeed,' grunted Bob. 'Doesn't look as if their skins see much soap and water. Thank God, here he comes. Hope he's fixed it.'

The Indian came loping up the dirt track, wiping his hands on a rag. He moved at the same tranquil pace until he was in front of them.

'How you feel now, pretty good?'

'Just fine. What's up with the car?'

'Ah. I think it's losing oil. Not too fast though. So I topped it up. Put some more water in too. It'll get you to Shiprock at least. Pity my brother-in-law ain't here, he coulda fixed it for you. All that's his junk down there. He get wrecks and strips them for parts. I don't know much about that stuff, prob'ly break it if I try and fix it.'

Bob stood up and took out his wallet. 'Well, we certainly appreciate your assistance today. What do we owe you?'

The Indian put up his hand. 'It was just some oil. My brother-in-law won't even notice.'

'We'd better be going, then.' Bob shook the Indian's hand. Mary did the same. The Indian repeated his offer of food and Bob declined. Mary was feeling hungry but said nothing. They had imposed enough. The Indian went with them to the car. Mary offered to drive but Bob insisted that really, honey, he was quite all right. The Navajo watched as they drove off.

'What a nice man!'

'Yes, very helpful fellow.'

They proceeded again across the barren plateau.

Crossing into New Mexico, the land became greener as the road followed the San Juan into Shiprock. The San Juan flowed into the Colorado. The Colorado fed a chain of reservoirs, which were headed by hydroelectric power stations. There were still old people in the reservations who could recall the time before the Colorado was a chain of stagnant pools, when it was a fertile vein cutting through the arid plateau from the Rocky Mountains to the ocean. The moon would paint out the line of the sandbars where the animals came to drink. Birds nested in the reeds where the river curved. Those days were gone.

The imposition of the newcomers was unjustifiable, said the old people. They had defiled the land, and given nothing. The power stations produced energy for the lights of Las

Vegas, to the north, which burned all through the night, and for the air-conditioning unit in the home of Bob and Mary Hamilton, in Scottsdale, Arizona.

The air-conditioner reactivated itself, adding its noise to the sound of Bob's voice. He was talking about the United Nations.

'They can't come up with a sensible programme for birth control or the Catholics object. It's impossible to do anything now without some group getting offended. If it's not the Catholics it's the blacks or some other group.'

Dick raised his eyebrows. Nancy attended carefully between spoons of ice cream with Kahlua. Their attention hadn't faltered throughout the meal. Bob Hamilton's learning was boundless, his experience global and on every important issue he had trenchant words.

'There's no doubt in my mind that we're heading for disaster. Look at the Chinese. Even they can't control their population growth, and they make it a national priority. Can you imagine what a strain on the land that must be? And with a growing middle class with an appetite for meat they'll begin to use the land less productively. Well over a billion of 'em already. What will happen when a country the size of China becomes destabilized?'

Dick and Nancy shook their heads at the prospect of a billion unstable Chinese.

'Sure is scary to even think about,' said Dick. 'That many people.'

Mary had stopped contributing to the conversation. Each time she had tried to do so, Bob had resumed with even greater force, contradicting her outright or picking at some aspect of what she had said and not letting go until she had been forced to concede her error. She tired of his hectoring and she tired of having to tiptoe around him, and she was afraid of aggravating his ill humour in front of the guests.

'And that's not to mention the rest of the world. Africa – chronic misuse of the land caused by overpopulation. The deserts are expanding. I forget by how many miles a year. And even if the UN came up with a decent birth control programme you'd have a devil of a time selling it to those people. They believe in having lots of children. Swarms of them. The most humane thing would be to sterilize them, save them from dying of starvation, but then you'd be called a fascist.'

Bob took his final spoon of ice cream. Mary rose and asked who wanted coffee.

'Decaf. Two decaf. Everybody? Well, that makes it very simple.'

'And the really crazy thing,' continued Bob, 'is all these people come knocking on our door. Every war, famine, natural disaster, they come expecting a green card. What I'm saying is, how many immigrants can the US keep taking in before we're paying the price for overpopulation in other countries? We can't let it go on for ever. It has to stop some time and it might as well be now.'

As the coffee arrived the sky cracked with thunder and the lights went out. In the darkened room their attention was drawn for the first time to the window, through which could be seen a second fork of lightning dancing its electric fingers across the jagged saw of the mountains to the north.

Power returned. 'I think I hear the four horsemen,' quipped Bob as he stirred his sugar. Dick and Nancy laughed at that.

'That certainly was loud,' said Dick.

'There's plenty of electrical activity in this area. If you get any rain whatsoever you get lightning.'

They went to the window and watched for a while the shapes of lightning splitting the sky.

Shortly after eleven Dick and Nancy made to leave. 'Thank you so much, the meal was delicious.' 'Quick, don't get wet! See you again!' 'Of course we will!' 'Bye!' 'Sleep well!'

Dick and Nancy would invite Bob and Mary once for dinner, in reciprocation, and that would be it. That was how it went.

Bob scraped the plates and Mary loaded the dishwasher. All through dinner he had never stopped talking. Now, alone with her, he had no words. It was suddenly so quiet that Mary felt sad and tired, though she had frequently felt uncomfortable during the meal. Just to say something, she asked:

'Sweetie, can I get anything ready for your breakfast?'

He scraped the final plate, handed it to her.

'Honey, you oughta know you can't eat before a medical. Not before blood tests anyway.'

'Oh, I forgot.'

It was the wrong thing to say. She had not forgotten about the hospital, only that he could not eat breakfast. He retreated back into silence.

The storm was subsiding as they lay down to sleep in their parallel single beds. The thunder became a dull rumble in the distance, no more disturbing than the air-conditioner, and they slept until one great bolt of lightning, deep in the night, wrenched Bob awake. He found himself standing by his bed, terrified, as though electrocuted.

'That was very close,' he managed to say. Mary was watching him. 'I'd say that struck only a few yards from the house.'

There was another explosion of thunder and lightning, this time like a bomb going off in their backyard, and in the white merciless light Bob caught his own frightened reflection in the mirror: eyes wide, his open mouth a black tunnel. His face was a skull, with the skin stretched over the ridges of his eyebrows, his cheekbones and the bare dome of his head. In the returning darkness the image lingered momentarily like a negative burned into his retina. His own reflection horrified him. He was disgusted at how old he looked, and weak.

'Go back to bed,' whispered Mary.

For a moment he wanted to go to her, like a child going to its mother. He wanted to lie close to her warm body, but he feared seeming foolish and returned to his own bed. He lay for hours without sleeping, staring at the ceiling.

As his appointment wasn't until ten, she let him sleep and drove to the supermarket. Along the side of the road groups of Mexican workers in identical green uniforms and caps worked in the dawn to restore the pristine façades of the housing developments before the heat of the day took hold. They raked the gravel around the shrubs and the cacti and gathered up the dried reeds and branches that had blown loose in the storm.

When she arrived back Bob was already up and wrestling with a stepladder in the backyard. She hurried out. The last time he had used the ladder, some six months before, he had slipped and ended up breaking two ribs. She had made him promise not to use the ladder any more.

'Sweetie! What are you doing?'

He pulled the ladder into position.

'Well, take a look, honey. I'm checking out the damage.'

The wind had whipped several sheets of weatherproofing off the roof and into the pool. He shook the ladder to determine its stability.

'But what about last time, dear?'

'I'm sorry, remind me,' he said sarcastically, and began to ascend.

'I thought we agreed you wouldn't –'

'No, honey, *you* agreed!'

'But –'

'Ah, dammit to hell! Would you look at that, what's in the pool is nothing.'

He was standing on the apex of the ladder surveying the wind-ravaged roof.

'Shit! Well, it's in another state now.'

'Honey, come on down now!'

He did, and much faster than she expected. He seemed to step into the air and then, realizing his error, grabbed at the roof. This manoeuvre failed and his flailing legs kicked the ladder from under him, so he fell on top of it as he hit the ground.

There was a sharp pain in his chest and his breathing caught. It was no heart attack: it was his right side. He had broken his ribs again. When he opened his eyes there was an old woman standing over him.

Her stricken face, upside down, open-mouthed with violent red lipstick, black-rimmed glasses, reminded him more of some grotesque insect than of his wife. She was gathering her scattered wits to say something. He waited. It was coming.

'Honey! Are! You! All right?'

In a rage of agony, searing words like caustic bile rose to his mouth. He would not be responsible for what he said next.

But the pain in his body was so great he could only gasp one word.

'Honey!'

Walking to the Danube

I

It was evening and I was walking between rows of poplars down a gravel road that rose and fell gently, the low sun coming in hard shafts between breaks in bruised clouds. The fields were shades of yellow – corn and wheat and grass – and in the distance were the black hills. I was walking to the Danube, forty kilometres south. I was alone and my feet were moving and the landscape was moving and I felt well enough. But I had no water and had to think about a place to camp.

I came to a well. I lowered the bucket down and as I raised it all the water spilled through the holes. By my third try I was able to raise it fast enough and drink from the metal cup chained to the well. Then, walking behind a hay cart, I entered the village.

Ilidia was one long cobbled street fronted by a row of solid houses. I had time to make the next village, but an old woman I asked directions from told me I could pass the night at her place. I entered the courtyard expecting to pitch my tent behind the house, and then I was in the house, her grandchildren preparing me a room. Andrea, twelve years old, talking very quickly as she made up the bed, was sharp and curious. Her sister, a year older, blonde and plump, watched us, giggling.

The girls showed me the village as it grew dark. They were at home in their place, proud of their animals and fruit trees and streets. Adults learn to be ashamed. They learn that they are poor, that the place they live in has been left behind. One little girl remembered me. She said she had been on the hay cart when I entered the village. She pointed at the stream and told me she was afraid of it because once she had seen a snake in the water.

Inside, night fallen, the grandmother gave me bread and onion and home-made cheese and butter and warm milk. The grandfather asked if I did not mind travelling alone. He asked why I was walking. Was I not afraid of wild animals? Then he said:

'The Swiss do a lot of work with gold.'

I nodded. I did not know what to say.

Andrea showed me photographs. Grandad had always had that blank look. He was good for cutting hay. Grandmother held things together. There were pictures of a man: 'Father, who left us.' In the wedding photographs Father had a vague, unfocused expression. A man who likes a good time. The bride, big eighties hair, plain and apprehensive, due to be abandoned. It is all very clear afterwards, in a snap. There was a photo of the couple outside the Miners' Restaurant, where the reception was held. It all happened in the nearby mining town of Anina, now depressed as the industry collapses. In the summer, Andrea told me, she and her sister went back to the grandparents and the village.

There was no toilet and I was shown the backyard. It was a starry night. The goats watched me with their green demonic eyes.

In the inner courtyard the old woman was drawing water and I asked what I owed. But she did not want my money. She wanted me to thank God, and for the girls to grow up well.

In the morning she fried me an egg. It was the feast of Saint Ilie, the patron of the village, and nobody would be working. She had been good to me and I felt like acting holy to please her, so I went down with Andrea to look at the village church. When I went she pressed a bottle of milk and cheese and peppers on me. I was accumulating food; the day before, the grandparents of friends had given me cheese and peppers and a big slab of *slanina*, salted pork fat.

So, down the dirt road to Socolari, where there was only one shop, then to Potoc, even more remote and straggling. There was no shop in Potoc and many of the houses were abandoned. It was a dying place. The only people left were old. Then I was in open country, and heading upriver along the banks of the Nera. In the early afternoon the weather turned bad and I pitched the tent for the first time.

II

The next morning I followed the Nera. The river is not big but the hills on either side rise steeply and for a long stretch the water cuts a deep canyon through the rock. My route upriver was a two-day walk along which there are no roads and no villages.

After several hours' walking the track ended, the gorge deepened and a mountain of rock stood in my way. I began to climb. It became steeper as I ascended. It was tough work, scrambling through the scrub, my pack snagging branches, loose rock underfoot. The place to break an ankle or get bitten by a viper. The rock rose too steep on my right so I veered left, away from the river. Then it was too steep on the left also. I rested briefly then began the slow descent.

Back at the river, I took the pack off and wrung the sweat out of my T-shirt. I strung my shoes together and hung them across my neck and hung my trousers across my neck and crossed. The water came nearly to my crotch and in the swift current I had to test each step until I was the whole way across. Then, satisfied with the fording place, I crossed back and brought my rucksack over. I rested on the bank and ate some bread and cheese and a pepper.

The next obstacle was a gap in a ledge carved into the rock, which at that point was the only way through the gorge. It had collapsed into the river, some distance below. I tested holds to climb across but judged the weight of the pack would send me into the river. So I took the pack off to swing it across, as gently as I could. If I did it wrong I would lose it into the water. It sat there looking tempted to slip off the ledge. Then I was across.

The gorge widened upstream and there was a wooden suspension bridge, a prop from a wild-west film, dangling rotten across the canyon. Well, I reasoned, this bridge would not be here unless it were going somewhere; this is the route I will have to take. The cables were good but the boards were old and loose and so many were missing you had to plan each step, decide between two especially rotten boards positioned together or one which was healthier but very narrow. It was no joke. The cables were strung low and to hold on I had to lean forward, making the heavy pack more awkward. But I had to hold the cables because with each step the bridge was bouncing like a trampoline. It was a long way down and I would have preferred not to look.

Further on the canyon opened out and I was walking through a meadow of mint when I met a helpful man with no teeth. He had no right hand either, just a stump. He was looking for his cows. Had I seen any cows? He waved the stump as he talked. I was heading the wrong way, he said, and he showed me where to cross the river. I took off my boots and rolled my trousers above the knee. I felt pretty silly about the bridge. He said he only used it in the spring when the water was high.

For a long stretch the river was slow and broad and the banks wooded and I could see big fish lazing in the shade by the banks. I wished I had a rod. I could have watched everything that happened under the water, the big fish hanging in the current, sniffing the bait. Nick Adams on big Two-Hearted River, onion sandwich in his shirt pocket. 'His muscles ached and the day was hot, but Nick felt happy. He felt he had left everything behind, the need for thinking, the need to write, other needs. It was all back of him.' Poor Hem. One day it wasn't fun any more. Not any of it. His wife said it sounded like a couple of drawers banging shut.

The trail rose until I was on a height overlooking a large area of wooded country. It was late afternoon, and the sun had cooled a little and the light was not so glaring white. Colours had deepened and shadows drew out the shapes, and distant objects appeared very close and detailed and clear. There were steep gorges ahead and behind, which I sensed converged at some point out of sight. It was that good feeling you have in your blood when you have climbed to a height and can read a wide area of land.

The canyons turned out to be one, created by the river looping around a crag. My vantage point was a saddle in the crag, the narrowest point of the loop, and I cut across and descended to the river again. It was a fine place, the river curving through the gorge, trees clinging from all but the steepest faces of rock. I camped on the floodplain between the forest and the river, on a patch that supported a little grass. The sun went down and I washed my clothes in the river, then washed myself, the current rushing past my body.

I felt rather holy after it, my fire burning, light fading from the sky. I heated a tin of meatballs on the fire and ate it with some bread, the pleasure of the food even greater knowing it was another half-kilo I would no longer carry. Then it was completely dark, and luminous sets of eyes watched me from the forest. Or was it my imagination? I was very tired. I crawled into the tent, under my blanket, and fell asleep.

III

On the next morning, my fourth day of walking, I continued following the river upstream. The gorge opened out and the land again was cultivated in the river valley and a dirt road connected the scattered houses from which dogs would bark and children appear as I passed. It was pleasant country and easy walking and I stopped only once, to eat some old bread and *slanina* and peppers in the shade of trees by the river.

I met the old man in the village of Şopotu, in a dip in the hills.

We ascended a steep cart track through woods – mostly beech – back into the hills. We went very slowly on account of his heart condition. His son was in Greece, he said, earning money. There was a whiff off the old fellow so I tried to keep upwind of him. He told me he had been in Bucharest once, years before, when he did his military service. We talked of recent history.

'Ceauşescu, he wanted to take the people's animals away and make everyone live in apartment blocks. That's what made people angry. Then they shot him.'

'Did he deserve it?' I asked.

He thought for a second.

'He deserved it.'

Once, above the tree line in the Bucegi mountains, an old shepherd sitting shoeless in the grass, watching his flock, told me things had been better under the dictator. The sheep had got a better price.

'Ravensca,' said the old man, referring to the place I intended to camp, 'that's a village of Czechs.'

It was a long way to Czech lands, but what the man said was not impossible. For a century the area had been a depopulated battleground between Turks and Austrians, after which it was resettled by the peoples of the Habsburg empire.

'Czechs or Saxons?' I asked, unsure I had heard right.

'Czech, Saxon, what's the difference?'

He had no idea how they had got there. They had always been there.

We came to a ridge, clear of the trees, and sat down to rest, looking across the hills. I sat upwind of him. In the sky above a larger bird was being harried by a smaller. We watched them and when the old man had caught his breath he began to talk about the gold.

There was gold hidden somewhere in the area, he said. An old man had hidden it in a well in the hills. But in which well? That was the problem. Somebody else said it was under a tree. Once a man had come round with something in a sack, he said, asking strange questions, and in the morning the earth was hollowed out beneath the roots of a plum tree.

When we reached his house he invited me in. I accepted a drink of water but when I declined food he made a face. I was eager to move on, to walk at my own pace again, but there was nothing for it but to accept his offer. The old woman went outside to an outhouse to prepare something. She called him Old Man, he called her Granny. It was a two-room house with a good view, interior walls freshly whitewashed, but there was no running water and it smelled bad. It would have been fine had he left the door open, it being a hot day, but he was trying to keep the flies out. It must have smelled good to the flies. I ate the fried cheese and meat the woman gave me and set off on the road again with the old fellow. He insisted on accompanying me.

'You'll remember me if you find the gold?' he laughed. I said I would. He was joking. And he wasn't.

Up the road the old man met a neighbour, lying in the grass, and they struck up a conversation. He had silver teeth and a familiar smell. I shook them off and headed across some very beautiful country. I could see the cart track undulating ahead like a ribbon in the wind along the crest of hills until it curved left and slumped and was lost in distant fields, and I walked swiftly, eager to unravel that track, alone at last and moving freely.

After an hour I felt my gut tightening. The food was not going down and I was becoming weak. A man stretched in the grass watching his cows told me it was twenty minutes to the village. I walked for twenty long minutes and hailed two women in a field, harvesting with sickles. I had never seen anyone using a sickle before. A scythe, certainly, but not a sickle. How far? Twenty minutes. It seemed cruel, that the distance should double at such a time. But coming into the village a hay cart stopped for me. The two horses wore bridles decorated with coloured woven cones that projected from their foreheads, and red ribbons hung from the sides of their heads. Dream horses, royal horses, unicorns. And the driver was smiling at me. I threw my pack on the cart and lay in the hay for the last kilometre into the village.

The village of the Czechs was the intersection of three

cart tracks. I rested for a while in a little triangular green in front of a Catholic church, then camped by the cemetery just outside the village. I was weak with fever and pitching the tent took great effort. I took off one boot, rested a while, tackled the second. It went on like that. Then I lay down and waited to vomit.

When it was done I crawled back into my tent. Thirst made sleep impossible. I had been sweating while I walked but my poisoned guts had absorbed nothing I had drunk. Night had fallen and dogs were howling down in the dark village, and I did not want to go stumbling around looking for water. At sunrise I went down and drank from a tap above a trough beside the church. Then I slept.

IV

At midday I sat at the wooden table in the little green by the church while the Czechs sang inside. Afterwards they stood around on the road, talking, and the shop reopened and the men bought beer.

By afternoon I was strong enough again to walk. The rutted dirt road was thick with dust. There were many plum trees and the plums were the size of grapes and were falling on the dusty road. The road wound through the hills and nobody was working in the fields. It was Sunday, the countryside deserted. It was hot. I passed a field of corn and the leaves were beginning to wilt. It was a disastrous year for corn. But I was moving downhill and was in a good humour, and after several hours the road veered down into a valley, its sides steep and thickly wooded, a stream running through the middle, and a grassy plain on either side of the stream.

The valley was dripping and green after the parched hills. It was too good a place not to stop in.

I went upstream a little and camped on a flat grassy area. I was concealed there, away from the track. I had the valley to myself.

In the morning I washed myself in the stream, then made a fire and put on a tin of sausage and beans. I felt good, and I did not mind even when I figured out that I had gone the wrong way the previous day. My valley veered north, so to keep south I would have to retrace my steps uphill to the three tracks that converged on the village of the Czechs.

It was tough at first. My piss was still an alarming rusty orange. After the poisoning it was difficult to rehydrate with all the walking, and the heat. I made Ravensca in two hours, then set off south-west.

This time the track became very rough, even for a cart. Sometimes it disappeared entirely and I would be walking across a field, guessing where it ran, until it reappeared. There were other tracks going other places and I could not be sure.

A woman was watching two cows in a field. Good day, I said, and she stared idiotically.

I had to stop and explain myself. I was on the watershed of the hills, the land used as a last resort by those who had nowhere else to go. Not even the people of Ravensca, or the other villages, went there. There was no reason to. It was beautiful for me to walk through once, by accident, but I would never go there again. So I stopped and talked, and she asked who I was and what I was doing, and I told her I was doing nothing, just walking, and perhaps she believed me, and perhaps she thought I knew something about the gold. I looked across the hills. From there the streams flowed to the north or to the south, but all ultimately joined the Danube. In a distant valley

I could see the misty gleam of what was perhaps a river.

'Dunărea?' I asked.

'Dunărea,' she replied.

Close enough to walk to with what was left of the day. And the mountains of Serbia on the other side. All within view. I wanted to walk, walk, to that great river. It was miraculous, that my moving feet could put this great river beneath me.

I must have walked an hour through fields, meeting no one. Then two men were lying on the ground nearby in a field of stubble. Their horses were grazing, still hitched to the cart. They called me over. There was nothing for it. I walked across the field and sat down.

They smelled like the hospitable old fellow who had poisoned me. They looked like brothers. The younger stuttered and had a speech defect and seemed touched. They had got drunk on a bottle of home-distilled *rachiu*. There was some left. The older brother's shiny red skin stretched over big rounded cheekbones and his big eyes were the strange green that some cats have. Neither had many teeth. Bits of metal held together what was left. They were both around thirty and in those parts nobody got that old without their teeth dropping from their head. They bellowed at the horses whenever they began to wander off. They passed the bottle. I declined. No hard stuff in the sunshine until my piss was fixed.

Their talk revolved until they asked how I knew where I was going and I drew from my pocket a little tattered map I had drawn by hand, to save me digging the atlas from the pack. My map had villages, rivers, a couple of Xs and other marks. The younger brother crawled over the stubble on his hands and knees to get a better look.

'Where's the gold, then?' asked the older brother.

'The old man put it in the well, a long time ago.'

He took a slug.

'And where's the well?'

'The well is in the hills.'

'Which hills?'

We sat and looked at the hills. There were so many, many hills. At the horizon they were hazy with distance.

'Do you have an old map?' he asked.

I told him I had, and an instant later realized he was still on about the gold.

My atlas was from 1981, before the regime became so paranoid that production ceased. And since 1989 nothing better had been produced. So I dug this book out of my pack to disappoint them.

Or maybe they thought I was being clever. The older one started telling me I was a sweet, sweet boy. It was time to go.

I walked away across the fields and left them dreaming about gold, though all the gold in those parts is in the mouths of the people. Those that can afford to hold on to a few teeth. Working a few parched upland fields for enough corn and hay to keep some animals. No running water, the well iced over five months of the year – spring comes and then you can wash every month, whether you need it or not. Your matrimonial prospects the dregs. If you were lucky. Because anyone who had the chance to leave had taken it.

Then I was descending a steep track through woods, using my legs as brakes and trying not to slip. I could not imagine how carts made it, but judging from the ruts they did.

At the bottom of the slope was a stream and the track widened and in time became a wide gravel road. Within an hour of reaching the valley floor I was coming into the town of Sicheviţa. I passed two women and they didn't even look at me.

In the town nobody cared who I was. Everything was wonderful. Dogs lying in the shade, minding their own business.
Cracked concrete. A girl in shorts. A truck with six wheels.
Music coming from a house with an open door. Gypsies
sitting on their doorsteps, eating sunflower seeds. A man
wearing a straw hat, driving a tractor. It was a long street of
house fronts and they were painted different colours. I felt I
must be near an ocean.

In the centre was a police station, post office and bar. I sat
on a bench and waited for transport to Moldova Nouă. A
Gypsy girl sat beside me. She was visiting relatives. Nothing
in Sicheviţa, she said. 'Naşpa.' Crap.

She was right. It was good for ten minutes.

A big truck came. The rear had windows and benches
along the sides. A truck had fucked a bus and this was the
offspring. I threw my pack on the spare tyre.

And then we were driving along the Danube, in the clear
tired light of evening. It was wide and calm and Serbia on
the other side, like an island. People fished the banks and
from boats and there were watchtowers at intervals. It was
magnificent, as if I really had arrived at an ocean at the end
of a long journey, a hard day. I wanted to walk and walk the
banks of the Danube, along that level road. Perhaps I told
myself that because I no longer had to walk.

When we got off the truck nobody paid. I offered the driver
money and he refused.

Moldova Nouă, a small city, a swollen town. Homeless
children. A couple of Gypsy girls picking clothes from a skip.
Four-storey apartment blocks. Hard-faced people. Men with
their T-shirts hitched up over their bellies, drinking bottles of
beer. Men repairing their cars. Women dressed like it would
all fall off tomorrow.

I got a place to sleep on the road out of town.

I was back in the world.

V

In the train station in the town of Reșița I saw my reflection but did not recognize my face at first. The fear had gone, for a little while, from the eyes.

I picked up a newspaper and sat on my bag on the platform and began to read as the people got uneasy waiting for the train. It seemed I had not missed much. The same things were happening but they looked slightly strange when you had stepped out of it for a moment, and I might as well have read Herodotus, or the Bible, to find out what was going on. It seemed obvious that everybody should have enough to eat, and enough space, to be satisfied, but it was never that simple. *All the rivers run into the sea; yet the sea is not full.* They should use that headline, on every newspaper, every day.

In the train from Reșița to Caransebeș it began again.

She was a fat middle-aged woman, huffing in the heat, fussing with too many bags, talking the entire time. She talked to nobody in particular. To everyone. It was a nervous condition. Watching her made me tense. There was so much of her, so little space.

She sat beside me.

It was very hot and cramped. The train began to move and she started telling the woman sitting opposite us about her husband. He'd taken up with a younger woman who was using him, obviously, and she wouldn't grant a divorce until she was sure she didn't lose financially. They were laying off workers and he'd taken early retirement and his pension was larger than hers. They had an apartment together. Then, gaining confidence in her confessor, she told of the husband's years of running with the harlots of Reşiţa.

The train stopped for no reason. The only view was a scrubby embankment to either side. The stagnant air grew hotter. I desperately wanted out of there, to make my way up the embankment and across the open fields.

But you learn to smother the living breathing soul, go deaf to it, and this violence to the self is what is commonly called sanity in the places where I have lived.

So I obeyed reason, which told me to sit tight. And still the train did not move, and I had no idea when it ever would.

Perhaps the woman's husband was not a good person. But at least he had not murdered her.

The fat woman's confessor sat with her handbag on her knees, her face pocked from old eruptions, some semi-active. She wore a black top with a silvery love heart across the front across which was written, in fancy script, *Natalie*, and below, in smaller script, *Paris*. It was sad, to look at her face, because you could see she did not want so much from life and she was not even going to get that. She gave Fatty advice from the problems page of a women's magazine.

But we all have plumbing, us townies.

Reşiţa, incidentally, depends on a machine-parts factory. The mad fellow built it up despite the lack of demand for the parts. This and other things he managed to do by effectively robbing the peasantry to feed the people herded into the apartment blocks.

Now the workers – the fat woman's husband – were being laid off because nobody bought what they produced.

It was a bad deal all round.

VI

I got back to my room on the tenth floor of a block on the edge of the city and let myself in. I stood in the middle of the room, looking at it. It was as I had left it after I had got up from my sickness, the days when I sweated and shivered through a heatwave, moving in and out of strange dreams, afraid of everything. They say that a room is the projection of the personality of the person who lives there. In that case I was nobody. My room was basically empty. The strip of foam and the blanket. And the stool and the table I wrote at. Bits of paper were scattered around the floor, poems and stories, all written by hand.

There was so much shit to buy and not much cash left, and I needed that for food. I did not want a job again. I had been through so many of them.

I had missed a spell of cool weather and strolled back into another heatwave, and some of my neighbours were going insane. I went to buy water and took the lift back up. One pair had their door to the hall open, hoping to catch a draught. The old woman told me off for letting the lift door slam.

I thanked her for letting me know. I'm a good neighbour, a decent citizen. I believe in peace.

Then the old man is standing there in the doorway in his undershorts, swollen naked torso, and he is screaming at me.

I try to say something but he continues screaming. An old man in a little room, nothing to do, going mad in the heat.

I turn and walk away.

He keeps screaming.

I keep walking.

Broken Teeth

Sunday morning. Radu went for four more beers. He brought them back to the room for himself and Andrei.

A first-floor room. Two beds, one on either side of the big window that faced onto the street. Between the beds and under the window was a table. They were ugly beds and it was an ugly table. It was an ugly room. The pipes from the floor above had leaked and the plaster on the ceiling in the bathroom was coming off in chunks and the walls were discoloured. The broken hot-water tap hissed a stream of scalding water down the drain. There was no toilet seat and the bowl was caked with history.

It was student accommodation. Andrei was a student, though he never studied, and it was his room. Radu had moved in after his wife kicked him out. He had a good job in computers and had had a good apartment until his wife caught him cheating. He didn't like living with Andrei and he didn't like the room. He didn't like the way Andrei slept late with both his sheets wound round him tightly, the vile stains on his old mattress exposed to the world.

But everything would change when Radu got his visa for Canada. He put down the four beers on the table, where a car magazine lay open. Models stood beside the cars, smiling. He was already planning how to spend his money.

Radu paced. He wanted to talk. Andrei was a good listener. He never interrupted. But he had no purpose in life. He never made his bed, for example, or cut his toenails. Radu wanted to explain to him the need for purpose. He held his bottle in his left hand and gesticulated with his right.

— Take me, for example. My nasty cunt of a wife is divorcing me and from now on my son will hear nothing but lies about me from her and the in-laws. I'll have to give her money for the rest of my life. I can't get back in my own apartment and I live in this shithole with you. You could say I'm pretty washed up, couldn't you?

Andrei said nothing. He just looked. He was sitting on his bed. He held the half-drained bottle of beer balanced on his knee and his mouth was slightly open. He felt a little dizzy.

— Well. How you respond to life's challenges defines you as a person. Someone else would limp along for years in Bucharest feeling bad. What's gone is gone. I'm going to Canada. Romania is finished for me. I'm going to start fresh in a new country. In a couple of years I'll have a standard of living you can only dream about. That's taking failure and turning it into success, Andrei, and you can't do that unless you have direction, an aim.

He paused, and was glad Andrei didn't try to confuse the issue.

— I think that explains what I was talking about earlier.

— I suppose.

— There.

Time passed and nothing happened except for cars and buses and a tram and a couple of trucks. It being Sunday, there was less of everything. Radu stood by the window and Andrei sat on his bed. Radu said:

— When I finish this beer I'm going to get sucked off by a Gypsy girl.

Andrei smiled.

— Do you think I'm going to treat you?

— No.

— You're right. We'll have a drink when I come back.

After the Gypsy Radu stood in the bright sun at the kiosk at the intersection and had a beer and a cigarette and felt pleasantly relaxed. Although she hadn't been much good he felt he had achieved something. She had cost the same as four beers. You got what you paid for. Radu tilted the bottle back and watched two fine young student girls go by in tight trousers. The summer's fashion was trousers so tight you got more than a hint of crack. Cunts.

An expensive car pulled up and all the men stared. There was nothing else in the street to look at. An expensive woman got out the passenger side and leaned over at the kiosk to ask for something. Cigarettes. All the men in the street looked at her. She got back in the car. The car took off for the centre. Its tyres squealed.

Radu put four beers on the table.

— Was it good?

— Oh yes. A lively little thing. Swallowed. If you had some money you could have gone too. But you don't have any money, do you?

Andrei swigged the beer.

— What are you going to do for beer when I'm in Canada?

Andrei looked around. There was no answer. They drank in silence for a while and listened to traffic. A tram rattled by. It was very monotonous. They finished the beers.

— You get them this time. Here's money.

The next beers they drank hanging out the window, looking at girls. It was a hot day and the girls wore tight clothing and those who didn't wore light flowing summer dresses. One girl passed beneath their window and when she was directly beneath she looked expecially good, the thin material clinging to her half-exposed breasts. Radu found Andrei particularly stupid-looking while drunk and watching women. His mouth hung open and his eyes were dim and glossy.

— Andrei! Here's the cunt for you!

It was an old lady shuffling along in the heat. She was carrying two bags. She wore a coarse brown skirt and her face was weary with her burden and the heat. Andrei smiled.

Then a slim young girl flowed by. She wore a white T-shirt and her nipples projected. Radu and Andrei both leaned out the window as she passed underneath.

— She's mine, said Andrei.

— In your dirty dreams. Hey! My friend has something for you!

She didn't look up. They watched her glorious retreating rear. A man who was walking by stared up at Radu. He stared up a little too long. He had a shiny red tan like a peasant and wore baggy trousers like a Gypsy and Radu didn't like the way he was looking up at him. He didn't like being looked at like that by a lowlife with his hair in a communist-era side parting.

— What? said Radu.

But it sounded like, Keep walking, Fucker. And the man stopped. There was another man just behind him. He had the same bad hair, too long on top, the same hard burned skin.

— You've got a big mouth.

— Crawl back up your mother's cunt.

More greetings, then the first man with the bad hair invited Radu down to explain.

Radu pulled Andrei from the window.

— Come on!

— I don't know . . .

Radu ran down the stairs, Andrei clattered behind in flip-flops. As soon as Radu hit the bright street it all felt wrong to him. He hadn't been in a fight since he was at school and the man was walking straight at him and clearly there wasn't going to be any shouting. Then he was on the ground.

It was the dream. The one where for no reason at all his teeth were crumbling in his mouth and he was spitting the fragments. The dream had occurred with regularity through the years and he had wondered what it meant. There were other dreams of course. The one where he was about to have sex but never could because of a chain of interruptions and distractions. The dream where he was in a public place such as a bus or a classroom and he was naked. The dream of trying to arrive somewhere and getting lost and the clock against him, a dream that lasted hours and only ended when he awoke exhausted in his bed to begin the day. But the dream of the broken teeth was the simplest and most consistent and now it had come true.

Cheap black slip-on shoes and white socks were in front of his face. The shoes were kicking him in the ribs and shoulders. Kicked to death by slip-on shoes! It wasn't funny. He saw specks of blood on the white socks. He closed his eyes.

He waited until he was sure the shoes were gone before he opened his eyes. He raised himself from the ground on his elbow. The old woman of the brown skirt was at the bus stop. She and Radu looked at each other. Her bags were on the ground at each side of her and she covered her mouth with her hands. She had seen something terrible. There were some young people also at the bus stop, also watching. People in cars were slowing down to look. The whole street was watching. Radu could feel the rows of windows of the apartment blocks squinting down at him.

— Andrei! Get up!

His voice was strange. His lips were mashed.

Andrei's flip-flops lay nearby. He got up painfully and put them on.

They went inside. They held toilet paper to their wounds. Radu's two upper front teeth were broken and his lip poured blood. His right cheekbone was grazed. Black grains of dirt were lodged in the skin. He kept sighing automatically and each time he did a sharp pain in his ribs caught his breath. Andrei had a small deep cut under his left eye. The eye was swollen closed. Also, he had sprained his left wrist. They sat for a long time, maybe thirty minutes, not talking. Two beers sat unfinished on the table. The street had grown quieter and they were sober.

When they got back from the hospital it was dark. Radu sat with a wad of gauze to his lip. Andrei lay on his bed facing the wall. The buses and trams and trolleybuses passed with less frequency now. They were winding up for the night. The cockroaches came out and patrolled the linoleum. Radu wished it were next week or next year. He wished he were far away. He wished he were someone else, another man entirely. It was not so much the pain – they had given him a painkiller at the hospital – but to have been beaten. Thrown to the ground and beaten like a dog. And by someone he would despise for his hair, his clothes, his job, his speech. Practically a Gypsy. And his broken teeth were the mark of his defeat. The strange dream had become reality. The two teeth they saw every time he spoke or smiled. He had had very fine teeth and had never thought about it until now. And so life passed, like a judgement. Teeth were supposed to be solid, stronger than bone. Nothing in the body stronger. People who had been in the earthquake in seventy-seven said that the most unsettling thing was that the earth had always seemed solid.

Beaten.

That was how it had been when he went to his apartment to be forgiven by his wife and the locks on the door were changed. She let him in and explained about the law. It didn't seem fair. If she had really loved him he wouldn't have taken advantage of a mistake in such a way. He felt she had been waiting the whole time for him to take a wrong step while he, credulously, believed their relationship had a solid foundation. He looked back at all they had done together, all they had said to each other, all the times they had made love to each other, and he did not know what was real. How could something real disintegrate so easily?

He uncapped a beer and drank. In keeping the bottle from contact with his injured lip and the gauze he had some spillage. A thin stream of beer and blood and saliva trickled down his neck and the middle of his chest, right down to his shorts.

— Andrei, drink a beer with me.

— No.

Andrei was wound up in his sheet, turned away from Radu. As usual the mysteriously stained mattress was naked to the world.

— Andrei, I'm sorry.

Andrei didn't reply.

Radu solved the problem of spillage by dismantling a ballpoint pen and using the plastic tube as a straw. He derived satisfaction from solving the problem. By confronting the challenges imposed by their environment human beings achieve technological progress. He remembered reading that somewhere. But getting halfway down the bottle he had to tilt it so the tube would reach the beer and he had another spill.

The gauze was heavy with beer and pulled at his lip. He poured the beer into a cup and drank with the tube from the cup.

— Andrei, these painkillers are no good. My lip is throbbing. I'm going to take another one.

— They said not to drink with it.

— They say many things.

— You won't have another for the morning.

— It's not like you to talk like that. Anyway, what did Jesus Christ say about tomorrow? Do you remember?

Andrei didn't reply.

— He said the birds of the air don't think about tomorrow.

Radu took the painkiller and started on another beer. In the end it was not such a bad day after all. A warm glow spread over his body. It began with a pleasant tingling in his limbs and expanded to encompass the table, the coffee cup full of tepid beer and Andrei, curled up like a child in his sheet. Outside, cars passed by smoothly, symphonically. The glow expanded with the minutes and spread across the sprawling exhausted city, over its citizens, now climbing into their beds. He saw into the rooms and apartments of the blocks, thousands of cells, an electrically lit honeycomb sliced open with a knife. The glow spread across the trams and buses and along the tramlines, which ran like a lacing of nerves across the city's concrete skin. It took in the crumbling houses of the Gypsies and the howling wastelands of the stray dogs between the blocks. It took in the phonelines strung above the streets and it took in roads with six lanes of traffic, wide as rivers. Neon signs atop the buildings in Piata Unirii blinked coolly at the House of the People.

The city was held together by invisible electricity. When Radu closed his eyes he heard it humming in his body, moving up and down his spine. He remembered the doctors and nurses at the hospital and gratitude for their goodness welled up in his chest and made him want to weep. They had not treated him with contempt for being drunk, for being beaten. They had been professional and kind. Nurses in white floated down silent corridors like angels. A hot tear trickled down his left cheek. It was beautiful.

He opened his eyes. He was in Canada. He was reclining in a large black chair, a dentist's chair. He was very high in the air. The transparent walls of the room overlooked a city of gleaming glass and metal towers and spires. Past the sky-scrapers a vast lake shimmered silver. White trails from jet aircraft criss-crossed the cold blue winter sky and the slow clear sounds of a violin concerto issued from somewhere in the ceiling.

A tall man in a white coat stood with his back to Radu, contemplating the city. His hands were clasped behind his back. He exuded calm. This was the dentist. The city was Toronto and the lake was Lake Ontario. The dentist turned slowly to face Radu. He was extraordinarily handsome. His hair was grey flecked with black, his beard black flecked with grey. His eyebrows were black and well defined and these, with his piercingly intelligent dark eyes and his slightly hooked nose, gave him the look of a hawk. He spoke gravely, in English:

— You know, when I was a boy, in Armenia, on just such clear cold mornings as this, when frost was on the earth, I would leave my father's house for school and, looking west, would see the snowy peak of Ararat, clear in the distance.

The dentist paused, and looked again over the city. He turned and spoke again:

— I can remake your teeth. In fact, stronger, with the ma-terials and technology we now have at our disposal.

Radu tongued the jagged gap where his teeth should be. The dentist continued.

— The way science is progressing, with enough money it will even be possible to arrest and reverse physical decline.

The dentist turned back towards the window. He nodded slowly to himself, the great city spread beneath him.

Radu woke with the hard light breaking through the window. He looked at his watch. The face was cracked. He was sick and his mouth hurt. He found Andrei's second painkiller on the table by his side of the bed. Walking to the bathroom to piss he was unable to stand straight. Low down at the back of his head was a terrible pressure. He took the painkiller with water.

The bathroom had not changed. The ceiling continued losing chunks of plaster, the walls were stained, the hot tap ran and ran and hissed down the sinkhole. He remembered he had an interview at the Canadian embassy at nine. It was ten. He stared at his face in the mirror. Bad news all over.

And his teeth were broken.

My Life as an Artist

We mulched the shrubs and trees, edged the brick walkways, cut the grass. There were thirty of us on that job and the place was enormous. The grass in the vast field in front of the corporate buildings had to be mowed in straight lines in alternate directions so that the motorists rushing past on the highway would see neat bands of alternating shades of green.

I was forking mulch into my wheelbarrow when José made the announcement.

'*Oye, Felipe, anoche pisé mi mujer.*' (Last night I fucked my wife.)

He looked really pleased with himself. Great, I said. But not really news.

'We share the room with six other people. It isn't easy.'

We were all immigrants, most of us illegal. José had been nearly swept away by the current of the river he had to cross to enter the United States. He was very skinny. That morning he had been suffering terribly from the cold wind. It was spring but those early Virginia mornings were still sharp. Only weeks before there had been ice on the handles of the shovels and forks first thing in the morning when we picked them up.

'*Lo hizimos muy tranquilamente.*' (We did it very quietly.) José wheeled away his barrow of mulch, still looking pleased.

The supervisor called lunch. We sat around on the grass, eating.

Some of the office workers came out and exercised. It was strange, while resting, to watch them, now wearing white trainers, performing rapid circuits of the industrial park, the artificial harmony of which we had laboured all morning to maintain. Peculiar to see those people walking at such an unnatural, forced pace. It looked like work. Wound up, always intent on some object, unable to stop.

It was their country.

The supervisor, Bill, was eating a sandwich, and everyone else had corn tortillas and rice and beans. He told me he wanted me to teach him Spanish. He was new on the job and he wanted us to like him. Sometimes he had me translate for him. His top lip was hidden by one of those drooping moustaches you see on pictures of Wild Bill Hickock, or General Custer, or one of those other Indian killers. Though he was perhaps thirty, the skin on his face hung slightly loosely and had many fine lines. The lower lids of his blue eyes were rims of red. Trouble with drugs once, he told me. He said that in his youth all he cared about was having fun.

In any case, it was over now, and here was Wild Bill Hickock – after his crazy years of smoking marijuana, fornicating, driving his pick-up truck intoxicated, having minor confrontations with the law – now supervising the labour of illegal immigrants, perhaps even finding them a little exotic, and asking me to teach him Spanish.

Of course I said I would, but it never happened. It was not much of a college environment and the inter-cultural studies did not flourish. Partly as a result of our employer robbing us all. More about that later.

You got made supervisor and earned $1.75 an hour more if you spoke some English and had a driver's licence. I lacked the licence.

Eddy drove me into DC one afternoon. We'd got time off

so I could do the test. Eddy looked seventeen but he was maybe ten years older. He had a wispy little moustache. They all grew moustaches if they could, even bad moustaches. No facial hair meant pure Indian. A subject race. A thick moustache meant big balls and the blood of the conqueror.

The test centre was a few prefabricated shacks set down in a lot. The staff were the usual surly types. Their ancestors had been brought over in chains in the holds of ships from Africa and now they were employed behind desks as public servants of the District of Columbia and they were not happy about it. A curt woman with a clipboard sat beside me in the car. She had been doing the routine for years but to her it was centuries. Bored or not, she looked good. She told me to start the car. I glanced at her legs as I let off the handbrake and put it in gear and slipped out of there very smoothly. I had a decade of driving experience behind me.

She jerked the handbrake up and stalled the car. We had not even left the lot.

'You have failed the test.'

I had broken a stop sign where none had any right to be, several metres back before the turn on to the road. I was supposed to halt there and look left and right like I needed to exercise my neck. Rules of the road.

I wasn't going to be a supervisor. I wasn't going to get a pay rise, and now she could go get herself a coffee.

She went back into the prefabricated shack, the hemispheres of her impatient backside twitching edgily in her slacks as she walked away, happy as an angry person could be. Eddy and I went back to work. We drove through the depressed black neighbourhoods of south-east DC. There were stop signs everywhere. Before they had been invisible and now I saw them everywhere.

'*Hija de puta*,' said Eddy.

'Yeah.'

It was America. Around that time I had the feeling that everything I tried to do there was doomed.

When I eventually got past that stop sign and got made a supervisor, months later, life was a little better. I got my own truck and crew and drove around the electrical substations of northern Virginia. Mostly we cut grass, with enormous motorized mowers. The machine was master, always pulling you forward faster than you wanted to go. It wasn't a run, but it wasn't a stroll either. You steered using the brakes on the handles. I had a cartoon image in my head of a skinny human stretched out horizontal, gripping the handles of one of these mowers, flying above the ground, teeth bared in a mad comic grimace.

And when you slept at night your hands seized up like claws. I have small hands. When I woke my fingers would not move at first, not even to grip the toothbrush.

The alarm clock went off at 4.45 a.m. It was dark and you only wanted sleep. So your day began with this tiny act of violence against a tired body. You forced yourself up, got stiffly into your uniform, the tan pants, the green T-shirt and green sweatshirt with the company logo. And down the stairs in the dark house where the others were sleeping for many hours yet. I would get breakfast and make my lunch, then at about 5.20 Eddy came round.

Eddy ferried about twelve of us to work in an old minibus and charged us a couple of dollars a day. If you were lucky you got to sit on the spare wheel. Nobody had much to say at that time of morning. We drove through the centre of town, through the deserted business district, and over the bridge linking DC and Virginia. From there you could see the Lincoln Memorial, brightly lit as we left the capital at dawn. Abraham sat there on his stone throne, alone, through the small hours, contemplating liberty, and sacrifice, and the other things that make America great. It took most of an hour to get out to the Company. The office buildings were prefabricated wooden shacks. Time being short, I was regular as clockwork, and as soon as we pulled in I headed for a throne of my own. I enjoyed it immensely. It was clean and quiet and meant for those office workers who would not arrive for hours, and a few minutes later I stepped out, a little lighter and more spiritual, to meet my working day.

The work teams formed up, a supervisor and crew to each vehicle, and we loaded our trucks with wheelbarrows, shovels, rakes and forks and whatever else we needed. At about seven we would leave for that day's site, which could be a drive of half an hour or more.

But first a stop for food at El Chino's gas station.

All those service stations served fast food – fries and sandwiches and pizza, always made in a factory somewhere, always suspect-tasting, always greasy and tempting – and coffee and doughnuts. And, if you were foolish enough, bean burritos in plastic wrappers with fifty ingredients and expiry dates months ahead that you would unwrap and put in the microwave and which gave you pariah farts that smelled like something had crawled up and died. But it was a long stretch from breakfast to lunch and it was all so tempting. At El Chino's there were always fat spicy french fries waiting, and sandwiches with salty rubbery bacon and eggs under hot lamps. El Chino must have got up as early as we did, poor bastard. Perhaps in a teeming Asian city, as a boy, he had watched his father wash and iron a thousand shirts a day in a hot room filled with boilers and steam, and was glad to have a gas station along a medium-busy road somewhere in America. I don't know where he was from – China or Vietnam or Korea – but most of his life was spent in that service station and over the years he'd even learned Spanish. He knew the numbers anyway.

The men from another landscaping company in the area would pull in there at around the same time and it was odd seeing them. Their uniform was almost the same, just a different shade of green and a different logo. It was unsettling, because they looked like us but they were strangers. Like looking in a mirror where everything was distorted, just a little. You felt you should recognize the faces but could not.

They did the same jobs as us and lived just like us. Only the company was different. We were not unique. We had joined an army, units scattered across the country, waging war on suburban disorder.

We serviced housing developments, those places that told you America was run by companies, was a machine. You were lost in the machine for a few dollars an hour. They bought the land, they put up the houses, and then they got in commando teams of illegals to landscape it to look pretty and civilized, and to maintain it thereafter. Then they sold the units and went off and bought more land and did it again.

Trucks would come and unload mountains of mulch. Back in the winter, in the dim frosty mornings when there was hardly any light in the sky, those hills of brown organic stuff would steam when dumped, and then steam again when you dug your shovel in, your shovel with the ice frozen on the handle, and if you had forgotten your gloves that morning you could thrust your cold hands into the warm fermenting heaps of it.

Well, spring arrived, and it wasn't steaming any more. No longer anything nice about it. Just a big brown hill on an otherwise pleasant day. For hours we pecked at the mountain, wheeling loads of it away in our barrows like industrious cartoon ants obsessed with an overwhelming turd dropped by some ponderous herbivore. And the sun would climb the sky and, possibly with some satisfaction, we would see that all the shovelling and wheeling and shovelling was having an effect. The mountain was getting smaller. There was even a little excitement as it seemed about to disappear. We began to shout out to each other more, and the work went up a gear. Now we *wanted* to get at it! We were going to defeat it! It would be gone before another truckload appeared. The barrowfuls were now taking appreciable bites out of the remaining heap. We were going to lie around in the sun and talk shit for a while.

But then, in the distance, turning off the highway, into the road where we were working, we would spot another truck, small as a toy, coming towards us. And we watched as it grew bigger. It was heaped to brimming with mulch, and it rumbled up and tipped its load exactly where the last mountain had been.

We never defeated the mountain. No matter how good we were there was always more mulch. This forking and wheeling and patting down mulch went on all day, every day, throughout that spring. Tantalus and Sisyphus and ludicrous. There was an infinite amount of mulch in America. It had been ordained when first the pilgrims got off their boats that as soon as they had dealt with their agricultural challenges they would have shrubberies in the suburbs and they would be mulched by

Indians. That was our life. Servicing fussy shrub beds, patting down the mulch so it looked smooth and pleasant to the eye and would prevent the appearance of weeds for another year.

All that labour. I would think, Why don't they go for a more natural look, why are my days spent shaping dough-nuts of mulch around the bases of young trees and saplings?

But it was a stupid question. The kind a man who can't get another job asks. It had been calculated. We simply did not cost that much. Everyone likes pretty, and if it's pretty cheap they like it even better.

And in the evenings as the sun began to angle and the mountain of mulch really was the last one, for that day at least, the Americans would be arriving home in their cars from their jobs in the offices of the capital to their landscaped homes, and life was beautiful. The sound of car doors banging shut, televisions going on. It really did look like a place where you might want to live. The sun becoming gentle, the day's work done, the gardeners in the background, tidying up, loading their tools onto the back of pick-up trucks.

The places we lived were different. We lived in the city.

The places where only black people lived were cheapest. There were also a few areas that were mixed. The best solution was to rent a big house in a black area and fill it up.

Don Pablo and his two sons lived with about fourteen other people in such a house. Once a crack whore came round. She needed only ten bucks, urgently. Several men came to the door but nobody was tempted. She was trembling like a sick dog. Finally Don Pablo took pity on her and had her, fol-lowed by his eldest son, then the youngest son, who was a few pesos short of the full *real*. All for ten bucks.

'*Bastante barato*' (pretty cheap), I said to Don Pablo's eldest, as we edged a shrubbery, the metal slicing the turf, then slipping nicely into the soil beneath.

He looked at me. 'Not as cheap as us.'

The immigrants had little respect for the poor blacks. Their papers were in order and they spoke English and still they lived in shit.

He asked me why I didn't go with whores. Was I stingy?

'Me? I've got a woman.'

He didn't consider that a reason.

It was March the seventeenth, and I was moving extraordinarily slowly. I felt I was due a holiday. There didn't seem to be many holidays in the United States. I think I was just very tired that day. And Wild Bill Hickock comes up and says:

'We need to move a bit faster. If – if that's possible. Reuben's team is kicking our ass.'

He said it politely. Apologetically, in fact. Another supervisor was eating the elephant turd faster, and Bill was nervous.

'It really doesn't bother me,' I said, wheeling away another load.

The funny thing was Wild Bill didn't even want the job. His wife made him take it. That's how he explained it. He'd invested in equipment. He could have been his own boss. That's what he told us one lunchtime.

We were sitting around speaking English, Bill and me and a big slow black guy from New York, another supervisor, called Stan. Stan was filling in time until he got a job as a groundsman in a school, where he wouldn't have to do too much. He had moved down to Virginia because his wife had got a better job in DC. Stan was the man who told me he wouldn't leave his wife at his age – mid thirties – because it was too late to get used to another woman. In some ways the perfect husband. He sat around in the evening smoking dope and listening to music. And Ramón was there, a fat Salvadoreño with big cheeks like a baby and Chinese eyes and a wispy moustache.

Wild Bill told us how the wife nagged him to take the job, because a steady cheque was the best thing in the world.

So he was up before daybreak, took his daughter from his first marriage to the day-care centre, and was at the Company at six-thirty to load up to get to the site at seven or seven-thirty to actually start earning money. He put in his nine hours of paid labour, got home and washed and ate. I suppose he watched TV for a couple of hours and listened to the woman complain about the office.

'And still she wants sex every night,' he said.

I looked at his red-rimmed eyes and saw him mounting her dutifully. Then leaving her snoring in the morning, trying not to make too much noise, hauling himself out of bed to go get that steady cheque.

Ramón told us that every evening he went to this woman, also from Salvador, and she gave him a top-class feed. Ramón had a whining voice and looked rather like a eunuch, a man more motivated by belly than balls. She wanted to marry him because he had residency papers, and she had none and had a daughter to think about. So Ramón was spinning it out, going over to her house every evening, grinning and filling his fat face.

'That's the only reason you should get married,' said Wild Bill. 'For food.'

Then he looked at his watch.

'Lunch over. Better get back to work.'

'But that was only thirty minutes,' I protested.

'Lunch is thirty minutes.'

All that time I'd been taking forty-five, on Reuben's team and Eddy's, I'd thought I was entitled to it. I'd been stealing from the company. Sometimes after I'd got my lunch in me I even had time to pull my cap over my face and doze a little. Those happy days were over. Wild Bill, the man who used to drink and drive and take illegal substances, was doing it by the book.

I filled my wheelbarrow with the fiftieth, or maybe six-tieth, load of mulch that day and headed for another tree.

I got married because I had no money.

The fifteen hundred dollars I had borrowed was gone, Rosa had borrowed another five hundred, bills were coming in and meanwhile I couldn't even get a job in the doughnut shop on the highway serving coffee to other losers at 5 a.m. Even the doughnut shop demanded my papers! I'd worked two days at a bookstore in a big mother of a mall out in the suburban wasteland of Montgomery County, Maryland. I'd lied about my status. They let me work two days while I stalled about giving them my papers. Then they sacked me and mailed my cheque.

We were sitting on the front doorstep. This was back in October and it was still mild. 'Let's get married,' I said.

It was a lot easier than buying a car, for instance. I went up to the county courthouse in Rockville with our passports and made a booking for several days later. On the appointed day, Rosa took the afternoon off work and I borrowed a jacket and took public transport up to Rockville.

We went for a coffee and talked about whether we should really go through with it. The coffee and talking was her idea. I had already paid the fee and nothing had changed. I told her I loved her and that seemed to settle her.

A woman performed the ceremony and we tried not to laugh when we said the words. It was like we were in a film. We didn't have a ring. Then we took a bus back to my place, a basement room in the house where I lived that autumn, in Montgomery County, and we consummated our union.

As it turned out, it would have been simpler to get fake residency papers, and cheaper, but at that stage I didn't know the people who could arrange that for me.

One day I was hanging around waiting to go home and one of the office workers calls me in.

'There's eleven men in there,' he said. 'Pick three.'

Sometimes they got me to do that kind of thing, the excuse being that I spoke Spanish.

I went into the room where the eleven men sat and stood. It looked like more than eleven people, because they were all looking at me, awaiting my decision. They had all heard maybe there was a job and somehow had travelled an hour from the city to find out. Some of the men were older. One had grey in his moustache and looked wise and kind. I wanted him to have a job. I felt life should somehow be getting easier for a man with such a face.

'All right. Who's married?'

I had seven men.

'Who has children?'

Down to five.

The three with the most children got jobs, among them the one with the face I liked. I had discharged my responsibility, though I wasn't sure about the criteria I'd used. Possibly I was discouraging the use of contraception. I brought their names to the manager.

'Photocopy their IDs, willya?' said the manager.

So I took the lucky candidates to the photocopier and they handed over their documents. They were all fake. Cheap fake. You ran your finger over them and the cut-out photo stood above the level of the card. I joked about the fake IDs. They laughed nervously, but said nothing. I was a company bureaucrat for that moment, somebody important. Grown men would laugh at my stupid jokes, scared, because they needed a job.

The photocopies came out. Proof, if Immigration called, that only legal residents had been employed. The Company had discharged its responsibility according to the letter of the law. The company was competing with other companies doing the same thing, so obeying the spirit of the law was not an option. It was springtime and the grass was growing and the housing developments needed their borders edged.

Immigration never called. Illegals are an institution. They get the shit done.

Eight men made a wasted journey and next day looked up rumours that a dishwasher was needed. From back doors they were admitted to the kitchens of downtown restaurants.

I went to the gas station across the highway and got a beer for the ride back.

We usually worked until five and were back at the Company and unloaded between five-thirty and six. Eddy, of course, couldn't leave until the last man had come in and unloaded, which meant the man who had worked the longest day or at the most distant site. So we would rarely leave the Company before six-thirty, and sometimes it would be later.

I would wait until we were at least a third of the way home before opening my bottle of beer so I would not suffer the discomfort of a full bladder. Discomfort was the last thing I wanted. The body felt good already, relaxing after the work. I was thirsty, and as we rode back through DC, everybody awake and moving now, all the busy successful Americans bustling about in the evening light, attending to their business, the beer would hit me. It was blissful. I liked to look at the city in the evening and all the people who were doing so well. No, it wasn't blissful. It was just a beer. It wasn't bad.

Which meant I got home some time after seven-thirty. Nine hours paid. Six, at least, spent travelling, loading and unloading and waiting around. Leaving nine hours per day, if all went well, for anything else, including sleeping.

Showering, at that time of my life, was a great pleasure. Hot water on the tired muscles, getting clean, then stepping into fresh clothes – sweats and a T-shirt – knowing you were free until you fell asleep. Which wasn't far away, once you'd fixed yourself something to eat.

The last thing you did was set the alarm clock.

Get up and do it again.

Seasons pass.

I got home and was getting something to eat which involved meat. This disgusted my housemates, who were all vegans and animal rights campaigners. I was there by some kind of accident. It was one of those houses in DC full of earnest young types who work for non-profit campaigning organizations. Mine were with the Pure Food Campaign, against cattle being coked up to produce more milk. In America the bread has twenty ingredients and is made in factory hundreds of miles away. Apples look big and beautiful and taste like nothing. The animals are drug addicts. It's an issue, but at that point I just wanted to get my dinner and these whining vegans were trying to persuade me not to contaminate a particular pan by cooking dead beast.

'We could go Jewish, have two sets of everything,' I suggested.

On the Lost Continent food faddishness is one of the many new religions. They don't realize that the only way to save the place is to give it back to the Indians.

'Why won't you cooperate?' they whined.

'Because I don't give a fuck.'

They considered me politically backward. Not 'progressive'. I considered them Americans. It was a tough job for them, being Anglo-Saxons, responsible for the fate of the world. It was a silly situation but the rent was low.

In fact, I had worked briefly in an office for one of the campaigning organizations. I was a researcher and very good at it. But the constant female American whining and bitchiness on top of the tedium of the work was rather more than I could stand and one day I said I needed some air and walked out and did not go back.

Then I got the labouring job. It paid slightly less. But there was no complaining. Just a job to be done. There was no ambition, no posturing, no ideas, no cause, and the people got along so much better.

I saw all seasons, from the freezing winter to the burning summer. In early spring a late snowfall disrupted work and we sat in a truck and watched it falling beautifully and hoped it would cover the world and end the day of work, and Luis told us stories about women he had fucked, and someone else talked about a man who had worked for the Company until he lost a toe to a power saw and got twelve thousand dollars compensation, which he drank away until his best friend stole his last three thousand and escaped back to El Salvador. We all agreed the friend did the right thing. You could buy land back home for three thousand dollars and set yourself up. One should not piss away one's chances. And we talked about what losing a finger would get you, or a hand. Accidents could be lucky. Then the snow stopped falling and the sun came out and the supervisors were shouting at us to get out of the trucks. If the job didn't get done they would look bad.

In the height of the summer, when I had my own truck, my crew would get the work done and, somewhere peaceful in the country, take a long lunch and lie in the shade. Once, in the north-west of the state, where the land is hilly and DC seems very far away, a huge vulture swooped down and stood in front of us on the dusty road. Luis told me that in Salvador the country had been full of such animals because there were always dead bodies on the roads. The Americans were supporting the government against the rebels and there were always bodies on the roads.

Some people do not want to work for other men. They know that the best thing is to have some land, because then you are independent. Such people are the true idealists, because they have a vision of the first step a human being must take to be complete. Those who work for others compromise this ideal. Those who work blindly for others and do not realize what they have surrendered are already lost.

Easter week, *Semana Santa*, is a week-long holiday in Latin America. In Anglo-America, of course, it is another week of labour. So we worked Good Friday and then came the news that we were to work also on Easter Saturday.

This was very bad news in itself. But it was also bad news

because we were not paid an overtime rate. On the contrary, for hours worked over forty we received *half* our hourly rate. Two dollars fifty instead of five.

There was a minimum wage, but that hardly matters. Our contract stipulated a weekly salary, but did not stipulate hours. So rather than robbing us, technically the Company was giving us a bonus for the extra time we worked. Since we worked nine or even ten hours a day this meant on a regular week we were being skinned for up to ten. Then, every second week we would have to do the whole thing on Saturday as well. This left you time to get drunk that night and fight with your wife, and sleep it off Sunday. Then you were back on Monday mulching trees again.

So there we were on Easter Saturday, wheeling our wheelbarrows and mulching more shrub arrangements and patting it down nicely and other acts of general fucking around in the prettifying department. Back at that same industrial park where Wild Bill had asked me to teach him Spanish. He seemed to have forgotten that idea. We were all in a foul mood. And with all the grumbling going on in Spanish, and none of us moving particularly fast, Bill started getting paranoid. He decided José, who he'd asked to move a little faster, had said something about him in Spanish. Maybe he had.

'José, you got a problem with me?'

José said he didn't. What else could he say? He didn't speak much English anyway, so it was hard to say anything.

I didn't like it. None of us did. He was telling José to mind his place. We knew our place. We'd been in it long enough. We didn't need to be told.

José came up to me first: '*Trabajamos hasta las cuatro. No más. Qué dices?*'

I was happy with that. The word went around our squad.

If we were not finished by four we were going to load up the truck and drive off. Four was the limit. We looked forward to it. We were glad we had decided something together.

So four o'clock we're loading up. José was the driver of that truck. But Bill, sweating, comes running up and says to me, because I'm the one who speaks English:

'*Hey!* What you guys doin'?'

'Loading up.'

'Job ain't done!'

'Yes, it is.'

I closed up the tailgate. José slipped into the driver's seat. We all climbed aboard. Bill swore. We drove off, left him there with a few of the men. I remember Ramón was one of them. I remember the sneaky look on his face, the look of a man who would never step out of line. We got back to the Company, unloaded the equipment and went home.

It wasn't much. But it felt like something to us.

That night I got drunk with Rosa and we fought. I don't remember what was said, but it was all very dramatic. It was just me, angry at my life and her. I suppose I liked to blame her for America. That's a lot to blame someone for, and I blamed her for other things as well. The details are unimportant, we were always coming back to something very old, the cause of the Trojan War, or something about an apple. Who did what to who and why. She later claimed I knocked her out of her chair. I recall something about her spinning on her backside on the floor. I was turning into a nasty person. All along I'd thought I was a decent person but something had happened and it wasn't true any more and I did not know how it had happened. I woke alone, early. At some stage she came into the room, already dressed, and stood over me. I opened my eyes. Everything hurt. She told me what a bastard I was.

'Fuck you,' I said.

My voice didn't sound like my own. It was a dry croak. My first words of the day, Easter Sunday.

She left. But we hadn't split. We were in love.

That was Sunday shot in the head and shoved in a hole.

On Monday Jesus was feeling better and so was I. I got up in the dark and went down and when Eddy pulled up I told him to tell them I was taking the day off.

I went to bed and when I woke again the sun was shining and it was good just to have long empty hours spreading ahead of me. No wheelbarrows, no mulch. I walked around my neighbourhood feeling happy, bought some food, went to the post office; the kind of things I didn't usually have time to do. And all the while I was thinking of them working while I was free and that made it even better. After lunch I fell asleep on the big sofa under the window. I had the big empty house to myself. The other occupants were out saving the world. Good luck to them. I was aiming to save a little of myself.

In the afternoon I sat down and I began to write a story. I hadn't ever written a story and I didn't know if I would be able. I didn't know how to make money in the land of milk and honey, and I didn't know lots of other things, and I certainly didn't know how to write. Yet there was something magical about how the words tumbled out, separate and connected, and became sentences and paragraphs that ran down the page and became, however clumsy, something more coherent than my life. This was freedom. The others are working, I thought, and I am sitting here at this table, with a pen in my hand, in this big empty house. I could write a sentence and if I didn't like it I could rub it out and make a new one. If you practised you could have the power to say things, even if nobody else heard them. A bound, dumb part of you began to move and speak, awkward and amazed.

Outside, through the door I had left open, I could see a cat, probably just awoken, its front paws stretched out as far as they could go, and its tail, high in the air, flashing.

Next day I was back on the job. Eddy hadn't passed on the message that I wasn't turning up for work on Monday, and for this and the Saturday incident I was brought into an office and had to sign a piece of paper admitting I was guilty of something. My punishment: I was awarded another day off work, no pay. Well, I needed the money, but I also needed to practise making sentences, and perhaps dozing off on the couch.

Back on the site, Wild Bill comes up to me. We passed words about what happened. It was polite enough.

'We decided we weren't working past four. That's all there was to it.'

'Listen, I am the boss!'

'I know who you are.'

I wanted to make peace with the man, but I was not going to submit to him.

'Working Saturday for half pay! Holy Week is a holiday in Latin America, the whole week is a holiday. It doesn't mean anything here.'

'It does if you're a Christian,' said Bill.

Then I saw it. He was a born-again. It's in their blood. You play around for a few years and then as soon as you get confused and burned out, which always happens in that bleak and lonely country, Jesus finds you and lifts you up. In the end Jesus gets their souls, and they're relieved when he does.

I felt sorry for Wild Bill. He wasn't so clever. He was like the rest of us, just trying to keep going, not sleeping enough, not earning enough, between his two households, keeping the woman happy and giving most of his living hours to work that meant nothing to him, that pushed him around and made him feel small.

I felt sorry that we had treated him like he was the Company man. He was just another man, not any luckier than the rest of us, and that is why I wanted to make peace with him.

And the truly incredible thing was that he kept insisting – while the mowers mowed the grass backwards and forwards to get those alternating bands of green that looked so smart to all the people driving along the highway to the capital – he kept insisting that he was the boss.

Colorado, moving south along the interstate towards the New Mexico border, dark outside, falling asleep, and the truck driver says:

'Hey! Your turn to drive!'

It was an articulated rig, and I'd never driven such a thing.

'So. Pull over and I'll give it a go.'

'No. I let the air outa the seat –' He pressed a button and the air hissed and the seat lowered. 'Now, you climb around behind me. Grab the wheel. I slip out.'

We changed places without slowing down, then I was driving. That was how I became a truck driver.

So I just kept going. I wasn't going back to DC. I wasn't going back to my wife.

First I had gone to New York to get a job. A friend had bought a car. We took it down the roads of Long Island, then we drove west, past the Great Lakes, across the plains, to the

Rocky Mountains. Then I was in the truck. We drove in shifts over the Rockies, across the south-western desert and into California.

North of San Diego the sun was going down over the Pacific. A couple of weeks earlier I had been looking at the Atlantic. I had crossed a continent by accident.

I had no idea what I was doing. I had no idea what would happen next. All I could do was keep moving, keep working. For the meantime it was better not to think too much.

The Beast

Two old men were standing in a vegetable garden. One of them was very big, and you could tell by his full head of grey hair and particularly by the grey moustache, long enough to curl at the ends, that he had a good opinion of himself. Ion could dress up and go into town and not let himself down. He always wore a shirt. When he worked by himself in his garden behind the house he might unbutton it and let the sun on his big gleaming bronzed belly. Only when it was very hot would he take his shirt off entirely. Ion liked to work in his garden. He had grapevines and plum and pear and apple trees. Then there were the vegetables and at the end of the garden was a stand of poplar trees, the leaves of which flickered in the sunlight when the breeze brushed through them. Beyond the poplars was the field of corn his son had planted with the tractor. Ion was standing with his friend Mircea admiring the progress of the beans, tomatoes and the other plants.

Mircea wore shorts. He was the only man in the village who wore shorts. He was bald. He wore a white T-shirt with 'Freddie Mercury' written on it. There was a faded picture of Freddie.

— You're dressed like a twelve-year-old, said Ion. Makes you look like a scarecrow.

— Is that a fact?

— And you don't even know who Freddie Mercury is.

— A singer from France.

— He's neither a singer nor French.

— If I had jugs like that I'd keep my shirt on.

— When you walk down the road . . .

Mircea seized Ion's wrist. He was pointing at a creature not more than ten paces from them, nibbling at the dill.

Ion had seen just about everything. As a young man, after the war, he had to sign away ten hectares of fine land outside Timişoara to the collectives. Then he cried. When they shot the dictator he laughed. By then he was too old to work the farm properly. His son, who lived in the city, bought a tractor and planted corn, and returned on weekends and holidays to the family's land.

But Ion had never seen anything like the creature that was in his vegetable garden that evening.

The two old men were very still. They expected the animal to flee at any moment.

Mircea pointed to a net by Ion's foot. It had been for protecting strawberries from birds. Now it was June and the strawberries were finished. Ion picked up the net and handed a corner to Mircea, all the while keeping his eyes on the creature. The old men advanced slowly through the rows of beans. They could not help feeling dramatic as they did this. This was hunting. They went very slowly. They were both nearing eighty and tended not to rush things anyway. But, in this case, with stealth called for, and under pressure, they managed to move with uncommon grace.

The creature looked up at them. It did not seem interested in escape. Perhaps it was a very stupid animal. The net fell on the creature. It continued watching them, twitching its nose. Ion leaned down to seize it behind its neck so that it could not bite.

— Careful, now! said Mircea.

The creature offered no resistance. They went to the yard beside Ion's house and disentangled it from the net and put it in a box and had a good look.

It was hard to explain. After all, they had both lived in the area nearly eighty years. In a hundred and sixty years you could expect to see just about every animal there was, even the rare and shy ones.

The creature had little ears like a mouse, and walked more or less like one, and had hair rather than fur. But it was the size of a young rabbit and had no tail. Its face was neither rabbit nor mouse. It did not seem upset at being captured.

— Maybe it's a cross between two animals, said Mircea, speaking what had crossed both their minds. Like a mule.

Ion harrumphed.

— Like a mouse and a rabbit? Don't annoy me. Maybe a mouse and an elephant!

They both laughed. This referred to Mircea's favourite joke. Mircea had no memory for jokes so he held on to just one, which he would repeat whenever he was with someone new and a joke was called for: a mouse is in love with an elephant and tricks her into letting him have his way. During the act a branch falls from a tree, striking the elephant, who cries out in pain. Take it all, baby! snarls the mouse.

Ion always considered this an inappropriate joke from a small man who had a very large wife, but had never said this to Mircea. Some things you could never say. Ion's wife was herself rather frail, so the conjugal beds of each of the friends took roughly the same cargo.

Finally they became tired of standing and the strength had gone from the sun. Mircea walked homewards down a dusty dirt road striped with the shadows of trunks of trees.

★

The bed creaked when Ion got into it that night. It creaked every night. It was that kind of bed and he was that kind of man. He was troubled. It was only a matter of time before Mircea started blabbing and his yard was full of people wanting to see the creature, all standing about and gawking and chattering like monkeys, and him expected to provide food and drink for everyone. He would have to be there to keep an eye on things and would never get any work done. The Gypsies from the other side of the village would come over his fence in the night and try to steal it. If they stole fruit off the trees at night they would be interested in a strange animal too. One that might be of great value. Of interest to scientists, perhaps. There might be a reward involved. A quite significant sum. Ion got out of bed and brought the cardboard box which contained the creature from the living room into the bedroom and set it on the floor at his side of the bed. He stroked the top of her head. She seemed to appreciate the gesture, lifting her head and twitching her nose. A gentle smell of warm hay and fresh droppings rose to his nose. It really was a placid, affectionate little thing, and possibly quite intelligent.

— There now, Brigitte.

He got back into bed. The name had come in a flash of inspiration. He had always been good at giving animals names. It was one of his talents. It was after Brigitte Bardot, a great star of his younger years and furthermore a great lover of animals. She had visited Bucharest a few years before, concerned about the stray dogs, and had even adopted one and brought it back to France. She was on the news about it. Still a fine-looking woman, Ion thought.

Along with the creaking of the bed there was also always much groaning and grunting before he settled. But this night there was too much going around in his head and he was unable to sleep. As well as all his other concerns, Mircea was troubling him. In fact, Mircea had been troubling him for over seventy years, since they were boys. Even then Mircea had been rather spindly and awkward and had tended to get in his way whenever there was something serious to be done. They had had their disagreements through the years. There had been patches when they had not spoken for months. But Ion did not consider a month or two a particularly long time. Certainly it was a shorter period of time than it had been when he was twenty. Yes, thought Ion, there was something flimsy and unreliable in Mircea's character. You could see it in the way he dressed. Who wanted to see his scrawny legs? And the way he spoke about Brigitte, as if asserting his rights as proprietor. He was probably already thinking about money.

— I don't know if we can trust him, said Ion to his wife, who had been drifting into sleep.

— Who?

— Mircea. He's not the kind of man who you can entrust something important to.

— You shouldn't have drunk coffee after dinner. Don't pester me.

Ion lay awake for what felt like a very long time. His mind whirred unpleasantly. A man could find himself burdened with responsibility when he least expected it. Then, just as he was drifting off, he was shocked awake by the strangest noise. It was a high-pitched bird call. Coming from Brigitte's box. He turned on the lamp and the noise ceased. His wife sat up, squinting in the light, her face crumpled with sleep.

— What was that?

— Brigitte! She sings!

The world was getting stranger.

★

Mircea, too, slept badly. He was troubled by Ion's attitude to the animal. It was clear to Mircea that the animal was half his by rights and it would have been nice for Ion to have acknowledged that. Ever since they were boys Ion had wanted to be the boss. Ion had been a year older and much bigger and they had always played the games he wanted. And Ion's family had owned more land. Even after the land was taken away the better families remembered who they were. Usually Mircea did not mind Ion taking the lead since there was no point arguing over every little thing. But in this case Ion would be figuring that the strange animal might bring in some money. Or perhaps attention from the media. Ion would stand in the garden in his best shirt telling the people from the television how *he* had caught the beast.

As usual, Mircea woke far too early because he had to get up and go outside to relieve his bladder. On this occasion he was unable to get back to sleep. It was already bright outside. He rehearsed the argument he would have with Ion. It was like playing chess. When he says that I'll say this, then if he says . . . At one point Mircea spoke aloud.

— Are you telling me straight to my face that –

His wife opened one eye and looked at him.

He got up and boiled some milk for his breakfast and after he had drunk it he fed the chickens and the pig. It was still too early to go to Ion's house so he fixed the fence around the vegetable garden where some of the smaller chickens were getting through and attacking the tomatoes and peppers before they could ripen.

— Up early! said Ion heartily, when Mircea appeared in his yard several hours later. Rather too heartily, thought Mircea. He's a little too eager, thought Ion, determining not to tell his friend that the beast sang. They walked back towards the garden where they had first found the creature, circling around the subject, each waiting for the other to begin. Finally Mircea came out with it.

— You know, I've been thinking. Perhaps we should involve the authorities.

— Authorities? What authorities? What are you talking about?

— I mean the animal.

— Brigitte?

— Brigitte, yes. Since we don't know what we have on our hands here. We have to go to town. Go public. The press. Or some government department which deals with unusual phenomena. And, of course, as you well know, there may be a sum of money along the line.

Ion, tight-lipped, dug his toe into the earth by the vines.

— We? What *we* have on our hands? I might have known. You probably didn't sleep a wink all night, thinking about reward money.

— Don't tell me it hasn't crossed your mind too.

Ion cleared his throat.

— I've always been happy with what I've got. This is a scientific discovery, not a lotto ticket. But if I receive any payment you won't be forgotten.

— How can I be forgotten? said Mircea, his voice rising. She's half mine and you know it! It's only fair!

— Don't get excited now! See this land? Mine! My father gave it to me and his father gave it to him. I had to wait forty years to get it back. And I caught her here so that makes her mine.

— I saw her first and then we caught her together, with that net there. So it makes no difference where she was caught. Under the law she's mine.

— I know the law. If my neighbour's apples fall on my land then that makes them mine. So she's mine, one hundred per cent, and if you get a penny it will be the result of my generosity. At right this moment I wouldn't count on it.

— We'll see!

— Indeed we will.

Ion escorted Mircea to the gate, where they parted.

— Guinea pig, said Ion's youngest son, who had driven out from the city, where he worked as a schoolteacher.

— Doesn't look much like a pig. She squeals though.

— They're from South America. The Indians in Peru eat them. Maybe that's it.

— Really? Think she's worth anything?

— No. And she's a he. Look.

— That would be a guinea pig tool, I suppose. What can I say, you've let me down, Brigitte. Or whatever your real name is, you Peruvian piglet.

Ion put the 'pig' back in the box.

They went inside for lunch. It was Saturday. It was always nice when one of the boys came home. Ion's wife became very lively and it was a good excuse to sit around and have a good feed and some plum brandy. Then Ion would lie on the couch in the afternoon, listening to the chickens scratching, and fall asleep.

Mircea was angry all day but by late afternoon he ran out of energy and was merely depressed. He turned on the television but was not interested in anything so he turned it off and sat quietly in his chair while the sun grew swollen and low over the fields, and he did not turn on the light, so the only light was the fading light through the window. In all

probability the creature was Ion's by law. But it was Ion's arro-
gance that offended Mircea. The way he had been dismissed
from consideration. A little bit of good luck and Ion could
not bear to share it. So much for friendship.

He heard the gate clacking shut. The footsteps were those
of a woman but lighter than those of his wife, who was visiting relatives in the neighbouring village. A head appeared
around the door. It was Ion's wife. She told him that Ion
wanted him to come round for a glass of wine a little later.

Mircea perked up immediately. He had been right to be
assertive, to show that he would not be walked over. It was
the right approach to take with one such as Ion, who tended
to get puffed up very easily.

As Mircea walked down the road the houses and trees were
silhouettes. The branches of the trees in particular, having
surrendered depth and colour, now stood out as an intricate
black lacework against the sky. Or if he looked at it differently, the light appeared as that which was solid, a mosaic of
a million irregular bright shards. You might live forever and
such things would amaze you, because always you forgot.
You could never really know things, because always you were
forgetting. If a man wanted to paint such a thing it would be
impossible. He would never have enough time. He would get
hungry, become sleepy, and finally discouraged at his lack of
ability. Behind the high wooden fences he could sometimes
hear sounds. The voices of children. Music on a radio. The
clank of a metal pot as a woman got a meal ready. The sounds
behind the fences were peaceful sounds. He saluted a neighbour taking a tethered cow back to its stable after its last feed
by the roadside. He passed a boy and girl. They had been
kissing and he had disturbed them. They separated and greeted
him politely and did not resume speaking until he had passed.

They were both perhaps sixteen. He knew the families they came from, knew more about their grandparents and great-grandparents than they knew themselves. But the knowledge of their grandparents meant nothing to them. The old were fading and disappearing and the world needed to be discovered again, for the first time. Only kisses on warm summer evenings, the first ones in the history of the world, were real to the young. And the young were right, he felt. Kissing a girl under a tree and looking at the road and not knowing or caring what it meant. Then you blinked and you were an old man, walking down the same road.

A bat flitted ahead of him. It was more a movement than a shape, an agitation in his field of vision, gone before he could focus on it. He had no wish to be elsewhere in the world. He did not know very much but somehow he felt it was enough. You were born, you died, and meanwhile life was often strange. He had a presentiment that he would die before his wife and he felt a little sorry for her. She had got very used to him. And Ion would die too. One of them would die first and then the other would be unable to visit, to drink wine and talk. There were other houses but it was not the same.

Ion met him at the gate and shook his hand warmly. So they were still friends and equals in any dealings concerning the animal. It was not about money. It was about respect. They sat down at the wooden table on the porch. Ion poured red wine from a jug. It was a better batch than the previous year's. They sat and listened to the crickets and talked of inconsequential things.

— I'm peckish. You'll join me?

Ion brought out a pot and plates and Mircea cut a loaf. They ate in silence until they were both full. Then they ate a little more. It was a fine stew of various meats and even some smoked sausage that had softened nicely in the cooking. It had onions, garlic, green beans, peppers, tomatoes, and thyme and bay leaf and dill and parsley – everything from the garden – and the sauce was rich with black pepper and paprika, and sour cream had been stirred in at the last moment. Mircea mopped his plate with bread and took a good swallow of wine to wash it down and leaned back in his seat and burped without restraint. Ion refilled his glass. Nothing better in life than to sit at the end of the day with an old friend and share a meal and a few glasses and talk.

— About Brigitte, said Ion.

— Yes?

— Everything you said. Quite right.

Ion leaned across the table and put his hand over Mircea's and clasped it, looking him in the eye.

— Fifty–fifty, said Ion, smiling.

— That's fair.

— Shared! Right down the middle!

Ion leaned back. He began laughing silently, his hands on his quaking belly. He looked ready to burst. His face was bright red. Then he laughed aloud until tears rolled down his red cheeks.

Mircea looked down at the little pile of bones on his plate. His mouth fell open.

Another Love Story

It was the end of summer and I was sitting on the terrace of one of my favourite bars, under a lime tree, feeling rather good, there was a light breeze, and she came over and kissed my friend Anton, an actor, and sat down at our table. He tapped his cigarette in the ashtray, it flashed, he introduced us, and she extended a long tanned arm. Her name was Ana. She looked good and smelled even better. She was dark, her eyes liquid and shiny, the movements of her hands graceful when she spoke. Had you said then that within a month we would be in love and living together I couldn't have believed it. I had long before stopped believing in magic.

But, to cut a long story short, that's exactly what happened.

One bright weekend in September we moved her things over to my apartment overlooking the park, from where by day you could always hear children's voices through the open windows, and from where you could see old people and young couples on the benches, immune for a moment to the harsh momentum of the city. Inwardly I breathed a sigh of thankfulness, that life could become so good, and I knew that it was because of her. I became more patient, gentler, with other people. I gave more time to my family, and my working days passed more easily. I even once suggested to my friends, slightly embarrassed, that it was not necessary to use vulgar language when they referred to women. They laughed at the difference in me and I laughed along.

In the evenings I would stand at the open windows, the

last warm light of the year falling across the park and over the people walking there, and I would think how simple life was. We made it hard for ourselves, by our struggling, our ambition, our stupid vanity, but it was in fact simple. There was nothing ugly in the world but what people did to one another. The warm air carried the sounds from the park, blew through the scented trees, washed my face. I was in love and the world had become pure.

We were good together, everybody said so, and women friends – particularly the girlfriends of my male friends – would tell me they always knew that in the end I would find the one. Everybody likes to see the loner hitched. It tells them everything is right with the world.

The first time I noticed the smell was one Sunday morning when we awoke together.

Sunday, the most beautiful morning of all, when there was nothing to do but lie in bed, make love, then shower, then lie in bed again reading the newspapers, books, and watching television until we got hungry. Then we would stroll to the market and buy food, for the fun of buying things and strolling as much as for the need for food. Then we'd come home with bags full of food, and unload them, and start to cook something good.

That morning we rolled over to face each other. She gave me a sleepy smile. I smiled too. My hand slid along the long hard line of her thigh, over the rolling curve of her hip, down the soft valley of her waist and finally cupped her uppermost breast, as much as could be taken in one hand, which I then kneaded gently. Then the head went down for a suck of dark nipple and the hand went down to caress the hemispheres of her backside. I wanted it all. I was greedy. This was not a prelude to any immediate sexual activity, there was no rush on that score, there would be a visit to the bathroom first and brushing of teeth and throwing water on the face. This was just by way of saying good morning.

I realized something was not right when I buried my face in her hair. She sensed my unease.

'What's wrong?'

'Nothing,' I said. I sniffed her head again, conscious I was behaving rather like a dog. 'Just your hair. It smells . . . different.'

It wasn't bad, or strong. But it was unusual. It was not her. There was a hint of staleness where her hair met her temple.

'Different? How?'

She was a little worried. People are always sensitive about smells.

'It's nothing,' I said, then kissed her lips.

We took a shower together and she washed her hair and it was gone. We had coffee and walked through the park then went to the market. It was one of the mildest autumns anyone could remember and the leaves were turning pale gold. They were turning bright yellow and rusty orange and blood red.

The next morning I rushed out to work. When I got back to the apartment that evening it was there when I entered, as soon as I opened the door. She took the flowers I had brought her – tulips – and put them in water. I opened a window. It wasn't a terrible smell. But it troubled me, and I moved about the rooms like a nervous cat sniffing at things. It was exasperating. It was everywhere and nowhere. It was in the dirty laundry, in the bedclothes. She came up to me and embraced me.

'What's wrong,' she asked. 'What are you thinking about?'
Most of all, it was in *her*.

'Nothing.'

We made dinner. Peppered steaks fried in butter, flambéed at the end with cognac – we turned out the lights to watch the blue flames – and then a little cream stirred into the frying juices. And a salad. It was excellent. We drank a strong red wine and I forgot my unease.

After several days the smell had not gone away. If anything it had got worse. The weather had turned colder and I had less excuse to leave the windows open. It was not overpowering. I can't even say for certain that it was unpleasant. But it was there, where it shouldn't be, and when I had nearly forgotten it she would walk past me and it would hit me harder. It didn't seem to come *from* her, exactly, but it was definitely stronger *around* her, and that made it more confusing. I was withdrawn and uncommunicative that week. It was enough to distract me, to take away my ease. It is like you go to a concert, are listening to beautiful music, but you have an itch on the sole of your foot, or the beginning of a toothache, or you can't remember if you left something cooking in the oven or a tap running, and the music does not work its spell. Ana repeatedly asked me what was wrong. I would say there was nothing wrong.

We didn't make love that week, except for once when I was rather drunk.

It had to be coming from her, I reasoned that Friday evening.

I sat on a bench in the park from where I could see our apartment, delaying the moment when I would have to go home. Leaves were falling around me. Winter was coming

165

and the days were drawing in. She was home and the light was on. It shone redly, warmly, through the almost bare branches of the trees, and I had that strange exiled, nostalgic feeling that I used to have when I was a teenager, when I walked at night through the lonely town, looking in the lighted windows of the houses, enjoying imagining the perfect lives of other people being lived out in those comfortable rooms. I loved her and I knew I was being foolish. Perhaps it was a medical problem and I had to overcome my awkwardness and talk to her about it. This was very difficult for me. For one thing, it would break down a distance between us that I valued. We were still a little bit of a mystery to each other and I did not want that stage in our relationship to end. But my behaviour was making her suffer. I walked home, resolving to speak to her the next day.

The next evening we were having people round. Arriving home, I opened the windows and made myself a strong gin and tonic and decided we would have garlic bread with a kick to it.

I was nervous about our friends arriving, embracing and kissing her, that they too would notice. Anton came first. He didn't comment on the smell, just started talking about a production he was involved in. After a while – Ana was busy in the kitchen – I interrupted him. I leaned over the coffee table: 'Anton, there's a funny smell. Don't you get it?'

He thought I was suggesting he had introduced something and looked at the soles of his shoes.

'Not you! Didn't you notice a strange odour when you walked in?'

Yes, he had smelled the aroma of the peppers roasting in the oven. It had reminded him of the autumn evenings of his childhood. And he was very hungry.

I leaned back in the armchair, confused, and he recommenced talking about the theatre. I found it hard to concentrate on what he was saying.

Next to arrive was Nick, an old friend of Ana's. He embraced her warmly. He had been drinking already and was in a good mood. Nick is very big, his huge torso is getting round, and every time you see him his facial hair is shaved differently, or else his head is shaved. He leads a successful rap group with aggressive lyrics. People are always very surprised how soft-spoken he is in person.

'Nick,' I said, when I'd got him alone, 'don't you notice something unusual in this apartment? An odd smell that wasn't here before?'

He didn't. He praised my garlic bread, though.

And so it went. It was a wonderful evening. When the others had arrived the six of us sat at my big wooden table and my friends devoured my food – I like to give my friends good food – and we were all in good spirits. We drank and laughed and I drank and laughed more than anybody. Ana looked beautiful. I put my hand on hers.

'You know,' I told them, 'I kept getting this strange smell in my nostrils all week, and it wouldn't go away. I started to think I was going crazy. And do you know what? Nobody else could smell it!'

Nick had built a big joint and it had gone around, and this seemed quite funny.

'What kind of a smell?' asked Anton.

I tried to explain. It was something sour, clingy, something gone a bit rotten somewhere. Mouldy blue bread. Damp, like a tramp's coat. Cheese. Smoked fish. Public transport. A common annoying sort of smell. Like lots of things but at the same time not quite like anything in particular. The harder

I tried to describe it the more ridiculous I sounded and the more they laughed.

'Really,' said Ana, 'he's been going around sniffing like a dog all week. He was starting to worry me.'

'It's gone now,' I said. I was relieved.

'There's this old woman who lives in my building,' said Anton. 'She knocked on the door and said she's being choked by fumes of toxic waste, that it's burning her eyes and throat, coming through the ventilation shaft and the plugholes. Says she can't stand it any more. She said she's going to get the police. It wasn't right, she said. It wasn't a civilized way to behave, please could I desist from dumping toxic waste down my sink.'

'Did she call the police?' Ana asked.

'Don't think so,' said Anton. 'Some kinds of mad people know they are mad somehow, know how far they can go.'

That night I think I laughed myself to sleep.

It did not make it any easier from then on, let me tell you, knowing that I was the only one who could smell it. Yes, it occurred to me that maybe there was something wrong with me, that I was a bit mad, but that didn't solve my problem, or make it any easier to live with her as the stink got worse. I would do anything to avoid sitting at home with her. I would come home late, already drunk, and drink more in an atmosphere growing heavy with rottenness.

Did I still love her? Of course I loved her, and of course I could have shown it if I had not been so distracted all the time by that odour that seemed to come from her pores and cling to everything. I began to love the cold cleansing wind of the impending winter, how it cut through my clothes, bit me to the bone, stung my skin, how it killed the stale organic stench that clung in the rooms I slept in. And I would sit down on the park bench and think: How can this happen to me? This is ruining everything. Is it possible that there is such a thing as a curse? Then this is it. And as long as I feel this person choking me I can not be happy. She can not be happy. Faith is necessary to maintain the spell of love. Doubt breaks the spell. I have waited and waited and it is not getting easier. Yes, I wanted to save my love. But I was poisoned.

Have you ever been sick in your stomach, feverish, waiting to vomit? And do you, in such a state, feel love? All a person does in a moment of suffering is to suffer. There is not room for anything else. And this was my position. All I wanted to do was to be free of misery.

I went to a bar and had a few drinks and went home. It hit me as soon as I came in the door.

It was becoming vile.

I had mentioned the smell several times but she thought I was just trying to change the subject and I was perfectly aware that all I could demonstrate was that I was not right in the head. I couldn't bear it when she touched me. I felt bad after I pushed her away. But I always had to push her away – it was an almost physical reflex – before I could create the space in which to consider how my actions had made her feel.

And then all those words! Having to explain what could not be explained. Talking increased my frustration until I could have cried like a little boy. I had violent fits of temper, which frightened her and which would fill me with guilt the next day when I was out of the house and in a more rational frame of mind. And then there were my absences, which filled her with jealousy. Why was I avoiding her? Why would I not speak to her? Why did I not love her any more?

I drank. Of course, I knew the conventional wisdom that drinking is bad if you are depressed. But in this case drink was the one thing that made it easier. The smell disturbed me less, then finally not at all, and sometimes we were able to be together like before. It was like surrendering, falling back into our love as it had been. And, at the same time, in a distant numb way, I felt it was dead and I was already living it through nostalgia.

Nobody knows where love comes from, or what it is, that magic. And nobody knows where it goes.

Thank God for bottles full of medicine, I thought, as we hung together a little longer.

Our sex life was dead. The last flowers I had given her had shrivelled and been thrown away. Where once there was generosity now there was only bitterness. I sat in the park with the shiny naked trees and the winter wind and looked at the window where the light of our home shone. Sometimes I would see her figure, or its shadow, move against the glass. To watch it from a short distance, realizing how close it was, was heartbreaking.

I went home, knowing that it was drawing to a close. I poured a straight vodka. It was very cold outside. I drained the glass and then opened the window a crack and leaned there and drank deeply from the icy foreign air.

I heard her behind me. Her footsteps on the parquet.

'I can't stand it,' she said. 'It's like you hate me. You don't even touch me.'

I turned round. I felt so sorry for her. For us both. It was easier to feel there was hope when we were further apart. I stayed by the window.

'You don't even say anything. It's cruel. It's cruel what you're doing.'

I took a big drink.

'You've changed,' she continued. She was pacing about. She was not the kind of woman who enjoys emotional scenes. But my behaviour over the past weeks had put her under considerable strain. She paced. There might be tears before it was all over. Perhaps mine.

'Look at you!' she said. 'Say something!'

I could not. The cold breeze grazed my cheek. I remained there, watching her.

'This can't go on,' she said. Her normally graceful movements had become disorganized. When she spoke her face and hands moved so quickly I was unable to focus on her.

'I'm sorry,' I said. 'I can't explain.'

She laughed bitterly that this was the best I could do.

'I'm getting out,' she said. 'I'm not staying here another night. Don't try to call me.'

My heart flipped. I had made it happen. I moved toward her. Rottenness was in my nostrils and still I didn't want to lose her. I hated her. My fists were clenched. I could have hit her if she said the wrong word.

'You rotten bitch! You rotten cunt!'

I pushed past her to the door.

I went to the park and sat for a long time watching the window through the black lacing of the branches, now bare and leafless. I sat there even after the lights went out and she had finally left and I had begun to shiver. Then I went back.

I opened all the windows. Clean air blew through. I was no longer forced to explain to another something I myself did not understand. I walked through the rooms, looked at the familiar objects, the furniture, pictures, books. It was all very concrete and simple. I was alone again, and it was a relief. Back to nothing. Back to zero. And at the same time I felt a dirty trick had been played on me. The icy air was cleansing the stink and already nostalgia and loneliness were setting in. I wanted impossible things. I wanted my life with her before it all turned bad. What I had been given had been taken away and now I was even less than before.

The cold wind blew everything poisonous away. Outside it had begun to snow. Huge flakes floated through the dark air, drifted to the ground, settled on the trees in the park. So much motion, and so silent! It was amazing. I began to cry.

As I Sink Down

I

Trapped in a taxi in the heat at the lights at Universitatea, heading south to Unirii. Traffic in its midday frenzy. And I'm sick. Poisoned. A rock in my belly and no good way to even breathe. Before the truck in front can move off the taxi driver leans on the horn, the way they do in Bucharest. Car behind does the same and it goes back along the line. Pointless chain of noise and the hot fumes through the open window. He accelerates towards the next light, edging out to see if he can overtake the truck, swerving sharply back into lane when he sees he cannot. He pours his anger into the machine and from the machine to me. I do not want to know him. A short swollen body under a shiny red sports vest, shoulders and arms covered with thick black hair. At the lights at Unirii he brakes hard and I pitch forward. We have reached the part of town razed by the dictator and rebuilt, new and terrible.

— Take it easy, I tell him.

He turns his head to me. I am looking straight ahead, teeth gritted, trying to hold it together. I can't see the look on his face but I can feel it.

Then it all happens again; the horn, the acceleration, the sharp halt.

— Take it easy or let me out.

And again the hard stare and on the other side the burning sun.

— If you've got a problem with how . . .

I lean forward and let go. A bucket being emptied. I'm surprised I contain so much. Not as surprised as he. I didn't mean to vomit in his car, but that is his problem now and I have my own. I spit, throw money in his lap and slowly get out. The lights have changed and the drivers behind are going crazy. The machines pulse forward to the next lights and I join a herd of people in the smoke waiting to cross six lanes of traffic. The day is getting hotter and it is still a long way down Unity Boulevard. That is where she is.

Meet me, I told my love, so that we can talk a final time.

No, she said, before the phone rang dead. You are being ridiculous.

This failure of a city. I am part of it again. I know I should give up but I cannot.

The lights change for the pedestrian crossing. We move forward.

II

The day before, I took a morning train from Petroşani. A journey I have made many times, but not once in the past year. It is a long trip and it is hot on the lowlands.

I went to the home of my sister, Loredana. She wasn't glad to see me. She knew I was coming but she stood at the door for a few seconds looking at me before she stepped back to let me pass. They haven't much space. She lent me money a year ago and she is waiting. She is an orderly, unhappy person and feels I have squandered my chances, am wasting my life. She resents my need for hospitality.

They have a baby girl and a boy of eight, my nephew

Ovidiu. He sits on a small chair by the door to the balcony to catch whatever breeze might come. It is the living room, which is also where his parents sleep at night. As I enter he does not rise. He smiles and I go and put my hand on his head. I ask him what he is reading. It is a book about sea animals. We are on the fourth floor and the tops of the trees outside sway gently. He is my only nephew and I am his only uncle. He is very clever, very patient, very observant. He's small for his age and listless and has dark rings under his eyes. A couple of years ago we thought he would die. It was something very rare which affected his liver. Supposedly he is better now but still my sister spends endless days in waiting rooms. I should ask her how he is. But I am unable to.

Loredana's husband arrives. We shake hands and tell each other we are fine. He turns on the television and sits on the sofa. On the screen two people are beating each other with huge padded sticks until one falls off a pedestal. It's on a beach. People stand around and cheer. It is fun. Everybody is dressed for relaxation. The commentator is excited.

Long ago my brother-in-law and I decided we were of no interest to each other and we have a habit of not speaking. He has a good job, gets good money. Computers, a foreign firm. For all I know he loves it. They have a car, private medical care. They can think about getting a larger apartment.

He waits sullenly on dinner.

I go downstairs with Ovidiu and we sit on a bench between the apartment blocks in the shade of trees and talk. They live in the west of the city, and it is just like everywhere else, row after row of blocks. It is back from the road, though, and not too bad. The kids run about. Some of them come up to Ovidiu and talk, but he doesn't join in their games. They are used to him. I smoke a cigarette and the smoke spirals up in the still air, towards the trees. I tell him that before the city was built, before people lived in cities, it was all forest from the Danube to the mountains. People who didn't know their way got lost in it.

Ovidiu says that one day he will work for the forestry department, cutting down trees with special machines.

— You have special machines, he says to me. Drills. Helmets with lights.

— Yes.

— Did you always want to be a miner?

— Never.

— Oh.

It's true. Growing up in a mining town, your father being a miner, you imagine your own life turning out differently.

— I'll give it up soon. I'll join the forestry department. We can cut down trees together. With chainsaws.

He smiles and I'm glad. We're only talking.

I am easy with children. I do not try too hard and they listen. I tell Ovidiu a story about a man who dreamed of treasure hidden in the forest. He left his village to look for the treasure. He went around in circles for a year but he could not stop because he saw the treasure in his mind. He saw strange things in the forest and met people he never would have known had he stayed in his village. When he got back home he had no treasure and the people laughed at him. When the people laughed he would remember his journey.

Back on the fourth floor we eat. Loredana is occupied feeding the baby. Her husband doesn't speak. Perhaps it is my presence. Perhaps he is always like this. A man resigned to his life, too worn out to be disgusted. My sister asks what I want in Bucharest. I tell her I'm out to stop a wedding. She snorts.

— You're wasting your time.

— I know.

— Then what's the point?

Her husband has a piece of spine in his fingers and he watches me as he gnaws and sucks over his bowl.

— I have to see it's what she really wants.

— Then what?

— Nothing.

There is purpose in what I am doing. It is something completely necessary to me. Even though it is futile it is necessary.

I do not want to discuss it with these people.

They watch more beach games on television. Then people sing karaoke, out of tune, in English. And the ads tell us what we need to buy. They have drink in the house, but they are not offering so I ask for a key.

— Don't wake the baby.

— I won't.

I come in drunk and kick the cot in the dark and the baby screams. I share the room with the baby and Ovidiu, separated from the adults by a pair of big glass doors with flimsy curtains. Lights go on. I'm sitting on the bed I share with Ovidiu, taking off my boots. Loredana stands with her back to me, comforting the baby, her silence more powerful than words. The same hostility as before but now it has found a focus and no doubt she is in a strange way satisfied. Ovidiu lies on his side, looking at me, eyes wide open as if he had been lying awake in the dark. His face is expressionless. It's worse than the screaming. Then it's dark again.

— I'm sorry, Ovidiu. I didn't mean to do that.

He is quiet and for a moment I fear he is angry with me too.

— I was thinking. The story you told about the man in the forest. It would be better if he finds some treasure. Then everyone can see his journey was a good one. That's a better ending. Don't you think?

— You're right. That's a much better ending.

For a long time I can hear them whispering in the next room, my sister's voice sharp and rapid, her husband's low and tired. I sleep for a moment and it is morning.

III

Unity Boulevard is a long straight madman's dream of perfection. Behind me in the distance, on a rise, is the nightmare House of the People. Old Bucharest bulldozed for a monument to insanity. And now it mocks us. There are no people to fill the space. Human scale has been lost. Another wasteland for mongrel dogs to piss on. The buildings glimmer in the intense sunlight. There is no shade and the sweat runs off me. At a kiosk I buy water, which I manage to keep down, and gum to kill the stink on my breath.

I march on towards the bank where Ileana works. I feel my feet sinking into the ground. I look back and it's no illusion. I have left tracks in a footpath of tar.

The bank is air-conditioned. I ask at three counters and find her in an office for foreign exchange. She is disturbed to see me, but now there is nothing she can do about it. She leaves her desk and comes to the door of the office, where I am standing.

— What are you doing here?

— You refused to see me. I had to talk to you.

We sit down in the lobby. She's dressed for work. Her face

is made up and she looks cool and elegant. I am the one who is out of my environment, still sweating from the street. It must look as if she is sitting with a stranger.

— So. What did you want to say?

All around us people count out money. There was a time when a little pile of money like that would have saved us. But what do I mean, saved us? She isn't lost. Mistakes happen, you forget, move forward. I am the one locked in the past, returning when I should stay away. I knew it would come, this moment when I see that it is finally useless. *What did you want to say?* I gesture with my hands. A thousand things I wanted to say to her and now nothing comes. Her legs are crossed and her hands rest upon her thighs. A diamond glitters on her finger. Coal and diamonds are the same stuff. It's a matter of compression. And then fine cutting. Some poor bastard went down a mine for that. I look down and notice my shoes are spattered. I put them out of sight, under the chair.

— I have a conversation in my head with you all the time. It shouldn't have ended when it did. It should have begun. I mean, when you were pregnant with my child.

She looks away. She doesn't want to be reminded of this now. She's starting a new life, a better one, where all the pieces are in their proper places. A home, a husband. She will have his children.

— I could come back to Bucharest. I'd do any work.

— No. It's too late now.

I'm disappearing. I ask:

— Are you happy?

— Yes.

It's true. I'm gone. I have no place beside her. She asks about the job.

— You said it was only for a year. It's a year now.

— There's not much else. I might give it one more.

A woman comes with something for Ileana to sign. She says she has to go.

— Go, then.

— You go.

I would like to sit in the coolness a little longer but I get up because she wants to see me go. We do not kiss or embrace. I walk from the bank. I have come to perform this act, and now it is done. The hot air of the street hits me like something from an oven door.

IV

I was a student once, at the University of Civil Engineering. There are no jobs for engineers since things fell apart and I didn't go to lectures. But Bucharest was new to me and it felt good to be free. Most of the students were like me, from the provinces, taking advantage of the free accommodation.

By the time I met Ileana I wasn't officially a student any more, but I'd done a deal with a student who didn't need the accommodation and paid off the block administrator. We lived in blocks, ten storeys high, four people to a room. I was in building seven, on the first floor. The refuse chutes on the upper floors got blocked so they threw everything out the window to the waste ground below. You never knew what would sail past the window. Bottles. Bones. Condoms. A television came down the night we got knocked out of the world cup. Wild dogs scavenged in the litter between the blocks. In the winter they howled with hunger.

It was a good time. The city was its grinding brutal ugly

self but it was still new to us and we were getting by and we didn't care. There was always plenty to eat and drink and there were girls. A decaying city full of the most beautiful girls. Trams rattling to a halt and their creaky doors banging open and girls stepping down to the street, hurrying to their lectures. Muddy autumn puddles with dancing circles of rain-drops in the cobbled sidestreets and a girl stepping over to spare her shoes. Mongrel dog standing dazed by snowflakes. A hatless girl runs past into the block, flakes settling on her black hair.

I had money. I went over the border to Bulgaria, came back with the goods on the train, slipped the customs officials their cut. Sometimes I even went to Turkey. When I got back from a trip I would go to where Ileana stayed, a room she shared with three other girls from her town. There was always a cloth on the table. Maybe flowers. The beds were always made, dishes washed and put away after eating. Patiently they would iron clothes for the coming morning, their talk unhurried. In that terrible city which wears you down there are women who know how to make things beautiful, to put grace in simple acts.

It is extraordinary to me now, that time, now that it is a memory. How at ease we were, that is what amazes me. Sometimes I even took Ileana on trips up to Predeal, where the mountains and pines reminded me of home. In summer the air was cool there and in winter the snow was clean. And we had a room alone to make love, and to lie together for long mornings listening to the sounds outside.

Everything changes.

The government brought in tax seals on tobacco to kill the black market and the kiosks were afraid to take the smug-gled cigarettes. I ended up going around the blocks from room to room, selling packs to students. They always wanted credit.

One morning I was brushing my teeth and wondering what work I could find when there was a heavy knock on the door. It was the police, demanding my documents. They were clamping down on people abusing student accommodation. I made up a story about being a visitor which they didn't believe, as they had already extorted the block administrator. They sat down and made themselves comfortable and talked for a long time. In the end it came down to one hundred dollars. I wouldn't hear from them again, they promised. I wasn't even in a position to bargain them down to forty or fifty. I only had about five, in lei, and gave that to them. Then they noticed I had a lot of cigarettes, which they decided to confiscate. I had to wrap up the cartons in old newspaper for them. They were shy about leaving the building with so many good cigarettes. They didn't comment on the fact that no duty had been paid on the tobacco but I knew they would have plenty to say about it when they came back. I had to get out.

I found a cheap place in the centre of town, little more than a closet beneath the roof, room for a bed and little else. The shower was down in the basement, a hosepipe above a concrete floor. Somebody gave me a hotplate. My friends came round and laughed at the place. But in general I had fewer visitors than before.

I got work on a building site. The first job was to knock plaster off a wall with a lump hammer. They were making a restaurant and there was good red brick behind the plaster. For two weeks I smashed at that wall with the lump hammer. I raised clouds of dust and breathed them. The dust floated out into the street. Girls skipped past the doorway waving their hands in front of their faces. We alerted each other to the good ones. When you're standing with a hammer in your hand covered in dust a fine girl is walking through a world that is not yours. She looks clean and light and very far away, and you know that if she met you she would despise you and your four dollars a day.

It was enough for rent and food but as time passed it got harder, those days of labour followed by tired dull evenings. You calculate pennies, frustrated at how mean your life has become. My friends would talk about the parties we used to have. We had rapidly become the kind of people we did not want to be.

Then I got offered the job in the mine. It was so unexpected, so extreme, that I grabbed the chance. I enjoyed the reaction of my Bucharest friends. To the people of Bucharest the miners are violent brutes who one day came and kicked about their more sophisticated betters in the capital. Men who suck the country dry with their high wages, which they receive because the government fears them. I planned to do the job for a year at most. Something else was sure to turn up. And, in any case, the pit could be shut down at any moment.

Ileana looked displeased but didn't say much. We parted ambiguously, and several days later I descended into a mine for the first time in my life.

Nothing could have prepared me for the horror of the first week. I was an outsider, always in the way. I laboured in a cramped chamber at the black rock, separated from the bright world above. That is what you can't understand until you've been down there: the distance from the world you've left behind. And you know any second you could be cut off from it for ever. I was in constant fear that first week of the roof collapsing. Many men had died sudden deaths in the pits. Others had time to wait for help in the silence and the dark, not knowing if it would come in time. Only my shame kept me going until the end of that week. The shame that I'd passed men on the street every day and their true lives had been hidden from me. I was ashamed because my father had done this work and I had never known how bad it was.

At the end of the first week she told me that she was pregnant. She needed money for an abortion. Had she had the money, I think she would have done it without telling me. She had just graduated and was living in Târgovişte with her parents while looking for work. It cost twenty-two dollars. The clinic wanted dollars.

I set out in the morning. I had the money in my pocket but still didn't believe I would have to give it to her. As the bus wound down from the mountains and on to the hot plain I rehearsed what I would say. It was a bright day and the mountains rose clear on my left. I always remember the road into Târgovişte, lined with rows of mature poplars, tall and straight, evenly spaced.

The bus emptied us out at the railway station. The walk from the station to where I was to meet Ileana led through quiet streets of houses set back from the road. It was early afternoon and the street was drowsy. Wooden fences hid the gardens and greenery spilled over the fences. It was a neighbourhood that had once been elegant in a town that had once been prosperous but had faded and grown old and now only wanted to mind its own business. I imagined it would be easy to be happy just to have a home in such a street, the only disturbance the tears of the children when the cat came back with a bird, slack-headed in its jaws.

We met in a park near her home. She wore a black summer

dress, black like her hair, with a pattern of red flowers. She looked straight ahead while I sat on the edge of the bench, turned towards her, telling her how I would leave the mine and get us a place in Bucharest, how we would manage together. She was pregnant with my child, and I had learned this at the end of a week when I had learned how easy it is to die, how little holds us to this life. I was in love with her, and I was in love with the trees and the sun and the future.

But I had been sinking for a long time in her estimation. When I finished speaking she shook her head slowly. After matters were dealt with it might again be possible to consider what we felt about each other. I had taken a job far away in a mine and she was no longer a student and needed work. We had no money, nowhere to live. Things were hard enough without a child. She was only starting out in life and with the country going the way it was nothing was certain. I promised her we would be happy. Again she shook her head slowly.

I was making her suffer by talking about impossible things. I gave her the money. She went to the clinic and I went to the station.

It was dark when I got back to Petroşani. Immense clouds were hurrying in from the north and it had rained and the ground shone slippery orange under the streetlights. I found a phone and at the far end of the line she sobbed, quietly and persistently. There was nothing more to say. We were at the end of something. In the long silences I stood with the receiver squeezed against my ear and my eyes shut, feeling ridiculous. I felt there should be something to say but nothing came. I asked her if it hurt and she said it didn't. She started to speak just as the phonecard expired. The beginning of a sentence hung in the air. I stood about for a moment stupidly. I didn't know who I was or how I had got there.

I had no money left so I went around looking for someone from Lupeni who could help me get home. I found my cousin Marius at the back of a bar, playing backgammon with some friends. They were drunk and cheerful and I sat and listened to them until they were finished. I was very far away. My real life had gone underground and could not be seen by anybody. The person at the surface that everybody saw was no longer me. I wondered had many people felt this way and I supposed they had. I thought of how I had never known my father, and all the men he worked alongside, until I had descended into a mine myself. I understood how it was them against the whole world. Nobody else mattered, nobody else knew.

Next day I worked. It was better than having time on my hands. I was no longer afraid. I worked well.

V

— You!

    — I'm getting my bag.

Loredana allows me to pass into the hallway. She follows me into the room and stands watching, arms crossed, as I collect my few things. As if I might steal something.

— So. Did you get what you wanted?

— Like you said, a waste of time.

— And money. Are you happy now?

I open my wallet and hand her two crisp hundred dollar bills, the money I owe her from over a year ago, when the police had robbed me and I had nothing. I brought the money in case Ileana gave me a reason to stay. Now I am on my way to the train station. I apologize for the delay with the money.

She is confused. She had nursed the money into a grudge. She is caught between pleasure at the surprise of money and discomfort at finding that I have turned out a little better than expected. I say goodbye civilly and the door closes behind me.

Halfway down the first flight of stairs I stop dead, my hand on the rail. I haven't said goodbye to Ovidiu. I could go back.

I go on.

The ticket hall is chaos. And the stink of people, impatient and nervous for their trains, crowds the hot air. Everybody has the same idea – to get out of the city – and this idea has funnelled us to the point of exit and we are almost clambering over each other like ants. I join a long frustrated queue and within minutes realize that it is a mutated creature with two tails, both winding into the same window. I join the back of another line. As it creeps forward arguments break out as people try to jump the queue. The inevitable pensioner bargaining on a show of feebleness. Then a man who pleads that he can't miss his train. A family of Gypsies lift the grandmother up the steps from the street outside. The old woman is sitting crumpled like a sack of potatoes on a board under which are castors. They pull her by a rope on this squeaking raft through the ticket hall, shouting noisily. It all must all look like a strange dream to her old eyes.

I make the train. The other seven in the compartment are older, from Petroşani. As usual, one begins to make conversation and they all join in. The one subject that everybody loves: the price of this and that and what was going for how much in such a market, the price of bread compared to last year and isn't everything gone to hell. It has been a long day and the pointlessness of such talk irritates me. The same thing has been going on in train compartments for as long as I can remember. Then as we leave Bucharest behind two old women start talking about all the different mine disasters through the years. This will take a while.

A man came from Germany once, part of a union delegation, and we stood around in a circle with the translator and he said, This is murder! This mine must be closed immediately! He appeared shocked. Then we went back to work. And he went back to Germany.

The joke is they don't even want our coal. It's poor quality and our equipment is obsolete. It would be cheaper to import. The government would shut us down tomorrow, but they are afraid the brutes will descend from the hills again, so instead they drag it out over years.

Open country, calm day's end. Strangely, the other passengers no longer speak, and it is better like that. I am very tired. Towards Piteşti the sun is bloated and heavy and shadows draw out across the land. With the white glare gone from the light, distant things stand out in detail. The hills, a cluster of willows at the curve of a stream. Everything appears close and urgent. The eye does not have to search, everything is immediately present. Something odd has happened in how I remember Ileana, however much I tell myself to let go of the past. The past as it draws away has moved into sharp focus. I know what occurred more clearly now than when I lived it. I can do nothing about this, no more than I can tell myself to look at this train window and not see through.

A line of men moves along a roadside lined with poplars, scythes balanced on their shoulders. The blades are folded in towards the shafts and wrapped with white strips of cloth, like bandages. Their work is done and they are satisfied at being released. I know that feeling.

A hand shakes my shoulder. I open my eyes. Grey dawn

in Petroşani. The people on the platform move past my window with that quick railway-station walk. They are eager to return to their lives.

I board the early bus for Lupeni as the colour is coming back in the sky. Exhaust fumes enter through a hole in the floor. It is not a problem on the level but when the bus labours on the uphill we choke and our eyes stream.

I walk through the single main street of Lupeni, which is also the main road through the valley of the Western Jiu. The road comes to an end at the head of the valley thirty kilometres beyond. Apartment blocks of naked concrete, ten storeys high, line the road. They are more or less the same as you see in the suburbs of Bucharest. A dead town where there should not reasonably be any.

I open the door to the apartment I share with my parents, the same one where I grew up. My father greets me. He has just got up and is in faded pyjamas and an old robe. He tells me my mother has gone to the market. He is in his early fifties but appears older. He moves slowly. His lungs are ruined from years of black dust. His eyes are heavy and the skin on his face sags. His gut sags. He is being pulled down. When he smiles it is painful, like he is fighting gravity. I want to take a shower but when I turn the tap in the bathroom it sputters and coughs. I sit down in the kitchen and he makes me coffee. He always keeps a few bottles of water in the fridge. You never know when the water will be off. He asks about the family and I lie. I say Ovidiu is growing well and looks fatter. His face brightens.

— That's good. That's good.

He asks how it went. He thinks I went to Bucharest to make some money. Something about tobacco. I make an excuse about them wanting too much cash up front.

— Never mind. You tried. You have the right spirit. Too many people, they just take what they're given.

I need to sleep but my shift will soon begin. I've had my rest days, and now it's time to go down again.

I board the bus with the others, and it takes us out of town, several kilometres up the valley to the pithead. A woman raises the barrier to let us through. She has done this job since her husband was killed in the mine a year ago. We change into overalls, boots, helmets. An earlier shift has just returned to the surface. They move slowly, spreading out, getting the feel of open space again. They are tired and smudged, and drunk on the light and the colour. It's always like that, when you are released, when you see sky and grass and mountains again.

We get into the lift. The metal gate is wrenched closed. The intersecting slats make diamonds. As we fall the air rapidly goes cold. We never speak at this moment. The first month or so my chest would always tighten, but now I am more used to it. When I come up to the open sky all kinds of strange and wonderful ideas occur to me. The world is created again. I might even say I believe in God. As I sink down my mind empties and I know only the labour before me.

I wake. I am lying on Ileana's bed. It is early afternoon, a Sunday, and nothing moves in the heat, nothing makes a sound. This is her room when she was a student. She is at her desk in front of the window, writing. Her back is to me and she is unaware that I have woken and am watching her. A white sheet hangs across the big window to shade the sun. A lower corner of the sheet stirs lightly in the breeze, and all I hear is her pen moving across paper. Her hair is shiny black against the brightly illuminated white sheet. I lie there, watching her.

The lift stops. The gate opens. We move forward.

A Performance

The applause died down and the performer stepped forward and took off his shirt. The auditorium went completely silent. The left side of his chest was atrophied, flat, artificial looking, and bordered on three sides by fresh red scars: a straight line just below his left clavicle, a straight line slightly to the left of his sternum and a line that curved slightly below his left ribcage.

He was an unattractive man, pallid, hair sparse on top, the facial expression of one who had received a terrible shock long ago and had never recovered. The kind of man who would say nothing at a party and you would not say anything to him.

He swabbed the scarred areas with alcohol and lifted a scalpel from the table. There was going to be no talking. Everybody had expected some kind of a discussion beforehand, an exposition of his philosophy, a frame in which the audience might place the spectacle they were about to witness. No; he was moving straight to the action, slicing his own flesh deftly along the lines of the scars. If you are going to cut yourself you must work swiftly.

The auditorium had the kind of seat which flips up automatically when pressure is removed, a standard in cinemas, and there was the noise of many of these seats flipping up as some found this already too much to stomach. It was more real than they had expected.

There was some blood indeed, but not so very much, the

flesh around the scar tissue having died back over the years. Now he was removing the staples which secured his ribs to his sternum and dropping the staples in a blue solution. Then a little more work with the scalpel and it was happening: he was putting his fingers into his own wound, near his heart.

Now that he was ready he raised his pale face to the audience. He was going to look at them while he did it. That was professionalism. He was doing it for them. He pulled at his ribcage and it opened. He unhinged the panel of his own chest.

He showed them a human heart, beating.

He stood there, sweat beading on his pallid face, blood dripping from his hands. His face showed suffering. Not the kind you sympathize with, necessarily. The suffering of a madman.

The noise of liquid spilling came from the back of the auditorium. That was bad. If one vomited it could set them all off.

Then came the sound of a man crying, crying as if he had not cried since he was a child, crying from long silent years of despair. The weeping spread. Soon many people were crying. They did not know why. Each person crying made a different sound. People do not speak the same or laugh the same and they do not cry the same, but the sound of their weeping flowed together like the waters of a river and became one sound.

He stood before them with his ribcage open and his eyes open and his mouth a little open and he raised his hands a little from his sides, palms open, trembling, as if to say: I am giving you my living heart. Now you see it. I cannot give you any more.

He held this pose for about half a minute, though it

appeared much longer, and was long enough for some members of the audience to wonder whether he planned to bleed to death in front of their eyes. He then closed his ribcage tenderly, and reinserted the staples that secured his ribs to his sternum. He no longer seemed to notice the audience. He had lost some blood during the performance and the flow now needed to be arrested. A man in a white coat came forward and assisted in this. Then, beginning with the uppermost part of the incision, the assistant began stitching the performer's severed flesh.

A fat man in a suit stepped forward on the stage.

'That's all,' he said. 'Show's over. You can go home now.'

This was brusque. Yet the people were glad to leave. They had seen enough. There was no applause.

'Say what you like,' said a woman in the lobby, 'but this shows there is still a role today for theatre.'

Outside, people began to discuss what it meant. There was general agreement that it meant something. After all, people had been moved. It had not been elaborate at all, but it had been affecting. Many thought it showed that theatre was getting back to primitivism, to the ritual which gave birth to Greek drama.

'It was extreme,' said a man in black, polishing his glasses. He was with a tall thin girl and another man. 'But is it art?'

The tall thin girl responded:

'Catharsis,' she said. 'Did you notice how many people started crying?'

'I didn't cry,' said the man, putting his glasses back on.

'Comfort isn't enough for people. They need to feel suffering,' said the girl. They stepped outside, buttoning their coats.

'The obvious parallel is Jesus Christ nailed up for our

improvement. A spectacle to last a couple of millennia. Maybe this guy has a messiah complex.'

A second man, the lover of the one with glasses, spoke: 'I don't know that the first one delivered the medicine.'

'That's because you're a stinking Jew,' said the first man.

'I showered this morning. But that's what I'm talking about.'

The girl laughed.

'I mean, what good is sacrifice?' the second man continued. 'So Jews kill Jesus. Christians kill the Jews. Now the Israelis kill the Arabs. The example of sacrifice is never enough. Or else it's enough, but it doesn't last very long.'

They argued Japanese against Mexican. Japanese was stylish, but what they really wanted was spicy meat, and melted cheese.

At the back of the theatre the performer was being bandaged and examined by his personal physician while the man in the suit looked on.

'You're getting weaker,' said the doctor.

'Rest up a few weeks,' said the suit. 'We're booked for two more shows, then we'd better call it a day, give you a good long rest.'

The performer looked unhappy.

'The people need me,' he said.

The doctor and the suit looked at each other. They were both earning big money, but they did not want any more.

'They need me,' repeated the performer.

The suit took a pill.

'People are fucked,' said the suit. 'You think you know what they need? Take your money and keep a little distance from the people. That's my advice.'

'You'll kill yourself,' said the doctor.

'They can never get enough,' said the suit.

Notes from a Turkish Whorehouse

I got her back to my room. She looked good. I just wanted to get down to it.

— Forty million.

— Thirty.

— Fine. Now.

— After.

— Now.

On the screen they always paid after. That's the screen. I gave her twenty dollars, about thirty million Turkish lire. She did a calculation, then indicated she had to take a little walk to check it was real, check if I was born yesterday.

— Right, I said, if you don't like it give it back.

She decided she liked it.

All this was a mime game – her only word of English was 'money' – until I said the name of the town we were in and pointed to her.

— Azerbaijan, she said.

Then we spoke Russian. I speak seven languages. Six badly. You pick things up away from home. Russian gets you by with whores in Turkey. They come from the ex-Soviet countries. Supply and demand.

— I have to give all my money to my pimp, she said. Give me five million just for me.

— All right. If it's good.

— It will be. Give it now.

— After.

— Now.

I gave her five.

I had met her on the street the day before. She looked like the Greek girl. Dark, and eyes a little slanting, the same small compact body. She offered me sex and a nervous muscle beneath my breastbone contracted like the cat crouching before it springs, but I was paralysed in Turkish and panicked silently as the shopkeepers watched us in the bright daylight. She tossed her head and walked off. I was a waste of time. I went back to my room and paced. How much to give her? The strings of zeros on the notes confused me. She was flesh and this was paper. She could have it all. I brushed my teeth and took a shit. When I was pulling my trousers up the top button went. I had no belt so I was literally running after a woman with my trousers falling down.

All day and night I looked for her, walking around the town with my hands in my pockets to keep the trousers up. At the end of the night I ended up in the whore bar, talking Russian to girls from Georgia and Azerbaijan and Moldova and Ukraine. By then I was drunk and worn out and talking was all I could do.

— Time is passing, she said.

She stripped off and got on the bed and spread her legs like she expected me to dive straight in.

It should have looked big and nasty and overfucked. It looked tight and neat. Her pubic hair was short, just a shading. No chance of crabs. Muslims are very clean people. She lay, propped up slightly, thick black hair spilling over the white pillow. I stood there in my boxers feeling like the sultan.

— You remind me of someone.

— To work, she said.

I lay down alongside her.

— Sorry, I said, I'm used to foreplay.

She was soft and scented. Rose petals. Of all the fragrant flowers in my harem, you I picked tonight. I put the rubber on. She whimpered and moaned like I was a big stud but when she realized I was in no hurry she started complaining.

— Finish! Time is passing!

I had a lot to learn about bargaining. She had been eating raisins when she picked me up and I reached into the brown paper bag and grabbed a handful and emptied them into her mouth. That shut her up. For a moment.

— Time is passing!

My reign was over. I finished up.

She ran into the bathroom. I heard the shower. She came back, drying between her legs, and threw the damp towel on the bed. She plucked the cigarette from between my fingers and smoked as she brushed out her magnificent hair before the mirror, getting ready for the next one. I watched her from behind. I gave her a couple of cigarettes and she left me a little hill of raisins on the bedside table.

That was my first taste of Sabila.

The Greek girl, back in Saloniki, had always been giving off about the Turks. Now I was at the Black Sea in a whore bar and Atatürk was on the wall. They had said there was nothing to see in the town so I went and the fish factories stank but nobody was trying to sell me a carpet. The whore bar looked normal enough from outside. That is to say, miserable, badly lit, a few men sitting around bored with themselves. The women sat behind the window that was shuttered off from the street. You could walk by and never realize. I'd go in and sit under Atatürk. Mustafa Kemal was everybody's daddy. He had advice about everything. If he told them to wash their hands before dinner they made a slogan of it and put it up with the picture.

I made friends with Yakup, the waiter. In summer he had worked on a bar on the Aegean coast. There were plenty of tourists. The British and German girls screwed the Turks for free, undermining a sector of the economy.

— But they say me, You old! Go away!

Thirty-seven, divorced, bald, small, and unable to afford the good twenty-dollar girls in the establishment. He could afford a two-dollar dirty fuck in the alley so he did without.

One day I said:

— Yakup, what's that stuff you're always writing when I come in?

He showed me his notebooks. He was writing what he called 'comic stories'.

— I look, he said, indicating around. I listen, I make notes.

Notes from a Turkish Whorehouse! I thought. Good title. Spicy yet Dostoevskian. Worth making a story just for a title like that. Might use it myself.

He joked about getting rich, winning the Nobel Prize, taking the girls out on a yacht. I respected him, though. He was where he was and he was getting it down. Whenever it was slack he was there writing, throwing something new in the pot and stirring.

And I was doing the same. The bones of romance are hard to bury so I put mine on simmer. My novel.

Winter came and rain poured in from the Black Sea and the boats tied up and the fishermen sat behind streaming windows and pulled their moustaches and played backgammon and smoked and drank little hourglasses of tea and there I was in my rented room with the wooden floorboards, getting up each morning and creating beautiful dancing prose, drinking buckets of tea, pacing about as the world in my head became brilliant, flashed, gave off sparks – sitting down again for lines that ran and flowed and surprised even me the creator. But that was the joy of it, I wasn't the maker. It wasn't me hammering it out, hacking at the reluctant material. I was the conduit for a magic energy. I was possessed of it, there to deliver it, deliver myself of it. The delivery boy. I was elated and humble. It was a holy time.

I was getting plenty of sex too and it freed me up for higher things. I trawled for trollops, tasted tarts, screwed strumpets, shagged streetwalkers, humped hookers and harlots. They were young and clean and rather good value.

I could never get enough Sabila. It was the bodily resemblance to the Greek girl, and something in her character, humorous and resilient, that impenetrable hardness just beneath the skin, that had me by the balls. In my dreams Sabila and the Greek became confused. I could have untangled it, been reasonable, stopped waking and crying, but reason could wait. The novel was almost finished. I knew I was fucking too much and the money would soon run out but I didn't want to break my rhythm. I got up each morning and made a coffee and took a dump and the words just rolled. I had even accumulated a stack of poems.

I developed a system whereby I got the best out of Sabila and she got the most out of me. I gave her a dollar for every two minutes. We swapped roles. She kept checking the time by the bedside clock.

— Slowly! she whispered.

— Jesus! I said, seeing what I had clocked up. Time is passing!

It was all going well until it went completely wrong.

This is what happened. She was combing out her hair by the mirror, talking continuously as she always did before and after, some nonsense about how her husband had a big car and was going to drive her home any day, and I went to my stash for her forty minutes' worth and there was no money. One of her bargain-basement sisters had cleaned me out. No matter how drunk you are, do not fall asleep before she leaves. Always see her out the door. Well, I wanted fun and now I'd had it. For one epiphanous medieval moment I worried that banging lots of whores was in fact A BAD THING and God was punishing me. I felt sinful. It was the shock of no money. I had a little in the bank, just enough to get me out of the country. That was all. I went back to the room. She was still chattering. About how she liked walnuts soaked in honey.

— Sabila, I'll have to pay you tomorrow.

She stopped in mid-brush. The smile fell from her eyes and then from her mouth.

— *YahachoomoydyengiseeCHAS!* (IwantmymoneyNOW!)

I explained the situation. She stepped up and hissed through her teeth. And lots of colourful language. I found it amusing until she fixed me with her eyes, now more slitty than ever, glossy black like wet coal, and slowly drew her index finger from my groin to my sternum.

— My boyfriend will cut you open like a fish!

I didn't know anything about her boyfriend or her husband or her pimp or if they were three in one like the blessed trinity but I have to admit this scared the shit out of me.

— I thought we were friends! Where's your heart of gold?

She actually clenched her fists and stamped her little foot on the floor.

— No free fucks!

It should have been funny but it wasn't. I tried to explain but her little calculator brain couldn't understand 'later'. She was ready to have bad things done to me and no mistake.

— You'll get your money. I just don't have it here.

— GIVE!ME!MY!MONEY!RIGHT!NOW!

— Listen, I said, opening my wallet with trembling hands. Look at this. It just looks like a piece of plastic. But this is Western technology. Magic. I put this in a hole in the wall and money comes out. So there's no need for your nasty talk. If you can't wait until tomorrow we'll go get your money right now.

This calmed her down a bit.

— Time is passing! she grumbled as she put on her coat.

I hadn't heard that one for a while.

We went down the wooden stairs, left, then right onto Atatürk Caddesi and straight down to the seafront and its rich pong of salt and fish guts, and the black shapes of the docking cranes against the sky.

I put the card in the wall.

— Time is passing!

I punched in the number and demanded all my wealth. Not that the rotten little whore would ever get any more of it. Teach her how to treat her customers.

It was cold. I rubbed my hands. The machine purred and clicked and messages flew across the ether from one computer network to another, the glory of global banking and information technology serving me, in my hour of need.

YOUR BANK HAS DECLINED YOUR REQUEST.
PLEASE REMOVE YOUR CARD.

I reinserted the card and requested a more modest sum. Same bullshit.

— You see, Sabila, this system depends on communication between a number of computer networks, linking a number of banking systems, and you know how computers are, sometimes the network is temporarily down. This doesn't mean I have no money. It just means I can't access it right now this minute, at the present moment in time. Please understand.

Her body twisted and jerked in anger, culminating with the little stamp of the foot. More obscene talk about my guts spilling on to the ground.

— All right, all right. Enough of that. If you don't trust me for twenty stinking bucks come back to the house and I'll give you something.

— Time is passing!

I knew that. Every time I looked in the mirror. And I was still unpublished.

We went back to the house but I had nothing but crap. Even the bedside clock was a piece of crap. I offered her an old radio belonging to the landlord. I even offered her my one pair of trousers.

— Ha! The girls call you the one with the trousers falling down!

I had actually hoped one of them would do a little sewing.

— What's this stuff you're always scribbling? she said, picking up my priceless notebooks from the table.

— Leave that. It's worthless.

She stuffed my novel and poems into her handbag, which she was then unable to zip closed. She muttered while she did it.

— No free fucks! No free fucks!

— Why are you taking that?

— Because you don't want me to! Ha!

Then she was gone with everything I'd written since I came to the town. There was no other copy.

I opened a bottle of vodka to settle me but by the time I was through I was ready for a knife fight with her pimp-husband-boyfriend. Fortunately I tripped on the rug and hit my nose on my writing desk. I got some toilet paper and jammed it up and tilted my head back. Then I fell asleep in the chair.

I woke very early and went to the cash machine. I felt like a scarecrow given a soul and sent to wander the badlands of the earth. There was nobody up but an arthritic street sweeper, sweeping in slow motion, and everything was sad and painful. A cold wind came off the Black Sea and stung my eyes and made them water. It might have looked good in the *National Geographic – Early dawn breaks over Turkey's remote Black Sea coast*, then statistics about sardines – but it looked like shit to me. And the idiot seagulls didn't help. As I keyed in my number a gang of them attacked a plastic carton. They were big as geese. A couple of them could kill a man. Luckily they were getting by on bits of fish.

Then a friendly whirring from my machine, the reassuring music of crisp banknotes being counted out. I inhaled the seaweed breeze, spiced with guano and things long expired.

PLEASE TAKE YOUR CARD

I did.

PLEASE TAKE YOUR CASH

I smiled at the seagulls.

The muezzin gave the daybreak call. It came crackling and

wailing over the loudspeakers from the minaret. How often I had cursed it as it woke me, and now it chimed so finely with my moment of salvation. I stopped at the steps of the mosque. It glowed inside with warm red artificial light. A few men were on the rugs, starting the new day by opening their hearts and giving thanks to God for life. I was pulling at my laces, my boots were off. I was inside, on my knees, my forehead on the carpet. That's it! All the way down! You Catholics have no idea! It was the hangover, the money, the hopeless motheaten dawn being banished by the rising sun, but my cheeks were wet. Let me be abject that I be raised again by your mercy! Abasing myself before the master of the universe and at the same time celebrating that he was on *my* side, O resurrector of my resurrection – my re-erection – O guarantor of my potency, O putter of bone in my meat! It was good while it lasted but then several of the worshippers were glancing at me. They were pretty reserved in their prostrations and I was fairly flinging myself down, my head uncovered. And I stank of drink and had a foreskin. I became self-conscious and shy of scandal. I withdrew. They would not understand my feelings.

So I went home and ran the bath and got in. The hot water on my balls was good and I took matters in hand. I felt independent of human entanglements. And I saved money.

By late afternoon I was frantic again, though. I couldn't find Sabila. The initial exhilaration of the money had faded and I was worried about my work. I knew she was a mercenary little bitch and would extort me if she had any notion how important the notebooks were. She would sell them back a page at a time and there'd be nothing I could do about it.

When the muezzin declared sunset I had made no progress.

I went down to the bar and sat with Yakup, but it was far too early for any of the girls and he hadn't seen Sabila. I told him about my notebooks. He looked at me with sympathy.

— I think you make mistake, my friend.

Those simple words! It was his authorial presence, his narrative voice. If the oracle of Amun itself had spoken it could not have been clearer that I was screwed. I wouldn't have the heart to begin the novel again. The way it flowed through me and surprised me and made me a servant, raw and open and humble in the act of scribing, could not be repeated. It would be like sitting down and making myself swallow big cold spoonfuls of yesterday's porridge. Telling myself it was tasty and wholesome would not help it go down. It would not work. And I might never have a good idea again. I would meet the muse but not get it up. Sabila had stolen my juice, left me impotent and poor. I was finished as a writer and a human being if I did not get those notebooks back.

It was nearly midnight when I found her, on Atatürk Caddesi where I had seen her that first time in autumn. I tried to control myself. I didn't want to seem too interested in the notebooks. I couldn't afford it. The end of my money was in my pocket. There was no more.

— I've got your money, so give me my books.

— I haven't got your scribbles. I'll give them to you tomorrow.

— I want them now.

— All right. Give me the money.

— Money after.

— Now!

Same old conversation. She had me. I gave her the money.

— Not enough. Last night-time was passing. Too many words.

I peeled off another note. She saw the wad this time and smiled. I was respectable again.

— Time for sex, she said, taking my arm.

— I don't want sex, Sabila. I want my scribbles back. Right now.

— I threw them away.

A strange sound came from my throat. A man being strangled, casually, by a stranger.

— Last night I was very angry with you, she said, wagging her finger. You are very bad!

— Can you find them again?

— Time is passing. You must pay.

— After.

— Now!

Screwed by a whore.

She took me by my arm and led me down the dark alley. She stopped and pointed at a skip.

— What? You threw my scribbles in there?

She nodded.

I leaped before I looked. For a moment I thought I had jumped among a load of rats but in fact they were cats, probably half the cats in town, and they scattered fast enough. My boots sank into a mulch of dead fish, cardboard, decomposed corpses, cabbage leaves, sodden newspapers and other stuff that stank. Actually I don't know what it was but the organic content was unusually high. I was gagging and I couldn't see a thing. I fumbled for my lighter. Even with the light it didn't make much sense. There were some papers there but not mine. I squelched about in misery looking for traces of art. It was gone. Buried in shit. Or never there in the first place.

— Sabila. I beg you. Tell me literature is safe in your room.

I forgive you for ruining my boots. I beg you. It was a novel about a girl who broke my heart and all I got was the story. It was the only thing that made it worthwhile. She looked a lot like you, in fact. That's the only reason you've earned in excess of five hundred dollars from me up to this point. Tell me art and love isn't buried in catshit and fishheads. Time is passing, I know as well as any. Speak to me! Sabila!?

The lighter got too hot and burned my thumb and I let it go. There were many stars in the sky and the longer I looked the more stars there were and it was lonely realizing I was talking to them and that already Sabila was gone. Maybe I would get a short poem out of it all. I clambered out of the skip. And went down to the bar to talk to Yakup.

— My friend, you smell of something not pleasant!

I looked down at my boots. We went outside to talk.

— I was disappointed with romantic love, Yakup, and wrote a novel about it. But I was unprepared for these whores. They're completely unethical.

— This is a comic story. May I use it?

— Take it. I'm finished with writing.

— No, it's like women, the desire always comes back. And when it comes you welcome it, because it says the heart is still beating.

— Very aphoristic, Yakup.

— You may satisfy hunger alone. But the desire for woman always needs one other person. It is never simple.

— This *must* be the end of the story.

— Just a little more, my friend. To tidy up. Unless we give to this chaos a form we suffer confusion, depression, and worse things.

The next night I was on a bus to Istanbul. The gamble had not paid and now I had to get back to somewhere and sell

207

my time. On the way to the bus station I saw Sabila. She was on the other side of the street, heading for an appointment. Those bouncy little steps she took. I knew she was on business because she was walking very fast, very purposefully. For some reason I felt nothing against her. In fact I admired her.

Some activities don't make much sense but then not doing them makes even less and that's when you're trapped, singing between the bars. As the bus pulled out I thought of Yakup. I wrote the title across the top of the page. And then the words began to come.

Philanthropy

Virgil wrote the article, then sat watching the smoke drift past his tenth-floor window. The smoke was from bonfires of leaves. The leaves did not really burn, they smouldered, and it had been going on for weeks. He had written about living with the smoke. He had tried to keep it amusing. He did not want to seem a crank.

A fist thudded against the door. He opened it. A hulk of a woman smiled down at him, gaps in her teeth. He handed her a single banknote and closed the door before she could speak.

For six years he had been lending her money. After several months she would return the money and several days after that she would come round smelling of drink and borrow it back again. For a couple of years this routine had amused him. But things had changed. The woman no longer talked about her varicose veins. He had told her sharply one day that he did not want to hear about her legs, or any other part of her.

Shortly after he had eliminated conversation from the creditor–debtor relationship she had bought a little dog which yapped hysterically every time he passed her door on the journey to and from his one-room apartment at the end of the hall.

He imagined handing her a fist of money: 'Here, sell me your dog,' and he would take the beast, still yapping, and toss it out his window. A little spin in mid-air, legs flailing, before it disappeared over the rim of the balcony. Tragic, tragic, and he'd only just bought it.

He could not look out his window at the smoky haze without feeling under siege. Besieged not only by smoke, which was bad enough, but by a general stupidity of which the smoke was just one manifestation.

Now, Virgil reasoned, in a city of grey concrete blocks, streaked with grime, were decaying leaves offensive? In a vandalized, brutalized city of wild dogs and aggressive traffic and smoke from old cars and buses and trucks, were leaves pollution? Yet if the city endured millennia, if religions came and went, if dynasties were born and died, if the city were pillaged by barbarians on horseback, riding in from the east, if all this and more came to pass there would still at the end be a little man in midwinter, dressed nearly in rags, bending over to set fire to a little hill of leaves. Here, neighbours, have some smoke! Let it mingle with truck smoke and the deranged music of car horns and the barking of ecstatic mongrels!

One year Virgil had gone down to reason with the bonfire-makers. Inevitably, voices were raised and a fat middle-aged woman who wore a scarf and about six skirts – she looked like she had just got off a train from somewhere in the country – shook a rake at him and told him to go fuck his dead mother. He replied in kind and some boys let off kicking a football and came to watch. The two men, with clothes and skin the colour of dead leaves, leaned against their rakes and grinned.

Virgil went to wash. The taps coughed air. Wash cancelled. But his hair stuck up in clumps. He couldn't go around news-paper offices looking like an idiot. You could write like an idiot and get paid for it but if you looked like one you were finished. He splashed water on his head from the bucket in the bath where his dirty laundry was soaking.

He walked down the hall and the hulk-woman's dog went crazy barking behind the door. As usual. He got in the lift and pulled the awkward doors shut and pressed the button. When you live on the tenth you spend more time in lifts than other people. Add up all that time, thought Virgil, going up and down, opening and closing doors, through decades, and you were cheated of a fair proportion of your life.

Thinking like that will drive you crazy, he told himself.

An old woman was leaving the building ahead of Virgil and, not noticing him, tried to tug the door closed. He held on until she realized her mistake. It took a little longer than he expected. She was one of those who have lived so long they have worn ruts to the shops and bus stops and navigate by looking at the ground. That's what happens, thought Virgil. You spend a lifetime without imagination or curiosity, cutting out the world, and you end up blind to what's in front of your face. The rest of her day will be just as beautiful. Dull young people become duller decrepit old people. Little children have more wisdom.

Then he was looking into a deep hole in the footpath. It had appeared overnight. Big enough to fall into. If you stepped in while looking at some sixteen-year-old wiggling her backside you'd be in trouble. The crust of the earth had simply collapsed and now there was a deep crater. He wished more holes would appear. Really big, deep ones, inexplicably, providing people once again with that secret joy they had experienced – the feeling that something extraordinary was possible – when the planes flew from out of the blue sky and into the skyscrapers.

Then he had to cross the frantic intersection. There was

always a lot of smoke and noise and car horns, more seconds of his mortal life ticking away while his frustrated soul consumed itself waiting for a pedestrian light. More crazy thoughts. Then scarpering across with the others.

He went down into the metro. He had just missed a train. The next batch of people was spilling down the steps to refill the emptiness. Standing around. Ten minutes. The tiles on the ground were dull yellow like something from an old urinal.

Somewhere, he knew, life was beautiful.

He got on the train and sat down. I understand, he thought, how people spend their lives obsessed with money and increasing their stock of material comforts and appearance of status, to be a flashier insect among dull insects. The truth is we despise each other. People don't respect people, they respect money. I'm the least materialistic person I know and if I had the cash I would put up walls and gates to preserve myself from these chattering savages.

The man next to him was reading one of the daily gossip rags. (Teach them to read and this is what they want.) There was a story about some man who had fallen down an open manhole, ten metres, and lain at the bottom for two days, moaning for help. The man didn't remember how he came to fall down an open manhole, which was understandable. Apparently people had been throwing rubbish down there for some time and the plastic bottles had broken the man's impact at the bottom, saving him from serious injury. Nobody responded to his cries. He was in complete darkness and lost all track of time. Eventually a pensioner, who happened to be walking his dog across the piece of wasteland where the manhole was located, heard moaning and alerted the authorities. There was a picture of the man lying in hospital with a drip in his arm and scabs on his lips. The man explained that he had no family and no job and only his faith in the goodness of God sustained him in his day-to-day existence and time down manholes.

Horrible. Good story though.

The first beggar got on. He held a holy picture, Jesus with a lamb in his arms. Little red lights flashed on and off around the picture. A battery-operated Jesus. Above the creaking and shaking of the metro, a scrap-junk submarine transporting invalids, came the monotonous pleading, the abject self-pitying drone. Father dead, eight brothers, mother sick with cancer, hungry, whatever you are able, God our Father. And then down on his knees, very low, blessing himself, the picture before him with the lights going round.

Christianity. Communism. Christianity again. Similar ideologies, though Christianity was invented for serfs and communism for factory workers and clerks. Under communism the worker, the drooling idiot, the sheep, are all presented as the innocent victims of history. The good guys in the film. And then the workers' state sets you free. From the obligation to do anything. Except work. The bovine element in man proclaimed most virtuous. Because Daddy says so. Then Daddy dies of a stroke and you're back waiting for Jesus, whining on a metro about your victimhood, imploring your fellow travellers in the name of common Christianity.

Then the Gypsies. The man played an accordion, the woman collected. Virgil loved the bright music dancing out from behind the machine noise of the badly fitting parts of the metro car, how the alert sounds battled through the clamour and briefly won, the sound of life rising above the beaten people, a flower in a crack in the concrete.

Virgil put his hand in his pocket. Funding the resistance.

Virgil believed that if you shared your money with strangers it should be on a rational basis. Did you wish to pay someone to display their deformities? Did you want a stump paraded before you? Was that an uplifting spectacle, for a man to drag himself along the floor of a metro car, trouser-leg rolled up, to display a dirty footless limb? Was that a good thing to pay a man to do, to display his own inutility in a way that degraded both you and him? Did you give your money to sad-looking waifs, sent by parents to work underground because it was more profitable than school? To some snivelling fool with a parody of a holy picture, abasing himself, thinking if he gets down low enough you'll throw a penny at him?

'OPPP-uuuuu-aaaaay-THUN! OPPP-uuuuu-aaaaay-THUN!' Virgil winced.

Operation Man had been working the same metro line for years. He hobbled through on crutches, bent low, eyes lost behind thick glasses, whining about an operation he was forever unable to make the funds for. Another victim. Of bad health. Which was not his fault. But that dismal whining voice. That was his fault. If you lived with someone like that eventually you would slap them and order them to clean the toilet bowl with an old toothbrush.

The metro stopped. The door slid open. Operation Man hobbled out. His progress to the next carriage was arrested by someone gripping his arm.

'Just wait a minute,' said Virgil.

'Attention,' said the automatic announcement, 'the doors are closing.'

Operation Man struggled towards the doors. The hand maintained its grip.

'I want a word with you.'

The tail of the train was swallowed by the tunnel and it was still and silent again, the platform deserted except for the two men under bad lighting.

Operation Man looked up, but his eyes were still down at the level of his shoulders, like a dog that's been kicked too often and keeps his head low to the ground, checking sideways for approaching danger.

'Let me go!'

'Now listen up. This is your lucky day. I'm going to pay for your operation, do you understand? I've money under the mattress and though I'm a stranger I'm going to fork out. I know it sounds incredible, but I'm not joking.'

Operation Man moaned.

'Snap out of it. This begging is inefficient. Most of what you get must go on food and other essentials, extending your career in beggary far into the future. So I'm going to do the rational thing. Besides, your voice has been annoying me for some time now. I don't think I have the words to describe the degree of unpleasantness your voice and all it represents has for me. The attitudes behind it, the complete disintegration of the human personality, beaten down by centuries of Christian and communist ideology. Now don't you dare cross yourself or I don't know what I'll do. I won't stand for it. As far as you're concerned I'm the Antichrist. And Raskolnikov. And Kurtz. Not that you've heard of them, you brute. The three little pigs is as much as you know of European literature. But don't worry, I'm not out to do anybody in because that creates more problems than it solves. I'm a rational man and I realize that. I'm not some stupid Nazi. No, I'm going to pay for your operation.'

'Le-le-le-eht-me-go-ooo!'

'Come on, let's get out of this hole and get to know each

other. I'll buy you a coffee and something to eat and we'll figure out how to proceed.'

Still gripping his arm, the benefactor extracted his victim from the metro station. Operation Man nearly fell over as the escalator ejected him into daylight. It was awkward with the crutches. He blinked in the light, his tiny eyes disappearing in a squint behind the thick glasses.

'You're practically blind, too. You look like a mole caught in a spotlight. I do believe you've never spent much time above ground. It's wonderful up here, you're going to love it.'

They had emerged into a wasteland. There did not seem to be anywhere that would serve coffee or anything else. Trucks, buses, cars moved down a big road. On a rise in the distance apartment blocks met the sky. A row of kiosks, each slightly lopsided, cobbled together, looking like they had been dropped from a height, faced the road. A few people walked up a dirt lane towards the blocks. Three dogs stood around in an odd, humorous pose, muzzles pointing in different directions.

'Stop behaving like I'm going to hit you. Be a man! Stand up straight! What's it going to cost, this operation? What's wrong with you anyway?'

'I-I have a k-k-k-k-uuuh!'

'O spit it out for Christ's sake! What? You have a speech defect too?'

'Kuuuh-kuuh-kuuh!'

'Constipation?'

'Kuhkukukuk!'

'O fuck me! What do you have?'

'Kidney thtone!'

Virgil looked up at the sky, where one bird flew. Then he kicked a crutch from under the mole. Then the other. The clattering of wood on concrete.

'It's a vewy painful condithion!'

'I'll give you a painful condition. What's the play-acting with the crutches, eh? You seem perfectly able to stand without them. And to think you nearly tricked me out of a fortune. I should punch your face in.'

'I'm almotht blind. C-c-can't work.'

'You know plenty of other tricks, you parasite. Swindling money from hardworking people. I know your kind, sucking beer round the corner while the kids hold cardboard signs saying "starving".'

'Leave me alone!'

'Get the hell out of here.'

Mole bent over to collect his crutches and Virgil gave him a generous kick in the hole.

'Work another metro line in future!'

That's when the police with the dead dog appeared.

'What's going on here?'

'Officer!' said Virgil. 'This ruffian has insulted me!'

Mole's protest got stuck on a plosive.

The policemen observed who was better dressed and came down on the side of decency.

'You filthy vagabond. Bothering this gentleman. Get lost!'

Mole scuttled back into the ground, both crutches under his right arm.

The police were too high-ranking to be patrolling a metro stop in a wasteland. The captain had a face like dough. The colonel was a little older, stern and handsome in a blank sort of way. They were both big. Guardians of the state. Any state at all. The captain held the small mutilated dog by its back feet, as if it were a rabbit he had shot.

'Ugh! What happened to its head?' asked Virgil, grimacing.

'Truck.'

'But carrying it around like that! Upsetting to children, I imagine. Upsetting to me, in fact.'

The captain, whose mouth hung always a little open, looked at the colonel, who continued looking ahead, sternly. The colonel was a bad actor who had mastered one expression – stern – and was going to stick with it no matter what happened in the play.

'The dog,' said the colonel, 'belongs to a senator.'

The colonel, though not the chatty type, felt his dignity compromised by possession of a dead dog and outlined the bare facts. A woman, a senator of the Greater Romania Party, had lost her dog and phoned the district station. The commanding officers in the area immediately went on the case and visited the senator in her large house, where a detailed description of the dog was given. The senator was distraught, obsessed with the idea that Gypsies had stolen it for some horrible ritual. All units were alerted. Some Gypsies were punched about but no dog materialized. Drive around, the colonel commanded all units, and keep a sharp eye out for an unusually small dog with no tail. Eventually Lucky, as the dog was named, was found in a bad part of town where his inexperience with vehicles had cost him his life.

Virgil agreed this was a bad way to wind up a case.

'I know where you can find a dog like that,' he said.

The dough-faced captain looked at the colonel.

'That may be worth investigating,' said the colonel.

'I'm not saying it's exactly the same.'

'Her eyesight is not good.'

'She put salt in our coffee,' said dough-face, speaking for the first time.

Virgil instantly knew they had drunk the coffee too.

Upon the colonel's orders the captain dropped Lucky down an open manhole. They got in the squad car, Virgil in the back. The captain started the engine.

'Siren?'

'Just drive,' said the colonel.

They parked outside Virgil's block. The fires burned and the smoke blew low in the breeze, too thick for comfort.

'Can't you arrest them?' asked Virgil.

'No law against burning leaves,' said the colonel.

'Take them in for questioning and slap them around or something?'

They went inside and crammed into the lift and got out on the tenth.

'Here,' said Virgil.

He knocked at a door. A dog yapped. The door opened. A big sloppy mountain of a woman, mouth opening in dumb alarm at the uniforms. Both policemen observed the dog.

'It'll do,' said the colonel.

The captain seized the animal.

'We're confiscating your dog, Madam,' said the colonel, sternly, raising his voice above the dog's panicked yapping.

'But –'

'Your dog is unregistered. From the police point of view it is a non-existent dog.'

The police left. The barking became more distant as the lift descended the shaft.

'They've taken my Muffin,' said the woman. 'My only friend in the world!'

'They have,' said Virgil, leaning his face close into hers. 'And if you try getting another one I'll have you arrested.'

He turned to go and several old neighbours who had spied on the commotion retracted their skinny chicken necks and closed their doors in fear. He walked down the hall to his room, went inside and locked the door.

He took off his coat and shoes and poured a vodka. He sat down and watched the smoke blowing across the window and looked at the glass of vodka on the table. When he had got all the satisfaction he could out of looking at the vodka he drank it down. He was one day older and the city was the same. Quite the Renaissance Man, thought Virgil. I go out armed with reason to serve my fellow man and I perform a Laurel and Hardy routine. There was nothing good or beautiful about kicking beggars, he knew. But it had felt pretty good at the time.

His article was still in his coat pocket. Somewhere two police officers were presenting a dim-witted senator with a dim-witted dog, insisting they had no time for coffee. Virgil poured himself another vodka. The fires still smouldered and the smoke still drifted across the darkening sky. He drank down the second.

It was good, very good, what the vodka did, and perhaps tomorrow would be a bright new day.

Reporting the Facts

I

Gara de Nord, Bucharest, leaning against an iron pillar waiting for Elena, a woman I hardly know. A fat old Gypsy hunkered to my left threshes sunflower seeds with her teeth. Check my watch and impatiently pick through the crowd. That's her, looking straight ahead, striding a direct path through the milling crowd, oblivious to those around her: ragged little boys with bags of glue, man with the sack of potatoes over-shoulder who nearly collides with her and then turns to follow with his eyes. Black lustrous hair pulled back and tied behind. Two young soldiers, faces raw with cold, see her break into a smile when she recognizes me. I see it all with satisfaction, a director who has drilled his extras and taken the perfect shoot. We kiss, a soldier shrugs. Cut! You can all go home. The fat old Gypsy, rising, vehemently spits. A corona of husks is left in the space where she has been.

— I'm late.

— Doesn't matter. Did you get it?

— I'm not sure.

— You didn't see him?

— Please. We'll talk about it later.

I plant a full bottle of rum on the little fold-out table by the window of our compartment.

— In the morning I will open my eyes and see a foreign land.

I turn and she is smiling at my words. We are at the stage in our relationship when everything that is said is interesting. As the train shunts from the station I kiss her. I have a feeling of something new beginning. Bucharest's grim apartment blocks slide by as the dirty evening light drains from the damp winter sky and in the half-light I catch my own satisfied reflection in the glass. The sensation of motion takes me from myself. I am happy leaving Bucharest and my tired life behind.

— You didn't say what happened with your uncle, if you got it in the end.

— I don't want to talk about it now. I'll tell you another time.

Not wishing to seem concerned, I drop it.

Her uncle, who had been a communist functionary responsible for major construction projects, has just been elected to the Romanian Senate. The scurry after privatization made him rich; money and old friends have made him a senator. As such he is entitled to a hotel suite and an apartment in Bucharest. The apartment he has promised to Elena and, having no fixed place to live, I have a personal interest.

The carriage attendant distributes bedding and the other occupants, a middle-aged Moldovan couple, soon make ready for sleep. I stretch along the seat with pillows behind me and Elena before me and am a long time sinking rum and talking, recounting tales of trains and travel, my vagrant life. Invisible towns slip by in the night and the beating of the tracks hammers out a metre into which my words fall. Elena is entranced by my talk, and indeed there is desire for her mixed in my speech and I wonder will I love her. Carried away with the romance of myself I tell myself I am right in the end, after all the self-doubt, to wait for pure rare moments such as these. I am right to be impractical, to have no home.

It is late and we recline, fitting together on the narrow bed, her head on my shoulder, my hand stroking her thick black hair, plans bubbling in my mind. I am at a threshold and I have so much to say that I overflow.

II

I wake with a vague feeling of shame, as though I have told a magnificent lie. The bottle is half empty and there's work to be done. Moldova, several chaotic years after emerging independent from the ruins of the Soviet Union, is choosing a new president. I must write a report; summarizing another poor country in a few hundred words. The sky above Chişinau is tarnished lead this last day of November.

In an unheated room on the eleventh floor of the Hotel International I take aspirin and disappear under a mound of bedclothes. Elena must write a piece on the celebration of Romania's national day in its severed province. In the street people are speaking Russian. I suggest she do something satirical, but that would get her fired so she rushes off to some ceremony in a graveyard. In the afternoon I feel well enough to get some work done. I buy the local papers, visit the offices of an international organization that is monitoring the election and then spend an hour being briefed by an earnest young patriot from the foreign ministry. He is alarmed when I tell him I am going to Transnistria, where ethnic Russian separatists have declared an independent state. Your safety cannot be guaranteed, he says gravely, and speaks of the rapacity of the border checkpoints.

That night, after making what is called love, Elena holds me for longer than I would have liked. She asks me what is wrong. Nothing, I say. There is the old disappointment that comes of getting what you long desire. The rum is gone and I'm too tired to go down to the street for more.

— What's her name? she asks after a long silence.

— What difference does it make?

— I just want to know.

— Her name is Ana.

I am tired, and irritable. It is as if I have watched the scene before and can hear the lines as they come. This is not Elena's fault, so I must control my resentment and speak my part. It is hard, watching myself like this. I remind myself that soon I will be in Transnistria, as if this were some kind of escape. Elena has charged my infidelity with a significance it does not have. I can feel her, as she lies beside me, trying on the role of The Other Woman, like a piece of clothing, testing its fit.

— Are you planning to leave her?

— Doesn't matter what I do. Things will unravel in their own good time.

More of this awkward style of talk, the details of which it is not necessary to relate, then, inevitably:

— This is what your fine talk comes to. You're not much of a man when it comes to the real world.

— I'm well sick of the real world.

— So what are you doing here, if you don't care about me?

— Getting the story. Reporting the facts.

It seems there has been a misunderstanding. Elena has planned another kind of film, one involving a real world and a real man. Naturally, I feel uncooperative. But we are getting argumentative and I do not want this fuss. It's not true that I don't care about her. I do care, just not enough to play this game. I don't want to fight, to say hurtful things. So I kiss her, stroke her.

We grapple again, better this time. Better, because we do it with anger and frustration that we are strangers. There is no pretending at tenderness and, strangely, moments of real tenderness appear like flashes in our struggle, inciting us further. Then it is a cold room again and we are covered with sweat and trying to organize the blankets we have kicked away. We sleep.

Election day. The talk is over, the sky heavy as lead, again.

Diligently Elena rises and as she slowly dresses I feel remorseful. She is going to the central election bureau and can't decide what to wear.

— I should wear a skirt.

— Is it so formal?

— No. But if I dress well men will be helpful.

— Up to a point.

She puts on a very short skirt and leather boots which come to above her knees, leaving a section of stockinged thigh exposed. I feel like pulling her back into bed.

I sleep for hours. When I wake the sky is the same as before and I consider getting the results from television or having a beer later with someone from a news agency. I take some aspirin and decide to make an effort. I can get a train to Transnistria, spend a few hours, come back that night.

Elena returns after lunch and is alarmed at my plan. I take the opportunity to find out about the apartment.

She tells how when she went to her uncle's suite at the Hotel Bucharest to discuss it, he tried to grope her. Apparently he wasn't giving anyone a luxury apartment for free. Which stands to reason. You don't get rich in a poor country with that kind of attitude. A picture is painted of a satyr chasing a young girl around an expensive hotel room.

— I couldn't believe it. He has two children my age. He's fat and old. He tried to pull me on to the bed. He said, I want to eat you.

— Greedy bastard. That's like something I'd say. Is he your mother's or your father's brother?

— No, my mother's cousin. They were at university together. I've known him since I was a child.

— Not really an uncle, then. Second cousin. Or once-removed. Whatever. I suppose he's got used to grabbing things that aren't his.

— It was horrible. I knew him when I was a child.

As we leave the hotel together she pleads with me not to go to Transnistria. It's gratifying that she thinks I'm going to do something dangerous. We hold hands and wait for her bus. There is a little boy of three or four at the stop. His mother hunkers down and rearranges his hat and scarf, though they do not need to be rearranged, and kisses his cheeks.

Elena says a child is the best thing in life; she would dress him up in funny clothes and hear him say 'Mama'. Elena's beauty is extraordinary but it has been of no help to her dreams, which are ordinary. All she wants is a good reliable man with a little money who will give her a child. Instead she collides with me and groping politician cousins. Well, bad luck. Basically she's a stupid cunt and I feel sorry for her. And I'm a stupid prick. And I feel sorry for myself. She tells me not to come back late as she gets on the bus and for a moment I actually regret that I am an episode without consequence in her life.

There is a stale odour. The people on the train east, Russian-speakers, are worn and poor. Hunched by the dirty window, cap pulled low, I watch the landscape drift by. Dollar bills are folded into tiny squares and hidden around my clothing so that the frontier guards can't take everything. Assuming they let me through. A man called Andrei asks me about myself and I reply in broken Russian. Did I ever see a place so poor? he asks. In fact I have, many times, and it is not interesting. He tells the same old tale; things getting worse, decent people can't make a living, the mafia run everything. I wonder will all this culminate in a request for money. I can give money easily but it is the listening, the waiting, which makes me uncomfortable. The terrain undulates and the horizon always presses close. A small tractor labours in a square field. The trees are shiny black and naked and the earth is leached of all verdure, patches of grey and brown grass waiting for the snow to fall and hide it. Do you have houses like that in your country? How much can you earn over there? A peasant leads a draught horse along a track, its hanging head bobbing heavily as it plods through mud. A woman berates Andrei for complaining to a foreigner. Others join in the argument. As their voices rise and grow excited I lose the meaning. When they tire an old man, previously silent, says calmly and with finality:

— A cow is what you need. You'll always have milk. And your own cheese and butter. Sour cream. Without a cow you have none of these things.

Andrei puts his face in his hands and rubs his eyes for a long time. Of course, there will be no request for money. He is just another man humiliated by his clothes, wanting to tell the stranger that the clothes are not the man.

In the end there is no check at Benderi, a town just inside Transnistrian territory. A flag waves lazily in the breeze above the platform. I discreetly ask the woman at the station café to change money and I am readily given a wad of local currency. A row of mafia types are sitting drinking vodka at the bar. She turns back to the television. I head towards the polling station located back on the Moldovan side of the border, crossing a concrete bridge over the rail lines with the wind whistling through its pillars, and follow a road which winds and narrows through the suburbs and out of town.

By coming here I've got away from Chişinau and Elena, where I'd gone to get away from Bucharest and Ana, where I'd gone for a similar reason. Transnistrian police stop cars at a checkpoint and I trudge through unnoticed with some locals taking bags of shopping home. Night is falling and mud is underfoot. At the polling station the observers say everything has gone smoothly. I watch a few old women argue about who is first to be behind the curtain to vote and that is all.

After eleven I get back to the hotel, cold and tired after the journey in an unlit, unheated train. Elena, relieved to see me, embraces the returning hero. I look at myself through her eyes and feel a little better than I have most of the day. She sets out food for me and pours a glass of vodka. I give her the remains of my Transnistrian money, over a million rubles. She examines my worthless money with interest.

I eat and drink, and the warmth creeps back into my legs. I feel a sympathy with Elena, the woman herself and not some dream of her, that I haven't felt before. She is glad that I am back, safe, and I am glad also, to be back with her. I tell her that I'm tired of freelancing. You have freedom, in theory, but it's a rotten way to make money, even if you manage to avoid paying rent. The vodka has gone to my head and I find that I am rambling.

— There was a man called Andrei, I didn't like him much.

They were all arguing in Russian, I couldn't follow it, and he was sitting there with his face in his hands, he'd heard it all before and he was sick of it. Life just going round in circles no matter how hard you try. Just then his daughter appeared beside him, maybe nine years old. She asks what language I speak and says to me in English, My name is Maria. He was looking up at her, his clever pretty little daughter, and for the first time his face came alive, like she was a light shining on him. That's what kept him going; not anything he'd thought or done or learned. It was this little girl who the world hadn't touched . . .

In another mood I might have said, it's odd what keeps us from drowning in shit, and left it at that. But now I am tripping over my words in my eagerness to explain. It is easy for me to create clever things with my speech, but in trying to uncover something simple I feel myself failing. It is something obvious and I am complicating it by putting it in words. But Elena is not listening anyway. She is turning the money around in her hands and making sentences in her head. She tells me she has been thinking, and it would be better if we didn't see each other when we got back to Bucharest. At least for a while. I receive a bad review. I am not unique, it seems. I am like many spineless men who have their retreat prepared beforehand. She goes on a bit. In the end I put up my hand. It's been a long day and enough to turn everything upside down. The struggle to be alone, overthrown by loneliness. I want to say, Elena, it would be simple for us to try to love one another! It is an easy thing to say, and even to feel for a moment.

I am starting to look dejected and as a result she has filled out and looks better, happier, stronger. Any pleading on my part would throw us into sharper contrast, and I have my

229

pride. So I tell her she is quite right, we shouldn't see each other, it would just cause trouble. I realize I am crumpling in my fist the millions I have brought her as a souvenir.

Midnight. The exit polls are coming in over the radio and the pro-Russian candidate has a clear lead. This is good for me; I can write about the collapse of the economy since independence and the need for Russian oil. 'Moldova looks to Moscow' is a good title. I make a few calls and write my article off. I conclude with something about the ideal of independence proving expensive. No matter how short or superficial the article, it's always good to have a bit of cheap philosophy at the end. It makes the reader feel he has really understood something.

I get into bed. It's warm. Elena is warm too. She wakes and embraces me and throws a leg over mine. For the last time, it seems. This time her tone is that of an independent woman taking her pleasure. I feel I have underestimated her, which makes me want her, and I am a little thrown off balance by my new part. I perform, and she falls asleep long before I do.

III

Now I've flown south and found my rest in Athens.

After returning to Bucharest I had to force myself to keep moving, keep the money coming in; economic collapse in Bulgaria, street demonstrations in Belgrade, unrest in Kosovo. The Balkans are burning! said a journalist friend, glee in his eyes. But I was worn out, and Bucharest was no place to rest. It seemed wherever I lay my head packs of wild dogs would howl beneath my window. (Half the city complained of being bitten, the other half fed them scraps – there was never a convinced majority for their extermination.) I stopped sending the stories. It felt nice, to give up. Ana finally lost patience with my apathy. I was sorry to have wasted her time. Winter always dragged me down. Spring is the season of migration.

One day in March I sat on a park bench wondering what to do with myself next. The money was getting low. The weather had turned inexplicably kind and the tiny bright leaves were bursting from the old trees. And then a strange thing happened: Elena, whom I hadn't seen since Chişinau, came strolling along the gravel path hand in hand with a man. She had a relaxed expression on her face that I had never seen before. She looked around, she read the ground, she raised her face to him, and she never saw me. I had the sensation – slightly too ghostly for my taste – of being completely invisible.

It reminded me of the scene in the railway station when I watched Elena cut through the crowd, except this time I felt more like an extra than a director. My moment had passed. I had taken my notes. I had filed my report. It was time to move on.

So I came to Athens, the city that has seen everything. The city that has died and been reborn several times.

I have a small room with not much furniture. Something is bound to happen soon but it will do no harm if I keep to myself for a while. Instead of watching Albania rip its heart out in a pointless civil war I spend my afternoons with two young women, aged nineteen and twenty-one. Their father, an owner of ships, pays me more to teach them English than I could have earned by chasing disaster around the Balkans. They dress fashionably and elegantly, as good-looking rich girls must. Their father has ordained that they will go to

California to study, that their idleness must end. They have no interest in anything I tell them about the world I've seen and nothing at all seems to impress them. We understand each other rapidly; they don't want to learn and I don't want to teach. In any case, their English is good enough for California. So, while their father sits in an office making fortunes, including mine, they take me around the town. We sit and sip on café terraces. They buy me cakes and ouzo. While I read ancient history, of the defensive walls Pericles and Themistocles built to keep out the Spartans, of ambition and treachery and empires long dead, they smoke menthol cigarettes and from behind mirror sunglasses impassively as cats watch the people as they come and go. Two sleek bored sphinxes.

I don't even know if they like me or if I am just part of the scenery.

Yesterday the elder of the two put her sunglasses on the table, her hands behind her head and, fixing me with eyes that could have belonged to Cleopatra, asked in Greek:

— What's the matter with you? Are you afraid of women?

I wasn't supposed to understand so I pretended not to and they laughed.

I replied in the language of my ancestors, to which I have a sentimental attachment.

— *Tá tuirse orm, tar éis do mháthair.* (Your mother wore me out.)

Not much of a conversation. She put her glasses in her hair, Italian style, like an extra set of eyes. I went back to Thucydides. The Athenian democracy debates whether to execute the entire population of a small island for backing the enemy.

Generations come and go and the world stays the same.

The wind blows north, the wind blows south, then back around again. Our eyes can never see enough to be satisfied, our ears can never hear enough. There is nothing new in the whole world.

There are days when I get sick of all this repetition and I feel like a dog running around in endless circles chasing its own tail. Other days I take a train down to the harbour and squint across the flashing water at the ships heading off across the sea and I feel life before me in the energy of the sun on the pulsing wavetops. It is that excitement, beginning all over again, in the spring, though the last winter has just told me it is useless. What next? What is over that sea? Is that boat heading for the Bosphorus? Quixote on his deathbed tells Panza, Forget those wanderings, I was mad. And Sancho weeps, But I loved you then! Just one more journey! The boat gets smaller and smaller. There is a bridge at Istanbul. I could walk to another continent, leave Europe behind. There is enough gold in my pocket. The boat becomes a point. I strain my eyes. It flickers. And is gone.

An Evening of Love

Dan had been standing in the angry sun all day, working. Now it was evening and he was ready for his reward. He got out of the lift on the fifth floor and stepped into a dirty dull hallway much like dirty dull hallways all over the city.

Irina opened the door to him. Her parents had gone away for the weekend. They kissed and he eased the door closed behind him. He slipped his hand under her top. She had just showered and her skin was smooth and cool, the flesh of her hips and breasts ripe and full. Such womanliness at the age of seventeen, he knew, must mean that she would be growing heavy as slimmer girls filled out. But for now everything was correct and in its place.

He detached himself from her and stepped from the hall into the living room. First he would smoke, then she would bring him something to eat and drink. Then it would be time for the bedroom.

Dan sat at the table and Irina embraced him from behind. He breathed the good smell of her freshly washed hair. She pulled it out of the way as she placed her left cheek against the skin of his right cheek. She rubbed his pectoral muscles, hard from working out with weights.

'Did you have a nice day at work, dear?' she asked playfully.

He snorted a half-laugh at her imitation of what bored old couples, so unlike them, said at dinnertime.

'No, dear, I didn't.'

'You sounded angry on the phone.'

'Several hunded kilos of rotting peaches.'

'Was it so much money?'

'Nothing I won't forget when I rip your little panties off.'

'You beast!'

She slapped his face lightly and jumped away. He let her go. They smiled at each other. He took his cigarettes from his pocket and she brought white wine and a glass from the kitchen. He heard the hiss of the gas cooker and a pot going on. The apartment was cramped and the walls had not been painted in twenty years and were yellowed. One day when he had earned enough he would give her a better place than this. The money would come. It was a matter of being steady and taking whatever opportunities came his way. He had been her first. That mattered. With older girls there was too much you did not know. He lit a Marlboro and watched the coils of smoke with great satisfaction. He felt like a man.

'Early for peaches,' came her muffled voice from the kitchen, almost as if she were talking to herself.

He knew it. They were imported from Turkey but no one else had been selling peaches so he had gone ahead and bought them and stacked them up at 7 a.m. in the hot morning at the stall at the intersection. The same as any morning, the anxious traffic revving at the lights, the trucks leaving expanding clouds of black smoke behind them, the crowded bus stops and tram stops, the people pouring into the metro station. The background scenery against which he made his money.

'It's not just the money,' he said, raising his voice so she could hear from the kitchen. 'It's that I hate making mistakes. They looked perfect at first. There must have been a lot of little cuts and bruises. And it was so hot. By midday they were turning to mush. Nobody buying.'

She brought him a bowl of soup and some bread. She sat down next to him.

'Not eating?' he asked.

'I've eaten.'

'And then,' he said, spooning soup and chewing bread, 'I had these crates of rotting peaches stacked up in a wall in front of the stall. I was serving this man, and the whole wall starts to lean forward. You know the way when something is about to collapse and break it moves in slow motion?'

She nodded.

'Like that. All I could do was watch it go. All those peaches, spilling across the footpath. I wanted to kill someone.'

She covered her mouth with her hands and laughed at hundreds of peaches jumping and rolling across the footpath. He too began to smile but the smile was quickly arrested by the image of crates toppling and people turning to watch hundreds of peaches in motion. The feet of busy commuters dodging peaches. Peaches tumbling into the gutter. A dog sniffing a peach, unimpressed. A car wheel crushing a peach and leaving a stain on the road. A little boy bending over to touch a pretty peach and being wrenched away by an impatient mother. And then all the peaches which had to be gathered up again by him and the boy he hired, going back into the boxes more damaged and dirtier.

'Did someone knock them over?'

He took a swallow of wine. It had been afternoon. The commuters were surging back out of the metro station like ants. The sun was angled in the sky, still hot but past its worst. He was serving a slim young man in a suit, the kind who looked well pleased with his job and his life. The man had not appeared to touch anything.

'Maybe they were just stacked wrong,' he said.

She stroked the back of his head and went back to the kitchen to fry a piece of pork and some potatoes. Talking about it had made him angry again.

She brought the food. When he finished eating he pushed the chair back from the table and wiped his mouth with a napkin. He folded the napkin over and wiped his forehead. He threw the napkin on the table.

'Too hot in this city.'

She got up and stood before him and kissed his face. He inhaled. She smelled cool and good.

'One day we'll have a place in the country,' he said. 'By a river.'

'I'm happy right now.'

'It's different when you're at school. When you start to work you feel time pass and you start to want things. You feel your life leaking away and you want something back in return.'

Gratefully, he began to kiss her face and neck. Then their tongues wanted each other. They did that until the moment to pause came. He stood up and picked the cigarettes and lighter off the table and put them in his trouser pocket. Then they went into the bedroom and undressed.

The evening sun through the window shone a broad patch of golden light on the bed and on part of the wall behind the bed. She lay down naked on the bed on her front and became herself radiantly golden. He straddled her and began to rub her back. He kneaded with his thumbs the muscles on either side of her spine, starting low down on her back and working up to her neck. She sighed as he pushed the tension from her body. Then with his fingers and thumbs he did her neck and shoulders. When he could resist no longer, he bit her shoulder. He bit a little too hard and she squealed and wriggled under him. He drew back and sat halfway down her legs. In the supernatural precision of the light her body was covered with very tiny golden hairs, too fine for his hands to feel, all down her arms and back and buttocks.

He frowned.

Her body, normally a paler honey-gold, had become deeper in colour. And around her hips was the narrow but distinct white mark which indicated how little had been withheld from the sun.

The summer before, when he was just starting the business, and when he had been seeing her for some months, she had gone for several days to the coast with her friends. She had not informed him before leaving, knowing that he had to work and would object to her going away without him. He had shown his anger by cutting her off coldly and waiting until she came to him, penitent and tearful.

She sensed something was wrong and turned her head to look at him. The sun had moved and now her face was in relative shadow. Her hair covered her mouth.

'What?' she said.

'That's a very good tan you've got.'

His voice was a little hoarse. She let her head fall back on the pillow. Her hair fell across her face, hiding it. He sat motionless, her legs pinned together beneath him. He watched her breathe. If he waited long enough she would have to say something.

'I told you,' she said, half speaking into the pillow, 'I went with my brother to visit some friends in the country. Old friends of my parents.'

He got off her awkwardly and sat on the side of the bed with his back to her and picked his limp trousers off the floor and took his cigarettes and lighter out of the pocket. She remained lying in the same position. She was very still. He was aware of each sound he made as he opened the packet and as he used the lighter. It lit the cigarette on the second go. He was aware that she too was hearing these sounds. Even with the window open it was very quiet. He could hear the cigarette paper crackle as he inhaled. All these sounds told him he was in charge for another little while. He did not know what he would say next.

He felt her body shift. He turned his head to look at her. She lay on her side, her head propped on her right arm, fingers lost in her hair. The sunshine was now just a bright strip across her breasts and midriff. His shadow fell across her hips. The light was narrowing and climbing the wall and would soon disappear entirely. He loved the shape of her uppermost breast when she lay on her side. He would rub his face against her breasts, take the nipple in his mouth for a very long time. Now, though she looked exceptionally beautiful in the strange light, the sight of her was troubling. He stared at her and exhaled smoke out the side of his mouth, away from her.

'Sunbathing topless with old country friends of the family?'

'It was a private place,' she protested. 'I was on my own.'

A high panicky note hung in the air after she spoke.

'I see.'

'I hate it when you get like this. Stupid questions. About nothing. About things that just aren't important.'

'When you love someone, really love someone, everything is important.'

He let the silence gather around them, to do its work.

'And you don't tell a lie to someone you really love.'

She began to be ashamed of her nakedness. Swiftly, in what could have been fear or anger, or both, she rose and picked up her clothes. She closed the bathroom door behind her. He could hear the rattling of objects and then water running. She was making herself uselessly busy. He put out his cigarette and stood up and put his trousers on.

The intercom buzzer sounded. Normally he would let her answer the intercom when they were alone at her parents' house. But today was different. He was already at the intercom when he heard the quick nervous sound of the bathroom door opening.

'Alex?' crackled the voice from downstairs.

It was a man's voice. Alex was Irina's older brother. He no longer lived with the family.

'Come on up.'

Irina was standing beside him. She had put on her shorts and top.

'Now you're being crazy,' said Irina. 'If it's someone my parents know I'll be in trouble!'

'In trouble! You sound like a schoolgirl.'

She looked about to cry.

'I *am* a schoolgirl!'

Dan stood with his arms folded over his naked chest as Irina opened the door. The visitor was young and slim and well tanned. He had expected to see Irina's brother and became confused as Irina told him that Alex was fixing his car. He turned to Dan, who made no move to introduce himself.

'But you said –'

Dan stared back blankly. His arms were still folded across his chest.

The man turned back to Irina. He explained that he did not have his bag and Irina told him Alex would surely be back later, at his place.

'I don't have shoes, anything.'

Dan looked down at the man's feet. He had the kind of plastic flip-flops worn at the beach.

Dan watched the side of the man's face. The man withdrew, heading for the stairs rather than waiting for the lift, and Dan closed the door without returning his goodbye. In the same moment Irina turned and went towards the bedroom.

Dan stood alone for a moment in the hall, staring at nothing.

'Who was that?' he called after her.

He heard her opening a drawer and closing it.

'O. A friend of Alex. When we got back the boot of the car was broken. We couldn't get anything out.'

'But why no shoes?'

'They were locked in the boot!'

She was very scared now. That was certain. The exposure of one lie would be enough to break her. It would be enough to unravel everything.

'You don't wear shoes in the country?'

There was no reply. He had spoken quietly and perhaps she had not heard. The light was fading. He turned on the hall light. It glowed pinkly. He hunkered down where the shoes were lined up by the door. He picked up one of the pair she usually wore and tapped it, sole downwards, on the floor. A dusting of fine sand fell on the linoleum. For a moment he did not rise. He put the shoe back in its correct place. He knew that the anger would soon come but for the moment he just felt short of air, as if he had been struck in the gut. Now that it had happened he felt it had been coming for some time. It had been inevitable but he had denied to himself that she could be like the others. He ran his index finger in a line across the little circle of sand, dividing it in two. He wondered was there something he could have done that she would have turned out differently but he could not think of anything.

The young man without the shoes bore a curious resemblance to the man at the stall. He had the same refined face, the look of one who dresses well for work and who knows where he is going in life. Dan knew that this was just one of those coincidences that attract the mind as it flounders. Dan saw the crates leaning inevitably, toppling in slow motion, hundreds of ripe peaches spilling on their individual journeys across the wide footpath, people stopping to watch him recover them.

He rose and flicked his thumb against his index finger to remove the sand. It stuck there. His fingers were wet. He had been her first. He had opened the door to trouble. His throat was tight. It had begun to hurt. He knew he loved her very much. He had no idea what he was going to do or say next.

He wiped his fingers against his trousers and moved towards the bedroom.

Crime and Punishment

BUNNIES COPULATING

Me and Diana were walking back to her place. Afrodite was with us. Two a.m. and the pussy cats were strolling, one of those hot summer nights when the concrete exhales the heat of the sun and the city hardly cools before the sun is back, burning.

'This way,' said Diana.

'This way,' I said.

We were drunk. The streets around where she lives are confusing and I never know the fastest way. So, sportsman's bet, she'd take her route and I'd take mine and we'd sort it out for good.

'Afrodite, go with him so he doesn't run.'

She didn't trust me. She'd got really into the game.

So I set off with Afrodite, a dark sullen cynical woman, tall and bony and long-haired. She kept falling against me, maybe because she was drunk. Maybe not. I grabbed her and pulled her into the alley.

'Hey, get your hands off me, you pig! Diana's my best friend!'

'Cut the crap,' I said. 'We don't have much time.'

We pretty much skipped the foreplay, but the location was sufficiently arousing, as was the elimination of excess chat. After you've fucked a girl fifty times, ten times, perhaps the second time even, there's no amazement in being there. The first moment you enter a woman is pure amazement. Before that moment it is purely theoretical, perhaps impossible, it is fantasy, but that first instant of penetration is the dream realized, sun cracking the clouds apart, the holy promise fulfilled, firecrackers going off, rain in the desert, sentimental music to the drunkard, the sacrament of communion, the first ripe apple, the snake in the grass, an explosion of meaning silencing the clever, making a child of the genius, raising the fuckee and rendering the fucker tender and humble. As I caught my rhythm there with Afrodite up against the wall the ethical dimension of our actions was not considered. We were elevated above ethical dimensions. I would not be so cheeky as to say that God was dead and all was permitted. I was raised in the light and I can say that what we were involved in was infinitely more important than petty mortal ethics and God our creator understood that completely.

I don't know if you've ever seen rabbits copulating but what happens is the male short-circuits his little brain when he comes; neurons go off like fireworks, there's a cerebral explosion, and he literally falls off the female, on his side, unconscious for a moment. Then he finds his feet again and shakes his head as if to say: What was that? Even for us higher primates sex is a potent narcotic, one that temporarily transforms reality. So I fell off Afrodite and back to earth, dizzy and disoriented and rather disgusted at being suckered again. That farting noise as the air goes out of the balloon. The zipping up and returning to the world, the time when your thoughts turn to transmissible diseases and unwanted children, to your wife and responsibilities if you have any, and if you have betrayed someone you love the knowledge of it stabs your heart.

We ran a bit and then walked quickly to the last corner,

which we sauntered around at a responsible walking pace, trying to catch our breath, because we were not cheaters. The collusion was instinctive. Diana was there at the door with key in hand and hand on hip and a clever-schoolgirl told-you-so expression on her face.

A GARDEN OF WEEDS

Finally after all the bust-ups and bad luck, here was a woman who said she loved me for who I was, who read my wretched scrawlings as if the lines cut her very heart. But I couldn't stand her and though I tried ditching her repeatedly she wormed her way back when I was weak, drunk and horny. I was very suspicious of anybody who said she loved me for who I was. I think the terms of any relationship should always entail a few qualifications. In this case there was the fact was I was using her disgracefully and she refused to take offence. All I had to do was put up with her and I was fucked and fed and housed.

Much to the disgust of the father, chief executive American somebody. The parents were divorced and the mother was cruising somewhere with a young Cuban with a big cock and Daddy, being the responsible one, thought a summer in Bucharest was just the thing for Diana, he would even give her an apartment. He barged in one day unannounced when I was stretched out on the sofa in my underwear, drink in hand, remains of a delivered pizza on the coffee table, reruns of *Beavis and Butthead* on the DVD. It was very embarrassing, him standing there in his suit, as I pulled on some trousers. He was very big and powerful-looking. This was the man who was ultimately supporting me, and being caught at a bad moment like that made me feel very small. I sympathized with his point of view. I found the situation disgusting too. But what was I supposed to do, starve?

I never really relaxed in that apartment again, knowing Daddy might burst in like a corporate superman.

'So you must be the poet?' he spat. He didn't extend his hand to shake.

And that was perhaps the most horrible thing, and what made me feel such a complete fake. She loved my unpublishable poetry, or the idea that I was a 'poet', so she was clearly a nut on that score alone. I'm pretty conventional in my tastes, I like women who are good-looking and perhaps a bit superficial. Practical women who like men with jobs and good cars, the kind of women who shun me.

Diana encouraged everything unworthy in me. My soul was a garden of weeds. It's like you start smoking dope one morning, then it's night-time and you've been watching MTV all day and you can't move and you don't even care. That was my month with Diana.

THERE ONCE WAS A BOY FROM NANTUCKET

I know what you're thinking. You're thinking I'm telling this story because I think it's clever and I get a little tingle in my balls recounting tales of sleaze. A quickie in the alley, putting one over on the dopey girlfriend. Well, hang on a minute, Rousseau already wrote that book. I know there's no perverted glory in these little games, and certainly nothing original in them. I'm not trying to be clever here, I'm trying to strip things away so that the plain truth shines through. I'm trying to tell you something about the human soul. I'm trying to tell you something about salvation. I'm trying to tell you something, if only you would listen.

We went up to her place, which was right next to the Swiss embassy. It was enormous, plush, modern. You could forget you were in the armpit of Europe. I was temporarily in Manhattan, away from the stink of humanity. And was I happy? No, I was not. I wanted to take out my dick and piss on it. This place had me trapped. I was trapped by comfortable beds and bubble-baths and a sound system and satellite TV and a well-stocked fridge and a drinks cabinet and I had to get away somehow but it was proving extremely difficult. I was the prisoner of a patron of the arts who even laid out paper and pens for me on the desk. I'd sit down reluctantly to produce and she'd tiptoe about. Life was perfect. There once was a boy from Nantucket, his dick was so long he could suck it. I wanted to cry, it was so useless, all this luxury and the company of an idiot. If I could organize myself to steal some of it and get away, that wouldn't be a bad plan. Of course what I really needed was a job and a place of my own to live and solitude – SOLITUDE! – and a return to order and decency, but I had grown so horribly lax. So this was why I was behaving shittily with other human beings in this unnatural situation instead of listening to the traffic in the dark in a little room on the outskirts of town, a place where I would begin to be happy again.

The basis of the good life is a principled existence and a certain degree of sincerity in our dealings with those around us, a concordance between our inner lives and our outer, social selves. But Diana would not allow this with her soft-hearted fluffy-headed permissiveness. Out of love she invited me to use her and I did and in the process became a worth-less parasite, a leech on her big left buttock. Above all avoid lies, for lies corrupt the soul as surely as rain rusts iron. Isn't that what Fyodor told us in *Karamazov*?

So you see, I was doing my best to provoke a ruction, to lance the boil, and we laid into the drink, the three of us. At one stage Diana had me read them a poem and she said it was powerful. I don't know, they always seem so much more layered and textured and pregnant when I'm shitfaced, and then my memory isn't too clear at all, it all got rather sloppy and I was alone in a room sending frisbees out the window at the Swiss embassy. But they weren't frisbees, they were compact disks of bastardized classical music, she had a whole collection of this classical music which they rocked up and put drums to. I couldn't stand it, whenever I heard her playing it in the background I felt like a suburban eunuch putting cans and packets in a trolley to neutered music, pushing it down a sterile aisle in supermarket bliss – hell! So I bombed the neutral Swiss, and gave them Celine Dion and Michael Bolton too. Then I came back and they were on the sofa together having a cry about something, something very emotional, and I thought, shit, women.

Then Afrodite is pointing her finger at me, tears streaming down her face, saying, 'He fucked me, the bastard fucked me!'

AN OSCAR NOMINATION

Something inexplicable had occurred. But I felt superbly clear and focused and glad it was happening and I lashed the whiskey tumbler against the wall in a fine show of manly rage. Was I going to let some worthless slut defame me? I certainly was not! I was ten metres high on a big screen, my shot at an

Oscar. Their squeals provoked me to kick over the coffee table too. I had taken quite enough. I shouted and waved my hands and they clung to each other like I'd gone crazy, which of course I hadn't. I marched down to the master bedroom – I could still hear their wails from the living room – and pissed on the bed, which was a disgusting thing to do but my soul was on the line and action was needed. I might even have to set fire to the place, I thought, putting my pecker back, yes indeed. I entertained myself with the thought but it was just entertainment, I wasn't going to do anything truly horrifically destructively illegal. I might break some small consumer durables however, such as the DVD. And with that in mind I marched back down to the living room. Afrodite was on the balcony retching, she'd overdone it on the Bailey's Irish Cream – a real cheap whore's notion of a fancy drink – and Diana was on the sofa, crying and trembling.

'Such a lovely evening, having a lovely time, and you have to spoil it. Always have to spoil it!'

'Yeah, same old story, always me to blame and you blubbering. And what are the Americans doing? Paying the Israeli army to murder Palestinian children is what. Putting a match to Colombia because Whitney Houston snorts coke. Propping up any little police state that lets them put an oil pipeline through, cutting down the rainforests and burning through the ozone layer. Look around you! Who pays for all this shit? Some woman with ten children working on a banana plantation in Guatemala. Insensitive bitch! Always thinking about yerself. I'm growing old. I'm going to die. I'm under a death sentence. Where do you think my poetry comes from but the exaggerated knowledge of my own mortality, watching the candle of my life on this earth burn down? And you're concerned with trivia, with ephemera, with your fragile wounded ego. With where I stick my dick!'

'You're right,' she whimpered. 'I'm being selfish. You need freedom to create. But you hurt me!'

'Now you're just trying to make me feel bad again.'

'I'm sorry. Forgive me!'

'Don't know that I can! You and your nine-eleven. You'd think you're the only people in the world ever took a bomb. What about Dresden and Hiroshima and Agent Orange and the Chinese embassy in Belgrade and a hundred thousand Iraqi conscripts who didn't even own their own uniforms? What about all the smart bombs in Afghanistan that forgot to wear their glasses and fried some shepherd instead? You know, I've always wondered what this golf club here was for but now I know.'

I waved it about. She cowered.

'Uncle Osama is an air traffic controller and I'm a golfing sort of chap.'

I let the DVD have it. Little bits of glass were all over the floor. Diana was sobbing. Afrodite heaved mightily in the background.

And next thing I remember I was in bed with Diana and it was very dark and quiet and she was very still and I was speaking very fluently, confessing to a murder.

CRIME . . .

Now you're going to hear the story I told Diana about a murder I committed, how I bludgeoned to death an old lady and her daughter for their money. While you read, please bear in mind that it is complete fiction. While there are credible details contained, consistent with my previous life as Diana knew it, the fact is I have never murdered anybody. I am simply not the murdering type of person. What happened is that in one of those intuitive flashes of drunken genius it occurred to me that if I could convince Diana she had been harbouring a wanted criminal she would give me a wad of money to put some distance between us and I could have a clean break and a fresh start.

I was fibbing my way to redemption.

'I wasn't in my right mind, Diana, I hadn't been eating decently and all I had to drink was this shit from a barrel at the market. It was clear but it had these strange viscous oily blue strands which used to float in it like snakes, used to hypnotize me practically. I was dreaming I was swimming underwater with Rimbaud in a tropical sea with blue seasnakes. Then who knocks on the door but this old crone from downstairs, tells me the water is coming in her ceiling.

'Now this had been going on for some time, her coming round, telling me about the ceiling, asking what I was going to do about my defective plumbing. Well, there was nothing wrong with the plumbing, it was the roof above me, I was on the top, the tenth, as you remember, and the rain dribbled down the ventilation shaft, damaging her ceiling as well as mine. Of course I explained this but she wasn't a listener, just a talker, and she'd stand there for an hour talking at me, it didn't matter what I said, round and round in circles, and she talked about other things too but it always came back to the ceiling. I thought she was a sweet old lady at first but eventually her ceiling was driving me demented. It's not stupidity alone which dements us, but the manner of its repetition, and the stupid each time demanding some kind of response, and that it be consistent with ideas of politeness and propriety. I think that's what makes some people finally snap, especially if they've been trying not to go under for some time and are under strain, as I was, let me tell you, because it got that she'd wait for me downstairs and I couldn't go out for a loaf of bread but she'd be pulling at my sleeve talking about the ceiling.

'And in fact she didn't even care about the ceiling, she was just lonely and needed someone to talk to. So this day she comes round, and me feeling a bit unhinged, the seasnakes and the food situation, and I'd been looking over the balcony thinking, it's really not that big a drop, if I landed on that bush there I'd probably survive. So I look at this old dear and think, well, she's practically dead anyway, and the rest of her life isn't going to be any fun, I could just hurry her along, that wouldn't even be a sin, would it?

'She had all this jewellery in a box. She'd shown me once. She'd come from an aristocratic family and the communists had expropriated everything, but she still had all this jewellery in a box and used to take it out and show visitors and imagine she was a countess or something. Well, I was tired of poverty, I couldn't even remember how I'd ended up in Bucharest, I only knew it was some kind of mistake, and I reckoned it was time for a change of scenery, maybe New York, maybe somewhere like Brazil. So I went down an hour later with a hammer under my coat, nobody in the hall, and she lets me in.

'Then I think, hammer, blood, that's disgusting! You're not going to bash anyone with a hammer, that's barbaric! So I smothered her with a pillow, it was just like going to sleep and probably less painful than whatever else was waiting round the corner for her. I could have gone out into the hall and told someone I'd gone down to check on her and there she was. Heart attack! I went to the box of jewellery and decided I was just going to take a couple of little things so as not to arouse suspicion. I thanked God I was finally thinking straight because if I'd done it the way I initially planned, all blood and greed, I might have got out of the country for a while but I might still have ended up in jail.

'But then in comes her daughter and spoils the whole thing. She was a fat nasty type, the daughter, never liked her. Schoolteacher, lived next to the mother, unmarried – who would? – very smug and aggressive. There's the old lady dead on the floor, my hand is in the ancestral jewels and there's a big brute of a lump hammer on the table. Looked bad. She comes straight at me, and I don't remember this bit clearly at all but I must have cracked her with the hammer because then I was slipping in the pool of blood as I made for the door. I'd grabbed the box of jewels and they went everywhere, even into the blood. Actually slipping on the wet linoleum and whacking my head against the wall – that was the big bruise I had when you met me. It was horrible.

'In the following days I felt I'd gone completely mad. I realized I'd murdered someone. I had moments of reason; the old woman had been euthanasia, the daughter had been an accident. The whole thing had been a mistake of course, I could now see that clearly, but I didn't want it to be the ruin of my whole life. If I could concentrate and stay calm and let some time pass – nobody who lived there knew who I was except in the vaguest terms – I could then slip out of the country.

'But how could I stay calm? What if I was caught? Recognized in the street? What if the cops were after me already? I couldn't think of myself as a murderer but then this image always came back of me running out, hammer in my hand, slipping in the blood. I got out of that apartment that night, dumped my clothes in a drain, even my boots. You think you know who you are and then you find yourself in a nightmare, you can't wake up, and you struggle for your sanity. The first step in undoing what I had done was to get rid of the jewels.

'One by one, I gave the rings, necklaces, brooches, earrings, bracelets, to beggars. All day I travelled the metro, trams, buses, criss-crossing the entire city back and forth until my route, drawn on a map, would have looked like a tangled length of string thrown down, a tortured senseless path, because it didn't matter where I was going. The only thing that mattered was to rid myself of my profit from murder, to render it a simple mistake, like accidentally cutting yourself with a kitchen knife, something that had happened that you didn't mean to do. I would spot a beggar, or just a poor person who appealed to me as I was swept through a passage with a herd of commuters at evening rush hour, and I would drop a gold ring in the hat and disappear before I could even see the reaction. Another time it was an old man playing a violin. Another time a street child, a very pretty young girl of about twelve, no doubt about to become a prostitute. And each time I would be making up little stories in my head about how I had changed the course of their lives. The old man with the fiddle goes home to his sick wife, tells her he can buy her medicine, they move to a small house in the country, he plays his fiddle, she knits scarves for the grandchildren. Awful sentimental drivel like that. You can't tell much of the time whether you're helping somebody or helping them destroy themselves, especially when it's a matter of money. You even see people who are in love ruin each other. But that's how I kept myself together that terrible day, through a chain of acts of charity, a feeling that I was divesting myself of the terrible fact of murder. And that is how you found me that evening, sitting in the bar, practically out of my senses.'

When I had finished the story I lay there on my back, very quietly, listening to her sobbing. It was very dramatic. The poor fellow, I thought, conscience burdened by such a crime, such sin, finally confessing in the dark, breaking a woman's heart. Then I remembered that I was that fellow and Diana was that woman and it was only a story. But not only a story, a damn good one, told in a rather hoarse tight voice, finally credible. Well done! No wonder I'd been acting erratically lately, with something like that on my conscience. (I particularly liked the bit about slipping in the blood, which I seem to remember from a murder in a Chekhov story – a nice realistic touch, and I *had* had a mark on the side of my face when I first met Diana, result of a late-night conflict with a wall.) Then I thought, You're just being a shit again, telling extravagant lies, what about *Karamazov*? Then I thought, Oh well, this scene has worn me out and she'll give me some cash and we'll be rid of each other, best thing for both of us and I'll have a clean start, ends justify the means. Then I thought, That was the Bolshevik philosophy, ends justify the means, and Stalin brought it to its logical conclusion, as predicted by Fyodor. Then I thought, Stalin murdered millions, I just made up a story about murder, is it my fault she'll swallow anything? Why are you always so hard on yourself?

I was just dozing off when I felt her move and I turned my head. She was sitting on the edge of the bed.

'Can't sleep,' she said, voice heavy with our tragedy. Then – 'What's this wet patch?'

I nearly told her. But it would have spoiled the mood.

. . . AND PUNISHMENT

It was far too early in the morning and far too bright and the room was full of people. Were we having a party? Why was I being poked in such an unfriendly way? Who invited all these security guards?

The cops were angry. I knew I was guilty just by their uniforms, shoddy as they were, and their anger. Hangovers make me feel guilty anyway and the cops putting the bracelets on before I could even take my morning slash made me want to sob and confess. Much of the night was an empty hole and I could have done anything. O horrors of booze, what is my sin? I remembered the DVD. Maybe Daddy had called round. He believed in justice. Or revenge, the American version. Recently every cash-starved little country was bending over backwards to demonstrate how exquisitely they felt America's pain and when America called for arrests they jumped. I was foolish to think I could fight the Great Satan alone. Diana was standing there with tears in her eyes.

'Diana, for Christ's sake get the cops off me!'

'I love you but you've done a terrible thing!'

'Foolish, yes, but I'll pay somehow.'

'I'll be an old lady when you get out!'

A police radio crackled. I realized what was going on and started getting agitated.

'You'll be bouncing off the walls when I get out!'

'Oh!'

We were speaking English but the violence of my exclamation provoked them to manhandle me down the hallway. I was being treated like the nasty bit of work I was. Of course, standard police procedure in a civilized country is to have a crime and then arrest somebody, but in this case they were just low-grade civil servants of the most obtuse kind responding to the stimulus of power. It was going to take a little time to sort out. I could tell them the murder was filched from a dead Russian writer but these men moved their lips when they read the sports pages, they thought Dostoevsky was a brand of vodka.

People watched me being shoved in the car. You know how in the films they put a hand on top of the head of the accused so he doesn't wallop himself against the car? Well, they don't always do that in some countries and I caught a stinging blow against my left eyebrow that made my eye stream.

In *Crime and Punishment* I don't believe it is the intrinsic evil of the crime itself which causes Raskolnikov to confess, to repent. It is the fear of being caught, exposed, and the tension caused by needing the score settled in the human world which he can not live apart from. In my case the thing was working backwards, with my arrest coming first, but the truth of the proposition was being demonstrated all the same. I'd been arrested for fiction and I felt guilty, just because of the handcuffs, car and uniforms and the serious-ness and the anger and the people looking. The external details produced a mood of guilt, even though I'd accident-ally provoked the scene myself through a bit of invention. It was my fault, causally speaking. I had been sinning for a long time and now they were on to me, something was going to be done against my way of life, offensive to the eyes of God. Guilty of a lack of principle, guilty of living off the American swine. I don't know. Guilty of wasting police time. Guilty of wasting.

Why are you always so hard on yourself?

'You are figments of my frenzied imagination,' I said, somewhat exasperated, to the cop beside me. 'Very shortly I will put a cap on my pen and you will evaporate.'

The cop looked at the nut and raised his eyebrows. Of course, it was all coming to an ultimately coherent conclusion. In narrative, as in life, there are only so many rules you can get away with breaking.

'Why did you do it?' asks the cop.

'For the money,' says the murderer.

The cop nods like he knows.

There is a camera shot of the police cars pulling away, getting smaller. You are shown the street with the crowd dispersing. Then the credits roll a bit and then the lights go on.

Some people cease to exist. Others pick up their coats and leave.

Life & Death & My Last $5

Two grand in debt, I got a labouring job. It ate my waking hours and started off costing money. My first morning I was down seventy-six dollars for the uniformed clothing they gave me, to be deducted from my first cheque. Clearly I hadn't got the wholesale price. Then when the weekend came I had to get myself a pair of tan trousers too, and workboots. I'd worked a week in the only footwear I had. They were what I suppose you call cowboy boots, but without the stupid heels. In fact the heels were rather worn down.

After the trousers there wasn't much money. I tried out some nice work boots, then some that were not so good, and finally I got what I could afford, a pair of clumpy clog-like things, made in China, and when I walked around I felt like a cartoon character with outsized feet. I looked forward to getting used to them so that I would not trip when I walked.

The soles of my 'good' boots were worn thin so I dropped them into a repair shop on Mountpleasant Square. It was a funny little place, a cubbyhole with a door to the street, and a rough brown wooden counter with a brown wrinkled little man behind it, and rows and rows of shoes on wooden shelves behind him and on both sides.

Mountpleasant, my home, was a buffer between two worlds. You didn't show your white face a few blocks over, past 14th Street. Even my Latino workmates who lived there for the cheap rent didn't stroll around for pleasure. They got a lift to work and got a lift back and kept their heads down the rest of the time. In the other direction were the people with money. Rock Creek Park separated us from them. It wasn't really a park, but a steep wooded ravine.

I went for a drink after dropping off the boots. Mount-pleasant was mostly Latino – Salvadorean and Guatemalan – and both the bars on the square were Latino. They sold cheap beer and played their music. The bar I entered had a brightly coloured mural all across the back wall, showing blue sky and a beach and palm trees, and straw houses and lovely girls with red flowers in their black hair.

At the bar Nolberto started telling me about one of his conquests, a girl from Papua New Guinea who he met in a supermarket. In the dairy section. When he said Papua New Guinea I knew it was a true story. You didn't make up something like that. He'd been sticking it in her a couple of months when one day she says, Nolberto, this isn't right, you gotta marry me! I canna marry you! says Nolberto, I already gotta wife!

I got shitfaced with Nolberto then left the bar in my clown boots with my last fourteen dollars in my pocket. It had got dark outside.

Two black guys were standing on the corner of 18th and Ingleside. One of them pulled a gun. I walked around him and crossed the street.

I did this because I had no experience in being mugged and was drunk, but my behaviour angered my mugger. He came after me and whacked me across the neck with the gun.

'You wanna take a walk in the park? You wanna take a walk in the park?'

I still don't know if he meant a walk in Rock Creek Park, a good dark place for an execution, or if 'a walk in the park' was what the black boys called death. Anyway, the metal was pointing at me. I gave him the fourteen bucks. The ones were wrapped in the ten. It was worth a Happy Meal at McMucks for the pair of them and the apple pie for dessert but it must have seemed a wad of tens.

'Run.'

I walked away.

This wasn't good enough and the gun started popping behind me. He fired off five and by the fifth I was clomping at high speed in my stupid Chinese boots across the snow and ice. I skidded and fell, cutting my hand.

Carmen was there when I came in the door, dripping blood.

'I was mugged, he started shooting –'

'*O Jesús o Jesús o Dios mío o Jesús o Madre de Dios o –!*'

She was blabbering and shaking her arms. This was very irritating to me.

'*Callate, ya!* Shut up for Christ's sake! I'm not hit!'

A few hours before we'd been going at each other, you're a bitch, you're a bastard, bla bla bla, now she was shaking her arms and making a lot of noise because I'd scratched myself.

Carmen was my wife. She was from Venezuela but had a US passport, and by marrying her I got papers to work. Getting married was a bad idea because we always fought but we had been broke and my back was at the wall and at that time I hadn't known the people who could make me a fake ID. Now I knew plenty of people like that.

I cleaned my hand up and told her I needed five bucks to get my shoes back. She presumed I was in shock but it was one of those delayed reactions. I set the alarm clock and went to sleep. I had to get up at 4.45 a.m. so I could put on my boots and get to the Company by 6.30, and maybe even begin earning something by 7.30.

The next few evenings I kept going back to the shoe shop but it was closed. You could see the shelves with all those pairs of shoes lined up inside. I beat and rattled the door but no one came. I walked home in my Chinese shoes. The corner of 18th and Ingleside always made me a bit nervous, but there was nothing I could do about that, I would just have to get used to it.

The next Saturday I went to the shoe shop. The door was open. A bell tinkled as you opened the door. There was nobody behind the counter, just the rows and rows of shoes looking down at you. I looked for my boots in the rows and didn't see them. I had time to think about how all those different shoes belonged to different people, walking around the streets of my neighbourhood, working, getting older. Yes, I contemplated shoes. It was a shoe repair shop. What else was there to look at? It was very quiet. I waited and nobody appeared. I called out. I was losing patience when a bowed woman came from the back of the shop. Her hair was tied back behind her head and was mostly grey and there were shadows underneath her eyes. I gave her my ticket. She disappeared for a while then shuffled back with my ticket.

'Not ready. Come back next week.'

It wasn't right to have to walk around in lumpy Chinese boots all week, for them to make you fall on your face, then have them for the weekend too. I was getting ready to say something but she got there first.

'My husband passed away.'

This was a very final argument for my boots not being ready. He had seemed healthy enough, but that didn't mean anything. What was I going to say? That he had been lucky to die in such good condition? She stood there, drowning in grief, and swamped by rows of unrepaired shoes and boots, all sizes and styles. I told her I was sorry. It was true. I was. It felt stupid to disturb her grieving for the sake of my boots. She shrugged, exhausted, into a row of shoes the dead man had left.

I went out on to the street. All the people were rushing around as usual, wearing out pairs of shoes. Some of them threw them away and got new ones, while others got them repaired if they were hard up. It was strange how human beings were always so caught up in what they were doing. Strange to die and leave a little shop, with rows and rows of shoes demanding to be fixed. Terrible to have your husband die and then to have to deal with all those shoes, just so that strangers could keep on walking around in them. And all the people still caught up in the world coming in, ignorant, the bell on the door tinkling impatiently behind them, expecting fixed shoes.

Well, I didn't have my boots but I still had five dollars. There wasn't much you could do with five bucks.

I took my clumpy Chinese workboots for a drink. Or they took me. They were well broken in. We were getting used to each other. I didn't recognize anybody there, which was fine, I just wanted a quiet one. I took a seat alone at the back wall, the one with the mural. Something about all those shoes on the wooden shelves had me rather reflective and I took the second beer slowly. So. Here I was from Europe, I was in the capital of the United States, and all these people with moustaches were from Central America, and a load of Chinese people in a factory had knocked my boots together. Before I could synthesize these facts into something that smelled meaningful Nolberto came in and stood me one. His shoes were black and shining. What's this shit he'd heard about me getting shot? 'Reports of me being punctured have been greatly exaggerated.' 'Fucking niggers,' he said, in English. He didn't know much English. Just a few phrases. He said someone had pointed out my wife to him. Good-looking woman. Was it true she had an American passport?

We sat under the palm trees and straw houses and the ocean and señoritas, and ranchero music played and the immigrants drank their beers and thought of untouchable North American women, or a woman back home, or the price of a whore. We all drank our weekend beers and it wasn't that good but it was much better than being at work.

Gone Fishing

He came up out of the ground, out of the metro station, and into the light. It was ugly and a little frightening, like looking inside the head of a madman. A dictator had razed and rebuilt the area, in an effort to create an impression, and shortly afterwards he had been put up against a wall and shot. They were ugly buildings and ugly cars and most of the people were ugly too. The young and good-looking ones were the ugliest of all, because they tried too hard, like the city had tried, to be something.

He had not wanted to see it all again, because he had been sitting in his room reading a story and he had not wanted it to stop. It was a story about a man who had gone fishing. But she had called him, and she would have been unhappy if he had not come, and he did not want her to be unhappy. When she was unhappy he felt bad too, so he kept trying to make her happy.

He was early, so he leaned up against a wall and took the book out of his pocket and began to read.

It was a beautiful story. In it nothing in particular happened. The man was on his own and he walked into the wilderness to find a good place to fish. The story described all the things that the man did. It described places he walked through, the heat of the day, the light through the pines, the weight of the pack on his back, how he made his camp, and the fishing itself.

What was beautiful about the story was the pleasure the

man felt, a sensual pleasure, in each of the things he saw and did. And his pleasure was heightened and his senses sharpened because the man was very much alone.

And that was what it was. It was a feeling for beauty that the writer of the story possessed. In the words he chose, in his intention to observe and report the world, there was something very pure and solitary. And when you followed the words and saw the things as the man walked and camped and fished, you too felt that the world was once again something new to be seen and noticed and felt.

He was in the story as he read, leaning up against the wall, and at the same time he was very conscious of the city, because what he was reading made him feel as if he was moving and thinking at a different speed from his surroundings. He was there in the city but he was also in the country. He was not escaping from the city by reading the story, because the story made him feel the city even more strongly.

His phone rang. He did not like to carry his phone, but she had asked him to. You made a plan, and then a phone let somebody change the plan. When people were together, always some of those people would be speaking on their phones to people who were not there. Nobody was ever completely where they were now that it was possible to speak to everybody all of the time.

He told her that he had not yet entered the cafeteria. Good, she said, and she gave him the new place to meet. He put the book in one pocket and the phone in the other and began to walk to the new place. When he caught sight of her he waved and smiled. Part of it was gladness to see her, and part of it was an act, jumping into the air to make her smile. That was something he loved, the way she smiled when she opened the door to him, or he to her. Once she had asked what he liked most about her and he had refused to tell her. If he told her that what he liked most about her was that smile, she would become conscious of it and it would no longer be the same.

They walked up the big road away from the metro station. It was still ugly but less so than what was behind them. They talked about where they should go and who they were due to telephone, and he said, let's just walk this way for a little bit. They would go someplace, probably a bar, and talk to various people, but what he really wanted was to open the book and be fishing with the man who had written the words that made you open your eyes and see the world again.

Her phone rang and she answered it and began to speak. They had reached an interesting place. To their right was a tramline and an old church with a garden. This was the terminus of the tramline. The tramline curved from behind the church and straightened briefly in parallel with the big road. At the straight section the trams made a stop before looping round the church and back in the direction from which they came.

He took the book from his pocket and sat on the low wall in front of the church and began to read about the man casting his line into the big flowing river.

When she had finished speaking on the phone, he looked up at her and said, 'Why don't we just sit here for a few minutes?'

It was set back a little from the street. It seemed a peaceful place for them both to sit. He could read the last few pages. He flicked through the pages to show her.

'You didn't have to come,' she said. 'If you wanted to read.'

He had hurt her again and now there was going to be a fight. Whether it was to be a big fight or a small fight was not yet apparent. He could change his mind and not wish to read, but it was too late, he would still have to find the things to say that would fix the damage and the things that would be said would be complicated and relate to all the complicated things said in all the other fights. Perhaps if he explained to her as simply as possible that he had meant no harm she would understand.

'I wanted to see you,' he said. 'But I was reading this on the metro, and it's so good, and I saw this wall here. And I thought it would be a good place to sit and read for a few minutes, and you wouldn't mind.'

'You didn't have to feel obliged to come.'

He controlled his anger, because it was not her fault that she did not understand, and if he did not try to explain, it would become his fault.

'It was just a moment,' he started. 'It was simple. I was thinking about this story, and you were talking on the phone and I saw this wall here.'

'Read if you want to.'

'It doesn't matter really,' he said, standing up and putting the book in his pocket. 'We can walk some more. It's not something to fight over. I really don't feel like reading any more anyway.'

'No,' she said. 'Read. I can walk down there, look in a few shops.' She pointed to a pedestrian street across the big road.

As she walked away he took the book out and sat down on the wall and opened it. He wondered if she had understood that he had wanted to see her and it was just that he liked the story so much. But now he found it hard to read because he was distracted by the fight, which was perhaps unfinished. He was angry at having been made again to argue, explain and defend. She had walked away to allow him to read but now she was between him and the river. He looked around. A Gypsy woman was sitting further down the wall, selling sunflower seeds, and on the path in front of the wall two barefoot children with thin legs were kicking a burst football. It was the edge of a Gypsy neighbourhood, an old network of streets and families, at the point at which it met the rushing artery of the big street, which belonged to everybody. He was sitting on a kind of border. He looked across the busy road, towards the pedestrian street she had walked down. It was a failure of a pedestrian street. Cars parked on it. It was just another parking lot. She could walk down that street, he thought, and I could get up and walk in the other direction, and that would be it. You imagined something and then it happened. Well, she had stopped the fight and allowed him to read. He thought like that for a moment and he calmed down and was able to find his way back to the river again. When the man stepped into the river to cast his line, the cold water was a shock, and then he could feel the current against his legs as his feet sought purchase on the gravel bed. He fished the smooth fast-flowing living river.

She returned just as he finished the story. He had fished and was satisfied and everything was right again. He rose and put an arm round her and kissed her face. He put the book in his pocket. They began to walk away together. As he was about to cross the tram tracks in advance of a coming tram, he heard her say:

'Was that some kind of tactic?'

He had crossed the tracks and she had stayed, and now the tram was rumbling between them and he was left with the word. He frowned. Tactic. That was what she had said. He wondered for a moment should he pretend that he had not heard. The tram passed and he crossed back quickly to where she was standing.

'No,' he said. 'It is very simple. I just wanted to read the story, because it was so good.'

He put his arm round her. Above the buildings the sky had become very big, with great broken clouds against the empty blue, and the clouds were colouring in the low evening sunlight. It was rare and lovely. He pointed it out to her. He thought to say, wouldn't it be good to be in the mountains, someplace silent, with a sky like that, without the buildings blocking off half of it? But he stopped himself, because that would have sounded like a complaint against the city rather than praise of the sky.

'Why isn't it enough for you to be with me?' she asked. 'It's like you're never really there with me. You just don't care enough.'

She was not looking at the sky. She was looking at herself.

It is never enough, he thought. And now some small nagging part of her is the only part that is able to speak. Perhaps it is my fault. Perhaps I am to blame again.

'Goodbye,' he told her.

He turned and walked away.

He walked back downhill towards the terrible square, and towards the metro station, and he felt the tightness under his breastbone, in his chest. When he had nearly reached the metro station he remembered that there was a tramline nearby that he could take and he was very relieved that he did not have to go back down into the ground. There was still plenty of light in the summer evening sky and the tram would rumble through old neighbourhoods before it brought him to his neighbourhood of suburban apartment blocks at the edge of the city, and by going above ground he could see it all.

The decision cheered him, and he walked up the street, eastwards, towards the tramline. The street rose gently and he enjoyed walking the incline. The sad pressure in his chest eased a little. He began to gulp air. His mouth opened automatically as if he were yawning, but it was not a yawn and he did not get enough air each time to satisfy his lungs. This happened four or five times as he walked up the hill towards the tramline, and it surprised him each time. It was as if he had forgotten how to breathe and were learning how to do it again.

The Retreat from Moscow

I wake up shivering. All I know is that I am facing a wall. I pull the blanket around me. The blanket is too small. It is completely dark. When I wake again it is light and I do not recognize the room. There are some empty bottles and a sickening smell comes from an ashtray, overturned, near my head. My left eye, the side I have been lying on, is gummed shut. The walls are painted but it was done a very long time ago, and the pale winter light comes through the dirty windows. I turn over to take in the room. There are two chairs, one on its side. The other sits squarely on its four legs and is looking down at me so directly it seems to have a personality, seems to be addressing me, like a fighter who has knocked me down and is challenging me to get up again. My ribs hurt. I am fully dressed and wearing my boots and am terribly cold, the kind of deep cold that goes right to the core.

I get up off the floor and stand before the window. It is snowing hard, falling thickly upon a strange white world. I am on perhaps the sixth or seventh floor and do not recognize the area. Apartment blocks the colour of ash, a small red car struggling through the furrows of snow. It could be anywhere in the city.

There are more rooms and I wander through them, not expecting to meet anybody, but moving carefully all the same. One room is empty like the one I have slept in, except for a single, stained mattress. There are several magazines by the mattress. I flick through them. There are two women's magazines. I look at the pictures of women. There is an article on how to have a better orgasm, and I actually begin to read it. The other magazine is a television guide from the year before. The next room is stuffed full of old furniture, draped in plastic sheeting. Mostly it is the massive kind with which people cramp their small rooms, with cases and shelves for displaying their things, their coffee cups and saucers and statuettes of Little Bo-Peep. In the kitchen the fridge is plugged in and humming, and I find this strange, that something is actually functioning. Inside are several jars containing what may be jam, probably plum jam, thick and black. My mouth is very dry. I find a cup and rinse it out and drink half a cup of tap water. I find loose tea also and there is a kettle but I feel uncomfortable touching anything. I feel like a trespasser. For all I know I, or the people I have been with, have broken into this place, and the real owner could walk in at any second. I will be unable to explain my presence. Also, everything is covered in a mixture of grease and dust, and now it is on my fingers. There is no soap. I rinse my hands and wipe them against my trousers. In the frigid air, my hands remain damp and cold.

I am dressed only in a T-shirt, and outside these unheated rooms the snow is falling so fast it looks like a film speeded up. I am not badly hung-over. It is that dense, careless fog when the alcohol is still in your blood and you have not slept, and my real problem is the cold. In the bathroom I find my shirt, bundled, damp and stinking in the sink. I drop it in the bath and rinse my hands again. I shake them nearly dry. They are red and very cold. I urinate. Though my bladder is full it takes several moments before I can let it go. The flush is unnervingly loud.

I try to organize myself to leave, but there is no sign of

my sweater, my jacket or even my hat and scarf. I remember us in the car, me in the back seat, wipers swiping madly at the snow, going someplace. I remember the girl sitting on my knee because there was no room in the car, my arm round her waist, her arm round my shoulder. I remember kissing her on the mouth, us alone in the hallway. I remember the one who drove detaching me from her with one hand, so authoritatively that I felt sure I had overstepped some decent limit. But that might have not been the case at all, and I realize with a sense of humiliation that perhaps I was simply too drunk to resist this more composed personality. Then they were kissing each other and I was watching. I don't remember much else.

My wallet is gone, and my ID, and my keys. I return to the first room and look under the blanket. Of course, there is nothing under the blanket. On the floor of the hallway, by the door, under a small table on which a phone sits, I find my wallet, empty. At least I still have my trousers and my boots. It seems important suddenly to get out of this place.

I lift the receiver of the phone, and am surprised there is a tone, and am about to dial for a taxi before I remember that I have no money, and in any case do not know the address. I try to think who I can call, who can help me in this moment. But there is nothing terribly wrong, except that I am temporarily lost. I am not injured or in any danger. It is simply that I would like to speak to somebody – a friend, for example. Of course, I have friends, I have numbers I have dialled many times and have memorized. But I am not sure what to say to anybody. I dial my ex's number and it rings and rings and when I get the answering machine I hang up. I would not have spoken to her anyway. Then I ring a number completely at random and a voice answers, a young woman's voice, and

I clear my throat and say, 'Hello, taxi?' 'I beg your pardon?' 'I need a taxi to the airport.' She tells me I have the wrong number and I apologize and we even say goodbye to each other politely.

The feeling that I must leave this place quickly is very strong. I hang up the phone, glance through each of the rooms again in turn, and open the front door. I look nervously into the hall and step out unobserved and the door seems on its own account to close. I press against it and am alarmed that I have locked myself out, that I am unable to get back in. I have a feeling that I have left something behind, like when you leave home and you ask yourself automatically if you have brought your money, your keys, your ID. And the answer in this case is I have not, and I must keep on going.

I take the stairs down. Outside the snow is lying thickly and more is falling. I stand in the lobby looking at it and wish I had a hat. Just a hat that covered my ears would make all the difference. It is the ears that always start to hurt.

Well, I still have the greatest asset of any free and independent man, a good pair of boots, and now it is time to get walking. I push open the door and head into the falling snow. The first few seconds are actually quite pleasant, and I think, it really isn't so cold at all, and choose to turn right and down the deserted street, crunching the snow, at a brisk pace. That's odd, I think, that snow can squeak when stepped upon.

I do not know where I am going and after walking for several minutes everything looks exactly the same – ten-storey apartment blocks, one after another. There are some trees and in the windless air the snow has gathered steeply on even the smaller black branches to a height much greater than the thickness of the branches, so that everything is written in bold white. I know I am looking for a large street which will give me a sense of direction of where the centre might be, of progress, and by now the first flakes have melted into my clothing and it is clear that a human being can die in such weather. I don't know how long it would take, to fall down freezing, but I cannot resist such cold indefinitely. I think of refugees crossing mountain passes, of Antarctic explorers who stepped out for a moment, of mountaineers in blizzards stepping over cliffs, of Napoleon's troops on the retreat from Moscow. Of course, history is full of people freezing to death, but that is not going to happen to me. At any moment I can admit defeat and step into the hallway of one of those anonymous apartment blocks, and perhaps even find a radiator. If I carry on and fall, the emergency services would presumably come, take me to hospital in time. But vagabonds, too, have frozen to death in cities.

I speed up, almost running, because I simply must make some progress out of this ridiculous situation. All I have to do is to find a big street, and public transport. Finally, I see someone I can ask, a short fat woman walking a small dog that, wearing what appears to be a padded waistcoat, is better adapted to conditions than I. The woman's face is almost invisible, under hat and scarf, but her eyes register fear as I approach her. Obviously I am a mad person, hugging myself and hunched in the cold, snow falling in my hair, teeth chattering, demanding, Where is the road, the road? Why is a crazy man in a blizzard accosting her, jabbering about a road, when she simply wants to take Fluffy round the block to do his poo-poos? Poor Fluffy, he can hardly walk, the snow is up to his body now, and rising fast! What road? she asks. The main road, I tell her, the big road! She points, and I set off running in that direction.

At the bus stop I stand in a corrugated-iron shelter. I no

longer care what the well-dressed people think. I brush the snow from my shoulders. My teeth chatter noisily. I see people who could do me an enormous kindness by lending me a scarf, perhaps, but people keep a distance. If it were so easy to help the poor, the deranged, the feckless, it would have been done long ago, obviously. The bottoms of my trouser legs are encrusted with snow and are frozen rigid towards the knee. My ears no longer hurt. My skin has become completely numb.

I take a back seat in the bus, and stamp the loose snow from my boots and concentrate on getting my hands dry. Now I am getting somewhere, I am out of the weather, and I will take care of one thing at a time, beginning with having dry hands again. I am huddled, looking out the window, as the city moves by swiftly. The snow ploughs have been through and have pushed up big banks of snow at the side of the road, trapping the parked cars. When I see a metro station I will disembark. Down in the metro stations the air is heated and I can beg a metro card and figure out my next move.

At first I don't understand what is happening, or what the man is holding to my face. I look up but already he is showing it to others, and people are digging into their pockets for tickets and bus passes and he is checking them, handing them back, and finally there is only me, going through my pockets, and he is waiting just for me. He gives a nod and then two of his colleagues are standing over me. The other passengers are watching.

At the first stop we disembark.

I explain to them I have been robbed, that I have no money to pay a fine, and that I have no ID to show them, for the same reason. I actually believe at first that they will understand, but they imagine I am standing there freezing because

I am obstinate, because I am a liar. Yes, these men have heard all the excuses. I am angry now at being persecuted, rather than helped, by three well-dressed ticket inspectors. They stand there in their hats and padded jackets, snow falling in our eyes, nothing in their heads but how much money I can give them. Do you think I'm joking? I ask. Do they think I'm standing around wet and freezing for some kind of joke? They smirk at each other. Well, then, says the big fat one, who appears to be in charge, you've broken the law, we'll have to get the police. I consider just walking away from them. What will they do? Chase me through the snowstorm? I decide to give pity one last go. One of them looks more intelligent than the other two, or at least human, and I address myself to him. Look, I say, have some decency. Can't you see I'm freezing to death? I've been robbed and I have no money. He is clearly a good man, I can see it in his face but before I can reach him the fat piece of human shit has his hand on my shoulder and is telling me to be reasonable, just hand over such and such a sum and they needn't call the police. I hiss something in his face, incoherent except for two words – *your mother* – and brush his paw from my shoulder with enough force that the other two think I am going for him and step in to hold me back.

My name is called. A woman's voice behind me calls out my name. She rushes into the middle of it, thrusts the coloured paper at the big one, then is pulling me away by the hand. She is taking me somewhere, through the snow, falling more thickly than ever, muffling the shapes of things, blinding me, forcing me to walk with my head down. We take a turn away from the blocks of big buildings, into a street, unexpectedly, of older two- and three-storey houses. Some of them even have wooden fences and gates. We seem to walk some distance.

She has given me her hat and scarf and her reddish hair is covered in snow and she is still leading me by the hand. I am about to ask her how much further when she stops and opens a gate. As we enter a small courtyard she tells me to wait and she goes forward and ties up a large black dog that emerges from a makeshift shelter. We pass through the courtyard, the dog snarling at me, straining at the end of a chain, and through a doorway into a hallway with a steep wooden staircase going up. We go down three steps, along a narrow passageway to the left of the staircase, and through a door and out the back of the building, again into the snow. There are trees and the backs of other buildings. It is all very old and tumbledown, this little corner which has somehow escaped the general destruction, the bulldozers, and is hidden from the city. We go carefully down several stone steps covered with snow to a semi-basement, and she opens a door with a large key almost the length of her hand. The door is stiff. She pushes it with her shoulders and it gives with a creak.

There is a tiny square hallway and two doors. The one straight ahead, slightly open, is to the bathroom. To the left we enter a small room with a couch, a dresser, a stove and an armchair. I sit on the couch and she removes my boots, my socks. My wonderful walking boots get confiscated. It is now time for me to avoid frostbite. From the bottom of a dresser she digs out clothing and a towel. She turns round and busies herself arranging wood to light the stove, allowing me to undress. The sodden T-shirt falls to the floor. My trousers I prise off with some difficulty, my fingers being almost useless. My member has gone into hiding. Well, that's how they avoid freezing off. I give it a good rub. The towel is rough but clean. The clothes belonged to a man who was much bigger than me – a pair of grey trousers that an office worker might have worn, a red plaid shirt with buttons missing from cuffs that dangle over my hands and a dark-blue wool sweater, smelling faintly of mothballs. I feel like a man who has shrunk. She lights the paper beneath the wood and soon the dim brown room is filled with shapes and shadows, hers wavering across the back wall as the sticks begin to crackle.

'It won't smoke so much when it gets going,' she says.

The circumstances of our acquaintance are unclear. She mentions the name of a woman I used to be with, of a club I used to drink in, years ago, and I know I have seen her face before, many times. But it is one of those faces that is always in the background, in the periphery of the group, one you nod to and nothing more, because you are just not interested. Her skin is very pale, and her hair reddish, and you cannot imagine colour in her thin lips. I feel a vague uneasiness that I had ignored her when things were going well, she who is my friend, who knows me and has helped me in this bad situation.

'How do you feel?'

I am still shuddering, but at this point it is almost pleasant. Sensation is returning to my limbs. My hands and feet hurt.

'Better.'

She arranges cushions and has me lie on the couch, and puts a blanket over me. I lie there, looking up at the one window, high on the wall, peeking over the lip of the earth. The light is fading and soon it will be night. Surely she is a little bit mad, I think, living in a place like this, taking me off the street and not even curious to ask what has happened. But now the fire is burning well, and in the reddish light I see some kind of a life around me – postcards on the wall, books and letters on the shelf.

'It has never snowed like this,' she says, rattling the grate. 'Like it is going to keep on going forever.'

Like it will drown the whole world, and just the two of us left.

She pulls back a hanging strip of plastic that serves as the cupboard door of a plywood compartment. There are potatoes, onions, carrots, salt, a plastic bottle of oil and a bottle of rum. She asks about the woman we both used to know and I tell her I have had no news for years.

'I could do with some of that rum,' I say.

'Oh, no,' she says. 'It's just the bottle. I keep vinegar in it. I'll make you a nice cup of hot chocolate. I should make it with milk, but I have none.' She boils some water. It is something from a sachet and in the end it tastes not much like chocolate. But in any case, it is sweet and hot. She peels potatoes over a metal bucket. She peels so that the skin comes off in one long spiralling strip, the way some people peel oranges, and she drops the potatoes into a big cast-iron pot of water with some carrots and onions.

When I wake, to the sound of the heavy lid of the bubbling pot repeatedly rising and clanking back in place, she is asleep in the armchair, mouth open, head slightly to one side, the reddish hair falling over one eye. It is almost warm. I still don't know her name.

'Hey!' I call. 'Hey!'

She starts and looks at me, with the odd blank look of one awoken.

'You don't have to sleep there,' I say. I shift over in the couch until my backside is to the wall, and raise the blanket. She gets up slowly, and slides the pot to a cooler place and places the lid at a tilt so steam can escape. She has her back to me and I am unsure whether she is ignoring me. With a special metal hook she opens the door of the stove and, crouching, stokes it with more split logs. She is wearing faded denim jeans and a sweater and I observe for the first time that her shape, silhouetted in firelight, is not bad at all. Then she walks to the couch and climbs under the blanket, with her back to me. The couch is narrow, her body against mine and, naturally, my arm goes over her. It has nowhere else to go. Her hair smells pleasantly of smoke. She is a woman I could have had long ago, who was waiting there, but I simply was not interested, there being better women to have, in better times. I will know how she kisses, the noises she makes when we copulate, before I leave this room. But not today.

'I need to stay here for a while,' I tell her. It is unclear whether I am talking about a few hours or a few months, but this seems not to trouble her.

'Oh, you can stay as long as you like.'

'Thank you. I think I will.'

I look at the window. There is no more light coming through it. A drift of snow now covers it completely, and probably it is still snowing hard, falling thickly, possibly harder than it has ever snowed before on this city, and it may continue all night, drowning everything in thick drifts, paralysing even the buses, even the trucks. Yes, such weather could kill a man, if his luck deserted him entirely. I let my head fall back upon the cushion, next to hers, my lips close to the back of her neck. I close my eyes and listen to the pot boil.